THE PURPOSE OF CAPITAL

A Progress Report

"Refreshingly thoughtful and reflective, in this book Jed blends his life-long fascination with how money can be used for good with a deep inquiry into the overall purpose of life. You'll soon delight in the road-map he unfurls slowly in this book—and the treasures he uncovers along the way—myth, mystery, meaning, religion, philosophy, spirituality, and ultimately, humility. You'll want to read this not just as a way to understand the core assumptions inside impact investing, but as a guidebook for a more personal exploration of how using capital for impact can ultimately shape not just the society we live in, but the meaning of your life."

—Cathy Clark, Faculty Director,
CASE and CASE i3 Initiative, Duke University

"In this mesmerizing and passionate intellectual tour de force, Jed Emerson takes on a several thousand year journey through money and meaning. Without judgment, Jed provokes us in the impact investing and broader finance communities to think about the why, more than the how, of what we do. But in the end, by doing so, I suspect Jed has re-ignited (or he would say evolved) a much needed discussion about the how as well, by reminding us that not only is value and meaning indivisible, but that our work and our personal lives, ourselves and our communities, and people and planet are all connected, and that to achieve good outcomes from investment decisions one must take a universal unified approach, not one that separates money from meaning. Oh, and there is a lot of good practical how in it too. This approach, if truly internalized by capital markets, promises to make the world a more just and equitable place, but also make us as actors in it more fulfilled as human beings. What could be a better call to action in a book than that? It's also vibrant, funny, challenging and deeply personal in an extremely charming way; highly recommended!"

—Jason Scott, Founding Partner, Encourage Capital

"Pulling from his own depth of experience and from wisdom traditions worldwide, this book is a true exploration and dialogue on the purpose of capital—A moment for all of us to pause, introspect, and question the very nature of capitalism and our relationship to it. Jed Emerson's authentic, poetic, and spiritual analysis of wealth and it's fundamental purpose is not only beautiful, it's compelling and is a call to arms for us all to see money not as an end in and of itself, but as a tool to be leveraged for a just and equitable society. Every policy maker, every wealth holder, every entrepreneur, every investor, and truly every one of us would be doing ourselves and society at large a favor by diving into this brilliant memoir on the purpose of capital. Jed is a reverent iconoclast, a conscious capitalist, and in my humble opinion, one of the great practical philosophers of our time."

—Daniel Epstein, Founder/CEO, Unreasonable

THE

PURPOSE

OF

CAPITAL

Elements of Impact,

Financial Flows,

and Natural Being

·····················

JED EMERSON

BLENDED VALUE GROUP PRESS

My intention is the e-book version of this manuscript be distributed free of charge to inform our public community's discussions and dialogue.

Please feel free to distribute this e-book to your networks.

While copies of the e-book will also be available for purchase in paperback and hardback format, these will be priced as low as possible to ensure wide accessibility to our global community.

Should any net income be generated from such sales, those funds will be donated to ImpactAssets, the nonprofit fiscal agent of this project, and used to fund future publications addressing this inquiry into the purpose of capital with such papers and future e-books also being distributed free of charge.

Those exploring these themes are encouraged to build upon and make use of the original materials included in this volume as long as you reference and give attribution to this author and source.

Copyrighted material presented in this volume is understood to fall under the terms and conditions of Fair Use and are not intended for commercial use by third parties.

....

Copyright © 2018 by Blended Value Group Press
Published by Blended Value Press, San Francisco, CA.

ISBN Hardcover: 978-1-7324531-0-4
ISBN Paperback: 978-1-7324531-1-1
ISBN E-Book: 978-1-7324531-2-8

Domini Dragoone, Cover Design and Book Layout
Dana Smith, Art and Illustrations
Herb Schaffner, Editorial Input
Front cover images: Pound Sterling notes © Bank of England, used with permission; Euro notes © Central European Bank, used with permission; water: © Ruslan Nassyrov/123rf; field: © elleon/iStock; graph: © winvic/iStock; mountain: © obencem/123rf; puzzle: © Thomas Vogel/iStock.

An Imprint of Blended Value Group Press

FOR

MIA HAUGEN

...the new generation of leaders rising from behind,
joining our ranks and moving us all ahead
as they find their purpose in the world
by being engaged with the world,

and to the honor of the many impact warriors, now our
field's elders, who have spent past decades innovating
in finance for our common good. There are many names
that might go on this list and you know who you are,
but in particular we recognize the late Tessa Tennant
for her life's work that was of benefit to us all.

MY SINCERE THANKS TO

Annie Chen

The Ustaoset Fund

and

The William and Flora Hewlett Foundation

for Supporting this Research and Reflection

If a man is fortunate he will, before he dies, gather up as much as he can of his civilized heritage and transmit it to his children. And to his final breath he will be grateful for this inexhaustible legacy, knowing that it is our nourishing mother and our lasting life.

—WILL AND ARIEL DURANT

TABLE OF CONTENTS

Part Three:
BEING PRESENT IN THE
CREATION OF POSSIBLE PASTS
AND POTENTIAL FUTURES

ADDENDUM

PART ONE

WHERE
WE CAME
FROM

CHAPTER ONE

WHY CARE ABOUT THE PURPOSE OF CAPITAL?

MOST HUMAN SOCIETIES ARE NOW DOMINATED BY FINANCIAL CAPITALISM—THE GLOBAL SYSTEM BY WHICH CAPITAL IS DEFINED, CREATED, VALUED, AND EXCHANGED. IS THIS WHAT WE WANTED?

We have become separated from capital and are now at its service, as opposed to it serving us, wherein our relation with capital comes to define our understanding of self, our value relative to others, our happiness and personal satisfaction, our prospects within this society, and the future prospects of our children. We live in a world in which we say we would like jobs, personal security, justice, opportunity, and a healthy planet, yet many of us seldom take time to pause and reflect upon our system of financial capitalism and in what ways capital seeks to determine how we may best be able to achieve those things we claim to want in this life.

Most Americans and many millions of others around the world, react to economic developments, engage in charitable giving, pay taxes, and consume goods and services, while operating within a superficial understanding of the nature of capital, the role it plays in our lives and its fundamental purpose. We work primarily within an understanding of capital as it has been defined and presented to us by others and not on terms we have had the opportunity to fully explore, reflect upon and modify based on our own life mission.

Our understanding of capital and its purpose is not solely one of individual definition. At its core, the notion of capital is itself a social construct and not an objective, economic rule of law operating beyond our societal bounds. It is a phenomenon that over scores of centuries has been spun out of our consciousness and collective experience, to become its being and force, acting upon each of us as individuals and all of us as a global village. Over the course of those centuries, many of us have lost sight of the fact that our approach to the nature and purpose of capital may be changed, expanded, refined, and applied in new ways not only in our own lives but within those of our families, communities, nations, and world.

We do not have to accept the definition of capital's purpose as developed in the last four centuries and which we have enthusiastically bought from Wall Street's firms of finance. The purpose of capital is about more than monetizing the economic opportunity represented by the mainstreaming of interest in sustainable, responsible and impact investing. The quest to discern the real purpose of capital is about each of us going deeper. That is, to seek to explore what capital is, the elements which make up its constitution and how we may work together to realize financial capital's potential as a tool for attaining our broad goals of life and meaning.

Each of us *is* the market just as we contribute to the creation of and give lifeblood *to* capital markets. We each have the possibility of embracing a new, deeper and more inclusive understanding of capital's place and purpose in our lives and in determining the future survival of this planet. That is why we should pause to reflect upon how we got here while reconsidering and refining our understanding of the purpose of capital and how capital should serve us all—human and non-human— over centuries to come.

AN EVOLVING UNDERSTANDING OF PURPOSE

The implications for our appreciation of the impact of capital—and how we might actively manage capital for the generation of positive change, a theme explored throughout this book—are many. In the context of our work, the process of becoming an impact investor is iterative, evolving, and developmental. It is complicated and convoluted. Seldom is it a process of being who we were at one point in the past or continually being the same person in the future. In listening to some of those new to impact investing, I smile when hearing them describe themselves as impact investors straight out of the gate. "I was investing in electric infrastructure, bringing light to villages in rural areas and didn't even *know* I was an impact investor, but here I am—an impact investor and *still* making serious profits!"

By way of example, I followed a journey like many of our colleagues. I began on my path in middle school as a peer-tutor in Spanish Harlem, a youth rights activist in my teens and a social worker in my twenties before moving over to philanthropy at twenty-nine when I began promoting what we called venture philanthropy and social entrepreneurship. The 2000s I spent as something of a "professional fellow," with faculty appointments at a variety of leading business schools, sustainable public and private equity firms, a foundation exploring how best to capitalize evidence-based nonprofit organizations and a sustainable ranching enterprise in Montana. I ended the decade working with, of all things, a fund of hedge funds group out of New York City. Today, I am a strategic advisor to asset owners and managers deploying capital through an array of approaches ranging from sustainable finance and integrated ESG investing, responsible investing, thematic investing and direct impact investing—all coordinated through a practice referred to as Total Portfolio Management.

I thought this journey was bringing me to a better understanding of how to create sustained change in the world through our allocation of capital. Now, I find it has brought me circuitously down, deeper—not higher—to a place of profound personal reckoning, greater humility, and quiet reflection.

I have enough trouble putting all this together—these experiences, lessons, evolving perspectives, the mainstreaming of "impact"— to be able to say I know much of anything any more. To paraphrase Kafka, I have enough trouble just *being*, much less being an impact investor.[1]

As the author Peter Orner writes—indeed, as *I* could have written:

> "Now more than ever I feel under siege by opinions masked as answers. I'm finding much of the talk I overhear—in the cafe, on the street, in newspapers, in magazines, online, and in too many books—more and more exhausting. Is it me? Or is there an epidemic of glib conclusions going around? Since when is everything so explainable? I've been rightly accused of early-onset curmudgeonry, but since when did everything become so coherent?"[2]

Perhaps we need fewer experts with answers and more openness to the fundamental questions and genuinely profound challenges of our own experience.

Perhaps we need more reflection and less advising and strategy and execution; fewer conference panels presenting "successful" strategy and a great deal fewer lightweight, blog posts presenting five-points to deeper whatever and promoting yet another formulaic understanding of the world.

Perhaps we need fewer answers to questions of the purpose of capital and more contemplation of the fundamental challenge of same.

Maybe we should shut up and listen to the world, to its various and diverse human and non-human communities and history of experience. Maybe we need to create greater space to hear from those whose lives we seek to impact? Maybe that will more effectively direct us to the life practice we seek to refine and realize in our own time. Perhaps it will be at that point when we may claim to be responsible fiduciaries of capital; prudent and impactful investors.

But youth in age or experience may both inspire us and serve to dim our path. As a youthful William Wordsworth wrote from post-revolutionary France,

Bliss was it in that dawn to be alive,
But to be young was very heaven![3]

In this present time of innovation and refreshed inquiry it is easy to envy those just starting the course of their careers or only now joining our community for they have before them a seemingly open plain of opportunity and a labyrinth stretching off ahead and around the bend. At the same time, regardless of our years, life is always open before us and directed by our choice. It is true "the years flow by like a bro-ken-down dam"[4] as we live with our choices and their consequences, but the mind may remain fresh, welcoming and accepting of what comes rather than fighting to defend what is known and thought to be true. Youth gives one time, but not always the wisdom to comprehend the fullness of the broader currents flowing around and potentially through us. If we are lucky, age brings the perspective we need to see around the upcoming turns of the river while recalling the churning torrents of the past. In this way, we come to understand our deeper self and forgive who we were as we continue our development and process of becoming what we're called to be or merely to accept we're called to be more fully present in our becoming.

The Buddhist teacher, Sangharakshita, once observed:

"Money isn't the most important. Success isn't the most import-ant…Knowledge isn't the most important. Religion isn't the most important. Meditation isn't the most important…. The most important thing in life, the most precious thing in the whole world, is contact with one's true self, between the surface of one's being and its depths. This is more precious than the whole world…this is the priceless jewel."[5]

Many scientists and other cognitive rationalists would see this path of development, the process of emerging as our true self, as one of log-ical steps, moving from initial question to insight to follow-up inquiry. And many a materialist might view it as less a personal quest than a natural process of connecting dots of matter, of learning how to thrive

in a material, living world. Neuroscientists would have us believe the
self, much less our spiritual self, is
merely a biochemical product of firing neurons and nothing more. This
could also be the result of scientists
focusing only upon those elements
of reality that may be measured and
described by their tools and within their conceptual frameworks. In
fact, there are many other aspects
of self as experienced by individuals
in community and society which are
products and outcomes not revealed

by scientific tools or rationalized metrics and thus not a part of our
calculus—much less included within successful conclusions about what
is in the world.[6]

> "Alexis de Tocqueville described the emergence in the Europe
> of his day of 'men who, in the name of progress, seek to reduce
> man to a material being.' He says, 'They look for what is useful
> without concern for what is just; they seek science removed from
> faith and prosperity apart from virtue.' They style themselves
> 'champions of modern civilization.'"[7]

I believe I know such men—and some number of women as well,
though I consider them to be fewer in number—who might fall into this
description and mindset...

One outcome of the scientific rationalism that has gained considerable attention and popular celebration in this present day is that it
eventually leaves the self alone, alien in the world, with no depth of
connection, meaning or transcendence.

> "The reduction of all forms of reality to invisible particles in
> motion threatens to denude the world of its beautifully ordered

heterogeneity. The replacement of the soul with neurons firing in the brain threatens to rob our ordinary experience of its
meaning. The proud declaration of human freedom and auton-
omy, on which we base so much of our political and ethical
thinking, runs the risk of leaving us placeless and alone," wrote
the historian, David Roochnik.[8]

The assumption made by neuroscientists is that there is no basis for
spirituality independent of the physical self for, being materialists, they
begin with this understanding of the world: a belief in materialism. It
is not that neuroscientists and others have proved this to be the case,
merely that they assume it to be so and go on from there.[9] Over time, we
each must grapple with this challenge of understanding our process of
experiencing elements of the spiritual and transcendent within a material world. It is a process linked to our development as a species as well
as our personal impact evolution as individuals.

We can take something from those who have gone before. Recall,
there were numerous others, in addition to Charles Darwin and Alfred
Russell Wallace, who in the mid-1800s were exploring theories of evolution and development. As the author, Mark Summer, writes:

> "That other men did not arrive at the same conclusion shows only
> how hard simple things can be. Natural selection looks sim-
> ple, and is simple, but out of that simplicity endless complexity
> can be generated. Looking at the world, most scientists (and
> non-scientists) saw only the complexity. The living world was so
> massive, so intricately interwoven, and so complex, that people
> looked for massive, intricate, complex answers. The real insight
> that Darwin and Wallace shared was that complexity could
> spring from simplicity. There was no need to go looking for a
> complex solution."[10]

The implication of this insight for us? When it comes to our journey to understand the purpose of capital and how best to deploy capital
through whichever means we're considering, we incline to make what

is simple, complex. Whether in an investment committee meeting, on a conference panel or at home with our partners, we should step back from our various mental, mathematical, and financial gymnastics to re-engage with the simplicity of our task and opportunity.

If we attain greater clarity in terms of how we approach the purpose of capital, we may be able to trace a process that begins with a vision of value which embraces material and extra-material elements of value creation. Then, secondly, we can design a strategy for integrating each with the other and, third, move to execute upon such an approach to realize a grand vision of blended value creation.

Along these lines, it is interesting to note that contrary to the perspective of some, Charles Darwin's concept of natural selection[11] did not impose a sense of "rightness" or order upon the world. He described a process in which we are all engaged as individuals, ecosystems, and societies across the planet. It is that simple; although this does not mean it to be quite that easy.

> "Darwin's discovery that all forms of life have descended
> from a common ancestor by a long process of modification
> over billions of years introduced a radical shift in biological
> thought—a change of perspective from being to becoming...
> by realizing that all living organisms are related by common
> ancestry, the Darwinian conception of life was utterly holistic
> and systemic: a vast planetary network of living beings inter-
> linked in time and space," says Fritjof Capra.[12]

As we reflect upon the implications of this process for each of us as changemakers in the world, we might consider adopting a systems change approach enabling us to evolve as individuals as we simultaneously promote change up and throughout the global and planetary system of which we are each a part. Accordingly, at the level of systems change, (which includes embedded personal change) there is a four-stage process wherein actors:

- Build a foundation for change and affirm readiness to engage in a change process.

- Clarify various levels of what the current reality is and one's respective responsibility for creating that reality.
- Explicitly choose to engage in the proposed change process.
- Begin to bridge the gap between what is and what can be by focusing on high leverage interventions, reaching out to additional actors and learning from ongoing experience.[13]

These four stages of systems change are fundamental; yet, as we engage in this personal journey of inquiry, each of us is also faced with the prospect of double exile in that as we are continually advancing what could be within a world of what 'is,' we will never become completely a part of any single community locally, nationally, religiously or professionally. One runs the risk of never being quite or fully comfortable in one's own skin for one is continually molting. By undertaking a path of questioning and inquiry one may at times assume a unique vantage point on society and life, but it is often a place only a single person may occupy at a time. The peak of the mountain we each seek to climb has a rock upon which we may sit, but no bench.

There are no doubt countless examples of this throughout history. In the case of the philosopher Baruch Spinoza, the price he paid for his commitment to the pursuit of his ideas was excommunication from his synagogue and banishment from his religious community, as well as rejection by many of those who would otherwise have been his intellectual and academic colleagues and social peers.[14] While it is no doubt overly dramatic to say so, in some ways this is the life of the truly committed social entrepreneur and impact investor. Our community of practice has thrived in recent years. While this is mostly a result of our creating a sub-culture of support that many of us have sustained while engaging the world, we must do so from a perspective that critiques the mainstream practices of modern business and financial capitalism. We must reject the community of which we seek to become a part. And while we may be one of many voices, ultimately I believe we do so on our own.

Alone.

As the historian Matthew Stewart has said,

"Some philosophers merely argue their philosophies. When they finish their disputations, they hang up the tools of their trade, go home and indulge in the well-earned pleasures of private life. Other philosophers live their philosophies. They treat as useless any philosophy that does not determine the manner in which they spend their days, and they consider pointless any part of life that has no philosophy in it. They never go home."[15]

I know many social entrepreneurs and impact investors choose the path of hanging up their tools at day's end. But the best ones never lose their passion and are continually striving for personal evolution and development by embracing new ideas, applying them and then abandoning them in favor of some greater insight or perspective gained from having stood in that place. These innovators experience how the *concept* of impact moves into the *reality* of impact implementation—and is ultimately found to be wanting. This inspires them to build upon that experience and advance into the future with yet one more new concept or idea to test, to bring from ideated conception into birth of material flesh. This more profound understanding of impact moves from ideal to material reality because of the quality of the vision of the impact innovator since it is a given that our practice is limited to the present as opposed to future expectations.

By extension, impact investors, while deploying capital and causing things to move in the world in real ways, must first and foremost be idealists rooted not in our present understanding of deals and funds and investment instruments, but rather being pulled irresistibly into a future we have yet to create and capital investment opportunities not yet formally realized. With this understanding of capital's extra-financial possibilities and expanded purpose, well beyond that of traditional capital finance and investing, many of the whines of some who might fancy themselves to be impact investors but discover the measureable, short-term outcomes challenging to realize much less capture in their portfolios, find their cries weakly fade into the wind, drifting off on clouds of unrealized potential for them and those communities and individuals for whom they profess concern. These are impact investors focused upon making themselves successful as opposed to of significance and deeper value.

In this way, the process of embedding purpose within one's life is not one of finding the right answer and promoting it as much as discerning better questions and exploring them. The best investors and entrepreneurs never achieve a goal of being successful actors in our space since the best understand themselves as always within a process of becoming. Ramana Maharishi said that just as you use one thorn to remove another lodged thorn, you use one concept to remove another idea, after which both are discarded.[16] Similarly, all this investigation helps you realize you're nothing if conceptual. You see this absolute experience when you're in total emptiness, and there's no second—no Plan B.

> "The expectation that we could or should be solid sets up a mistaken frame of reference that seems constantly under attack. So in the Buddhist context, knowing 'who you are' means knowing the mind is more like a whole theater than one character in a play."[17] (Layth Matthews)

> "Without your layers of decoration you are a person who is completely transparent…you cannot say who you are, because there is nothing there; no concept of you…When there is no concept of you…there is just transiency, just time. So you are not you, you are time. That is all! You may be surprised or upset. But if you just watch yourself with a calm mind, you can see the truth that everything changes moment after moment. At that time, you can realize yourself as a human being who exists in the domain of impermanence, attain enlightenment, and save yourself from suffering."[18] (Dainin Katagiri)

As impact investors, we must seek to be present in that moment of discovery, innovation, and evolution, not relying on any 'second' upon which we might rest, as we're then open to the new, to the uncharted, to what we see within that emptiness of experience. As our truth is evolving, our ability to understand truth is a function of our capacity to hold multiple shards of Burton's broken mirror, to grasp a crystal that is refracting diverse colors of a broad truth spectrum across the ground where we see them in their radiant fullness before us, or redirect our personal light spectrum up into the sky where it is itself captured in a rainbow spray of mist, becoming visible to others across the land.

It is only in such brief moments our capital, our sense of purpose, and the actions of our lives all become unified and aligned. In that minuscule moment,[19] we stand, spread out and in fullness, tentatively holding it all together—our understanding, the form into which we have shaped our capital, the flow between who we are, how we deploy our energies, and how our selves and our resources are received in the world. In this moment we come to manifest everything all at once, becoming only at that point the full, blended value we seek to bring to the world, promote into the future with our diverse forms of investment and *be* in that single, unique point of presence in community which then itself fades as we move on to the next exploration in our journey.

FREEDOM FROM ANSWERS, ENGAGEMENT WITH KEY QUESTIONS

One of the many challenges of the mainstreaming of sustainability and impact investing is that after what we assume to be some number of years spent reflecting upon the nature and purpose of capital, we are presumed to have thought enough about the topic and are now positioned to focus on solutions; moving from the why to how. And, yes, growing numbers of us sincerely believe we know how. Shareholders give fund managers the duty of directing capital into one opportunity versus another; as asset owners, it is presumed with a bit of training and guidance, we will make the appropriate decisions regarding the management of our wealth, and as thought leaders we're expected to consistently offer compelling commentary of profound insight and deep meaning. However, within our field, this has resulted in high expectations all the way around. God forbid a wealth advisor does not have the correct answer to a question for fear they look incompetent in front of a client!

This has led to a high degree of explaining within the impact investing advisory community wherein clients pay advisors to offer them solutions to the challenge of how best to invest capital for more than financial performance alone. When it comes to traditional approaches to financial advisory relationships, this practice of presuming knowledge is widely understood. In fact, it could be argued that many of those who lost funds during the 2008 downturn did so at least in part as a result of trusting the unquestioned, perceived financial understanding of their advisors.

In the context of investing capital for more than financial gain, this practice of reliance upon experts is especially challenging—and potentially damaging—since it presumes an understanding of why one is engaging in this pursuit. This rapidly shifts the discussion from an exploration of the why to one of how. I have played a role in this having co-authored/edited something on the order of seven books regarding what social entrepreneurship and impact investing are and how to do it, with this being my first book-length effort to engage with the more challenging question of why.

A central issue for many of us in impact investing is that we are operating within an assumption we've answered the question, *Why?*, only to find during executing upon the how that we, in fact, do not have an adequate grounding in the why to answer the how. To be truly successful, we must embrace a more cosmopolitan approach to the purpose of capital, for "A genuinely cosmopolitan response begins with caring to try to understand *why*...Cosmopolitanism is about intelligence and curiosity as well as engagement...It involves seeing not just a suffering body, but a wasted life."[20] Within impact investing, the body is the how—the life is the why.

As we grapple with the limitations of our present focus on how to do impact investing, we may look outward, blaming a lack of investible opportunity, poor metrics, "bad deals done by good people," impact investors who are all talk and no dough, and a host of other factors that relieve us from having to turn the camera on ourselves for our ultimate selfie opportunity, capturing a shot of our own shallow understanding of what it is we are actually attempting to do—our fundamental understanding of purpose—and the strategies we are attempting to bring to market, nay, to the world through our life's work.

When asked to compute the answer to the Ultimate Question of Life, the Universe and Everything, Deep Thought, the computer in Hitchhiker's Guide to the Galaxy (after calculating for 7.5 million years) states that the answer is "forty-two." And in response to the disappointment generated by this answer, Deep Thought then goes on to observe that, "The problem, to be quite honest with you, is that you've never actually known what the question is."[21]

Those who are attracted to the practice of impact investing are by nature smart individuals drawn to the notion that investing should be about more than simply increasing one's wealth but should also include consideration of various other social and environmental aspects of capital investment, return and portfolio performance.[22] However, of late, our field has become lazy. The question of why we are investing with this intent is rapidly answered with an interchangeable set of seemingly self-evident answers:

- To minimize negative impacts while creating positive impacts;
- To do well and good;
- To align money and mission;
- To respond to climate change;
- To advance a positive response to social/environmental challenges.

These are not, in and of themselves, wrong answers. But they are light responses to what are fundamentally deep and profound questions of personal meaning and purpose. They are responses to the "why question" offered with a lower-case "w." They require no further reflection or consideration. They are the easy, responses one would expect from a first round level of conversation on the topic at a cocktail party. They require no shift on our part or fundamentally new thinking, informed critique of current practices within financial capitalism or change in our behavior, nor do they require we reconsider our assumptions or understandings concerning the meaning of money, the true purpose of capital or the larger implications and real impacts of our investment practices. Such facile responses to the question of "Why?" allow us to drop off the hook of accountability, slightly modifying our investment practices and capital allocation assumptions so we may think all the better of our selves and sleep more soundly, knowing our capital is not creeping around in the dark of night, contributing to a world of moral and environmental decay, but is proudly parading in the light of day, bringing good things to good people—including bringing good, clean profits to our own good selves.

By rushing from the why to the how we allow ourselves to fall victim to a light definition and understanding of meaning, intent, and purpose. Such light responses to serious questions enable us to operate in an ahistorical context of capital, ignoring its pernicious potentials and confusing the good intent of our advisors, fund managers and our selves with the actual generation of sustained, relevant and transformative impact.

And one should never confuse intent with impact.

Some would argue all this is allowable and that by learning through doing, by getting to the why by executing more directly on the how, asset owners and the field at large may then bring more profound meaning and appreciation to the work and its challenges, as well as eventually discern the more profound aspects of why. While a commitment to conscious praxis—the process of engaging in debate, moving from practice to more informed thought to then better method—should indeed be our goal, overall, we are not asking ourselves or holding our field accountable for pursuing the hard questions and exploring the tough answers.[23]

As a practice, our approach is not adequate to the task before us. Such a justification of light inquiry and reliance upon the straightforward explanations and rhetoric of our advisors and our positive self-talk prevents us from leaving the shallows of the lower case why to dive into the deep end questions of an upper case Why? Such an approach allows us to quickly validate our initial assumptions, ideas, and practices, to affirm who we already are and to think (just as we are in the eyes of our mothers!) that we are all quite fine and unique—especially now that we are attempting to do both good and well. It appears some of us are at risk of drowning in the shallow end having not adequately trained for the deeper end we each intuitively seek.

THE IMPACT PARADOX

There is a central challenge in this effort to "do well and do good" in that at its core is a commitment to making use of the very financial tools that have failed to create a just, equitable and sustainable world in the pursuit of creating a more just, equitable and sustainable world. As impact investing continues to go mainstream, we now see a plethora of traditional investment strategies, tools and practices applied with ever greater complexity in the name of impact and a decreasing amount of innovation in how capital is structured to transfer the actual power of money to the objects of our influence. Over generations, we have come to embrace a notion that the engineer, the technician, the expert at navigating financial analysis and handling an investment tool knows best what the purpose of that tool is. In truth, tools are merely means to ends and nothing more. Unless we are clear on the ultimate use and goal of the instrument, its capable, even artistic, manipulation will still not create the end we seek. And so we are presented with the first of many paradoxes to be explored in the following pages:

1. What is the process by which we will rise above our limited vision of finance while at the same time draw upon its utility to help build the world we seek?
2. What must we do to operate as effective socio-financial engineers in our world and life while remaining grounded in the broader vision of what we long to create?
3. And, as Christians used to say, what is the path to our remaining in and yet not of this world as we serve witness to a society we are creating, to a world yet to come?

If we are indeed to transform capital markets, if we are to make them not slightly more just but significant vehicles for the advancement of economic justice, social change, and a verdant planet, then we need to go more in-depth into an inquiry not only of our perspectives on the purpose of capital. We must agree how we, as a post-modern culture, have evolved our understanding of capital—understanding where it came from to then better understand where it needs to go. And we must realize the very system of financial capitalism that created the problems we seek to address may not be easily modified on the edges merely to accommodate our conscience, but must be reassessed at a fundamentally more profound level.

Albert Einstein may mistakenly have been reported as saying,

If I had an hour to solve a problem and my life depended on the solution,
I would spend the first 55 minutes
determining the proper question to ask,
for once I know the proper question,
I could solve the problem in less than five minutes.[24]

Regardless of whether the words are his, the implication is clear:

Present deliberations and discussions at impact investing events, advisory and investment committee meetings, strategic philanthropy forum and so on, all tend to focus 55 minutes upon proposed solutions and promoting funds and deals while allowing only 5 minutes for reflections of more ontological, existential or theological/philosophical topics. And then, to our great frustration, we are offered the answer to our question of the purpose of capital only to be disappointed to learn the answer is "forty-two" and poverty remains, the planet continues in decline, and our children's future grows yet ever dim. But we can at least feel okay about our investing practices since we've done what we thought we could and may then call ourselves impact investors or responsible investors or investors in sustainable business practices. Our task, as traditionally understood, is completed, our defining label embraced. We may now rest.

I would submit our better, more profound answers will evolve as we cultivate a more contemplative and informed understanding of the questions.

As we look to explore new ideas and approaches to not only how best to structure capital to generate multiple returns but also enunciate this more in-depth understanding of Why we should do so, it is critically important we not prematurely lock in on early answers, inhibiting our potential for future evolution and development of both conceptual and practical approaches to our work. Our urge to define, measure, and comprehend in terms the mainstream will accept is understandable, yet it is only over recent decades we have begun to be formally organized as a unified practice at any real scale. While many in our field still grapple with the fundamentals, our work is rooted in many centuries past and has the potential to set a course for centuries to come. We must not risk prematurely closing the gates on our fortress of knowledge, much less practice, when we at this stage only barely comprehend the more celebrated traditions, experience and historical structures of which we are a part. While we may indeed have some level of knowledge, we lack in wisdom.

We have been here before.

During the first Millennium, in the early years of what was to be a Golden Age of inquiry under Muslim rule, Christian Europe "withered in the gloom, crippled by a lack of resources and a dearth of curiosity. St. Augustine had been positively hostile to the concept of investigation and research. 'Men want to know for sake of knowing,' he wrote scornfully, 'though the knowledge is of no value to them.'"[25]

We have modern equivalents. While many experts are publishing a surge of writing and research taking place within the broad areas of impact investing, strategic philanthropy, social innovation, entrepreneurship and a host of related topics, much of that work focuses upon refining and drilling into concepts and practices which firmly rest within what we have already come to define as our reality. And some of those promoting new impact investment solutions function within an even more limited understanding of our context. We operate within the boundaries of the current realms of nonprofit, for-profit, economics, investing and finance, and public policy as presently defined. The mainstream framing of "what is" threatens to direct our vision downward, toward what is immediately before us as opposed to up and beyond our present position of possibly positive development. As we focus on our various parts, we do not see the larger whole or our more significant potential to transform organizations, systems, and selves on a grand scale; much to our loss.

Before we lock in on any supposedly innovative and new under-standings of capital and community—much less, before we accept for a new generation the standard definitions of financial and other realities we buy from merchant bankers, fund managers, institutional invest-ment advisors and others—we need look up and move to stand astride the not so distant horizon if we are to envision what we are, at our core, called to create.

And then we must move beyond that horizon, leaving our peers, advisors, and experts behind.

To begin moving forward on that journey, we must understand more of our past and what brought us here. The exact origin of the why/how split is millennia old yet has its most recent roots in the devel-opment of relatively modern scientific inquiry. The Czech Economist Tomas Sedlacek observes that modernism is defined by embracing the how of life, not the why:

> "The era of scientific thought set a goal of pushing through a method of examining the world that would not allow doubt and would be free of any subjective, disputable dimension. Perhaps the most important character of the modern era has been the change in emphasis from the question why? To the question how? This shift is from essence to method. The scientific era has tried to demystify the world around us, to present it in mechan-ical, mathematical, deterministic and rational garments and to get rid of axioms that cannot be empirically confirmed, such as faith and religion."[26]

This question of how versus why is deeply rooted in our core expe-rience of Western knowledge and our supposed Age of Enlighten-ment and has been the basis of debate and discussion for centuries. For example, oddly foreshadowing developments within impact investing, in 1648, Rene Descartes argued the focus of debate within philoso-phy should not be upon more in-depth inquiry regarding metaphysical questions (the why) but instead should focus upon "physical and observable things" (the how). It is amusing to note that part of his rationale for this position was that he felt he had already addressed all there was to consider regarding the why and so everyone should now move on to focus on the how![27]

Later, Kant divided the philosophical schools into two opposing camps: the "empiricists" and the "noologists" (from the Greek word for intellect). Thus even today we have the empiricists and the rationalists, those who operate from a place of experience and observed reality as opposed to those working from a position of what is thought to be pure reason.[28]

Our current popular focus upon evidenced-based strategies and what we often take as objective financial truth in contrast with social or natural, supposedly subjective truth has its roots in our having embraced materialism and a form of reductionist, scientific rationalism as the dominant meme within our modern culture. This focus inhibits our understanding of truths outside what we already know—and, within economics, allows us to think there is such a thing as "externalities" simply because there are factors which lie outside our calculus but not outside a greater reality we cannot quantify. Materialism operates within an inverse logic model that states that "we must shun non-materialist explanations of human nature because they cannot possibly be right" since they cannot be proved within a materialist conceptual or experimental framework.[29] And by extension, as the neuroscientists Mario Beauregard and Denyse O'Leary wrote:

> "...even if materialist science does not offer satisfactory explanation now, we must stick with its unsatisfactory insights, in the hope that better ones will arrive someday. Philosopher of science Karl Popper has called this line of thinking 'promissory materialism.' In other words, if we adopt it, we are accepting a promissory note on the future of materialism. Promissory materialism has been immensely influential in the sciences because any doubt about materialism—no matter what the state of evidence—can be labeled 'unscientific' in principle."[30]

Our current challenge is rooted in the reality that the Enlighten-ment philosophers and scientists, "burned down the house instead of remodeling it." In their rejection of the answers of institutionalized religion, they threw out and denied many of the fundamental ques-tions that remained following the great Enlightenment, which then became its own new form of scientific High Church. As explorations turned from science to finance to morality, we then continued to create and operate within a positivist, reductionist framework that left huge swaths of reality, question and purpose unaddressed and alone in the shadows cast off from the bright light of our ambition and arrogance. The American poet, Gary Snyder, speaks to this point and suggests a direction for us when he writes that:

"Words are used as signs, as stand-ins, arbitrary and temporary, even as language reflects (and informs) the shifting values of the peoples whose minds it inhabits and glides through. We have faith in 'meaning' the way we might believe in wolverines—put-ting trust in the occasional reports of others or on the authority of once seeing a pelt. But it is sometimes worth tracking these tricksters back."[31]

One of these aspects of the trickster is the notion that humankind is and will always be driven by a standard, defining set of motivations. As Will and Ariel Durant observe,

> "Since we have admitted no substantial change in man's nature during historic times, all technological advances will have to be written off as merely new means of achieving old ends— the acquisition of goods, the pursuit of one sex by the other (or by the same), the overcoming of competition, the fighting of wars. One of the discouraging discoveries of our disillusioned century is that science is neutral: it will kill for us as readily as it will heal and will destroy for us more readily than it can build. How inadequate now seems the proud motto of Francis Bacon, 'Knowledge is power'! Sometimes we feel that the Middle Ages and the Renaissance, which stressed mythology and art rather than science and power, may have been wiser than we, who repeatedly enlarge our instrumentalities without improving our purposes."[32]

This is why, as we reflect on the future of capitalism, innovations in sustainable finance and potentialities of scaling impact investing, we need be clear concerning our own purpose, intent, and commitments. As we mainstream impact investing and seek to bring trillions of dollars of investment capital structured to advance positive futures we need to pause and reflect upon our actual direction, the fundamental meaning advanced over the course of our lives and the broader, transformative purpose of the capital we seek to deploy.

Descartes' setting aside mind from matter allowed him to focus upon the material[33] and what he understood to be the mechanical aspects of how the world functioned—without his then having to "clutter" his thinking with questions of deeper meaning and purpose. Similarly, our focus upon the mechanics of how to do philanthropy, impact investing, and sustainable finance allows us to, on the one hand, reduce and define our work to that of strategy and tactics, by maintaining an exclusive focus upon how we act in the world while, on the other hand, removing ourselves from the task of profound reflection and under-standing of *why* we operate in the world.

In the absence of this deeper grounding in purpose, meaning, and intent, we will grow impact investing by leaps and bounds while stand-ing at risk of reflecting the sentiments of this recently seen bumper sticker: *I'm lost, but boy am I making great time!*

In many ways, our focus within impact investing, upon the "how" of making an impact versus the "why" of our engagement in impact, is like the notion of operating within the letter, but not the spirit of the law. This idea plays out on both secular and religious levels. From within the Judaic tradition, with its guidance taken from the Torah and various passages of religious law and practice, Ira Stone states the following:

> "This emphasis on law, while a crucial factor in the survival of Judaism and part of its genius, is equally responsible for one of its oft-recurring flaws: the narrowing of focus from the purpose of the law to the means of achieving that purpose. At times, the study and practice of law (especially ritual law) has proceeded without regard to the perfection of the individual and without regard for the centrality of ethics. This tendency has been pres-ent in every age of the Jewish people: from the biblical prophets, railing against the legalistic belief that rote sacrifices devoid of proper ethical devotion could move God, to the Talmudic dictum that one must strive to do more than the law requires in interpersonal situations...".[34]

And, of course, the same is true of each of the major religions:

> "Most religions stay at this level of Leviticus and Numbers reli-gion, a first half of life religion. It is a good belonging system with clear boundaries and identity. It takes away most self-doubt, and thus people are often quite happy at this stage, if they can succeed at it. It is a largely patriarchal, authoritative, top-down religion...they become so invested in doing the task of Law and

maintaining social and personal order that they think that is what religion is for!"[35] the theologian Richard Rohr says.

Rohr also describes E.F. Schumacher's (as presented in Schumacher's book with perhaps my favorite title of all time: *A Guide for the Perplexed*; interestingly enough, a title he lifted from Moses Maimonides who wrote a book by the same title—if not with the same intent—in the 12th Century!) notion that religion moves through three levels of development: legal to prophetic voice to wisdom. The stage of wisdom is grounded in paradox (in our context, the notion of doing well and doing good and our assumption these are somehow two separate things) as well as grappling with the larger mystery (purpose, why, ultimate meaning), while the first stage demands total light (i.e. the answer to here's the metrics, here's the how one needs to operate, here is the definition of impact) as opposed to living in the dusk of partial light or even total darkness where one must take revelation on faith, along the lines of that old saying, "I don't believe there is a God, I know there is a God." This requires us to "dance between the inner and outer authority, reaching a new unified field that can include both light and darkness."[36] In this way, we should perhaps focus less upon the emerging laws of impact investing than upon our goal of optimizing the total, blended value potential of our lives and capital resources, broadly considered.

While the focus of much of the impact investing world is upon the how of execution, strategy, and tactics, we overly focus on these points to our peril. If we lose sight of the core and fundamental drivers of the value we claim to be committed to creating, we lose grip of the very reasons we are called to deploy capital not in the manner of traditional, financial capitalism, but in the greater interest of community and planet, in addition to our natural self-interests.

As Baruch Spinoza observed so well, "The mass of men believes they are free on this account only, that they are conscious of their actions and ignorant of the causes by which they are determined."[37] The deeper we delve in our efforts to create the perfect fund and investment strategy and the greater focus we place upon defining success as a function of fund size, the more likely we are to drift from our core motivations and values. Our ability to raise ever higher amounts of capital under the Impact Brand is not in question; our capacity to catalyze sustained, transformative change in our consciousness and awareness of self and Other whereby we then may become participants in social liberation and fundamental global change, is.

What is missing from the exploration of impact investing (much less from traditional, mainstream investment practice) is the power of the vision and myth within which our work and lives unfold. We have become obsessed with the how and the quantifiable elements of the practice—the metrics, the definitions, the financial returns—and in so doing have missed out upon the broader, truly more powerful aspects of the call to create impact through our capital and, most importantly, over the course of the trajectory of our lives. We must rediscover the mythology of impact, the power of the hypothesis we seek to bring to life using ritual, action, contemplation of its effect upon our lives and the pursuit of insights into the difficult puzzle of our world.[38] As Rohr said, "If we did not enter deeply the early learning process of 'how,' we will use our actions to defend ourselves, protect ourselves from our shadow, and build a leaden manhole cover over our unconscious. We will settle for being right instead of being holy and whole, for saying prayers instead of being one."[39]

IMPLICATIONS OF OUR TRUE PURSUIT OF IMPACT

These are admittedly dangerous waters. What I am calling for is that we inject our discussions of how best to structure capital with critique and dialogue regarding religious, moral and ethical concepts and the broader, political and social implications of same. Our philosophy of impact may be a "big tent" but it must be a big tent supporting the poles of countless small tents. We need to stay pointed in the same direction toward a more transcendent goal that grounds our commitment and passion for justice, equity (not in the financial sense of the word!) and commonly shared values and communitarian beliefs. The American political philosopher, Michael Sandel, directly addresses our need to go deeper in the public sphere of morality when he states,

"Some see in our rancorous politics a surfeit of moral conviction: too many people believe too deeply, too stridently, in
their convictions and want to impose them on everyone else.
I think this misreads our predicament. The problem with our
politics is not too much moral argument but too little. Our
politics is overheated because it is mostly vacant, empty of
moral and spiritual content. It fails to engage with big questions that people care about."[40]

One might say the same regarding much of the present discourse
on impact investing and modern financial capitalism. And so we must
reject the old German adage that "Money is not what one talks about;
money is what one has,"[41] in favor of raising what are for many asset
owners uncomfortable questions and considerations. To neglect to do so
consigns us, at best, to a dystopian future and, at worst, to the coming
extinction of both culture and species. But before we attempt to do so,
to move back from how to why, we need to recognize we must engage
not in a pivot, but a process of historically based reflection, group learning combined with more profound, personal contemplation. Moving
from the how to the why is in many ways a function of moving from
being smart regarding how we manage and invest capital to being wise
about the fundamental and long-term *purpose* of capital.

In the mid-1990s, elders of responsible investing would convene
annually in Mexico for a retreat to reflect upon issues of money, meaning, and purpose, so they were not the first, but in 2007, The Aspen
Institute hosted a retreat for a group of ultra-high net worth individuals under the theme of exploring an understanding of the purpose of
capital. Each person was asked to reflect on that question and engage
in dialogue with other asset owners regarding their knowledge of the
purpose of capital. While the setting was cool, the discussions were
hot with participants discovering as they stepped back to reflect on
the topic, each was hugely conflicted in his or her own appreciation
of how best to define the purpose of capital. They found that while
many might commit to such notions as doing "well and good" they
were not able to resolve more complex, deeper differences in meaning,

purpose and intent. Indeed, these are tricky conversations in that they are grounded in our shared, cultural experience of economics, ethics and wealth while at the same time being highly customized concepts that in many ways define who we are as individuals and how we value our sense of self-worth.

And so we must recognize that moving from "How" back to "Why" is not simply the topic of a retreat or a book well read. It is not a pivot in a new direction but rather a new direction itself that requires individual self-assessment and group exploration—but such a group process is worthless unless founded upon personal commitments to humility, doubt, questioning, learning, reflection, and inquiry. Exploring and embracing a deeper understanding of the Why is, for each of us, a deeply personal process, being an inner journey as much as one in which we engage with others.

By focusing on what others are thinking and doing—how they may understand their sense of the Why—we risk redirecting our energies from our quest to that of what fits with the pursuit of others (whether defined as clients, customers, advisors, our networks or Society itself). Indeed for those committed to working to bring about greater good within society and our world, it is easy to lose focus on our challenges and inquiry; it is easy to begin to pass judgment on others—their path, their understanding and their answers to the question of Why. While certainly challenging for me (as one known to speak his mind and regularly pass judgment on others!), perhaps we should heed the words of Menachem Mendel of Kozk who said, "Be concerned about your own soul and your neighbor's body, but not about your own body and another's soul."[42] We need to understand that moving back to Why is our own, individual yet socially embedded process. One may undoubtedly think of this as a Personal Journey, The Hero's Journey, or, as in Paulo Coelho, the creation of one's Personal Legend.[43]

JOURNEY AS BOTH PATH AND PRESENCE

The journey in which we engage is one of both past and present—or as we might also say—of Path and Presence. If we are to participate in explorations of the why and defining our understanding of the purpose of capital, we must recognize the path we move along is one of our current understanding as well as the end result of history and reflections on it. We are the product of not merely our personal experiences but our collective and shared experience, a product of our being fully who we are, who we are becoming and who we have been thus far on our shared, historic quest. Therefore, to be truly present on this ever so important journey, we must consider a host of factors.

First, perhaps what is our path is not a path shared with others. Gary Snyder writes:

"A path is something that can be followed, it takes you somewhere. 'Linear.' What would a path stand against? 'No path.' Off the path, off the trail. So what's off the path? In a sense everything else is off the path. The relentless complexity of the world is off to the side of the trail. For hunters and herders trails weren't always so useful. For a forager, the path is not where you walk for long. Wild herbs, camas bulbs, quail, dye plants, are away from the path. The whole range of items that fulfill our needs is out there. We must wander through it to learn and memorize the field—rolling, crinkled, eroded, gullied, ridged (wrinkled like the brain) holding the map in mind…For the forager, the beaten path shows nothing new, and one may come home empty-handed."[44]

Snyder's words reminded me of a time, some years ago, when I moved off the path, off into the deeper forest…Down the dirt road from our home in the Colorado Rockies is the trailhead of the Roaring Fork drainage, a sharp slash in a ridge of mountains connecting the Indian Peaks Wilderness with the area we call Rocky Mountain National Park. I don't know what the Northern Utes called this area before the mass genocides and being shipped off to a stark, barren reservation in what we now call Utah. As I understand it, a remnant of the Mountain Utes held onto a parcel of land in Southern Colorado which is still theirs, but in our parts the only Indian that remains sits forlorn and downcast as part of a motel sign in the next town over, Hot Sulphur Springs.

Back down our road, the trail heads up and up from Lake Granby, climbing along the creek that comes crashing down from over eleven thousand to eighty five hundred feet. This was the Ute's summer hunting range and I imagine this track was once theirs as well, though called by a different name I'm sure.

Moving up the trail, through the woods and on the path, after a time, one comes to a fork and must choose to head North to a mountain lake or South up to a ridgeline and continuing trail that takes you to another, Stone Lake. On one occasion, done with those choices, I opted to simply follow the flow of the creek and seek the source of the Roaring Fork, up above the trails, out of sight's way. I found myself cutting across small, grassy openings in the woods, following faint animal trails and breaking through the occasional stand of brush blocking the way, but not the direction.

The lack of trail and steady climb forced me into a slow, deliberate meander. Walking step-by-step, crunching upon groundcover dry from lack of rain, my foot froze in mid-air—Shit!! What?!!—I lurched left and came crashing down to the ground, wind knocked out of me, head turned right, eyes focusing on the object that had caused my radical turn—a roosting, dusky brown Blue Grouse. She sat, still as the rocks beside her, nestled into the earth, staring up at the one who had almost Vibram stomped her as she sat on her eggs, refusing to vacate. There we were, eyes locked, mine in wonder, hers with a calm peace, taking me in, waiting until I crawled away, slowly standing, moving on up the hillside.

And then, not minutes later, coming along the ever-narrowing yet still raging water, I glanced across to see—not five yards away, but across the creek—a full, mighty buck. Again, our eyes locked, him standing his ground and me withdrawing, pulling back into the brush and branches. Both encounters left me to mull over this world I had moved into where animals live, fully present and aware while I'm the intruder, stumbling along in search of place and presence, finding my way off the path but on my way.

For those who seek to move off the path, a second consideration one must have is that the journey on your path may not be a continuous path from before. When you step off the path you've been on, you may find a need to pause, to regroup, not to simply roll from conference to conference in quest of meaning and purpose, but rather to find space and place to shed what was and embrace what may be coming. "Every now and then the merry-go-round stops and there's a short break. The Tibetans call this interval between rides the bardo, after which you look for another vehicle."[45]

Third, as that old cliché goes, the journey to a deeper connection with Why is just that—a journey—and not a destination or place we find. This is a challenging notion for asset owners and financial advisors used to assessing their value and performance against short time increments of a few years, much less quarters or trading sessions. Understand the journey as an unfolding process of self-development, growth, and movement toward wholeness. The Norwegian Philosopher Arne Naess, who first coined the term and concepts of deep ecology, said:

> "The word in Norwegian is Selv-realisering: Self-realizing. It is an active condition, not a place one can reach. No one ever reaches Self-Realization, for complete Self-realization would require the realization of all. Just as no one in certain Buddhist traditions ever reaches nirvana, as the rest of the world must be pulled along to get there. It is only a process, a way to live one's life."[46]

Finally, there is the tension between who should lead and who may follow. Ralph Waldo Emerson said, *Do not go where the path may lead, instead go where there is no path and leave a trail.* This sounds nice enough, however, is this necessarily always the best path to pursue? First off, there is the whole concept of "Leave No Trace," which speaks to the notion that we should move on the Earth in the absence of damaging the Earth. Beyond that stands the reality that our path may *not* be one

others could or should take. The process in which we are engaged is ultimately our own, regardless of whether we are a forager or a person following the trail of others.

We must embrace the principle of setting to our work and moving along our path, with more humility and a broader vision wherein we recognize the ego and cultivation of our brand may not be the only things we should consider along our way. The field of impact investing and social enterprise is rife with those who celebrate the individual's vision, journey, and quest—and in this way, we have consecrated the social entrepreneur as deified individual instead of as part of a whole, dynamic social enterprise and impact eco-system.

We may be better served by breaking with that notion of personal, individual success and reconnecting with the idea that our success is a function of the success of—of being in service to—the Other. How about the idea of running up the path to help others find their way or running back down the path to help others along their journey? We must manage, chisel down, and balance our relentless focus upon the how, including any sense of righteousness in advancing our shared good works, to go more in-depth, deeper and further with higher significance in our pursuit of what I describe below as Mutual Impact.

IMPACT INVESTING AS A PROCESS
OF PURPOSE EXPLORED

Exploring the purpose of capital from the perspective of impact investing strategies comes naturally. Impact investing is rooted not merely in an 'objective' exploration of how capital is structured, how it moves in the world's markets and affects our planet's communities (both natural and human), but impact investing seeks to do more than make money. It brings us beyond the fundamentals of finance or economics to profound, more complex questions of meaning, intent and, yes, purpose.

Impact investing bridges various perspectives on how money itself operates in the world and how it *should* operate, functioning to advance both enterprise and justice. Impact investing flows from privately controlled capital to public funding streams and strategies, and on to philanthropy and charitable giving. It includes early stage crowd funding and individual donor campaigns. It is not simply invested, but *directed* capital seeking to be intentionally activated to explore various levels of financial performance with diverse forms of return while simultaneously addressing—and advancing solutions for—myriad social and environmental challenges.

Impact investing draws upon available capital and is best viewed at the portfolio level to see its potential for deploying capital across what is commonly viewed as the entire capital continuum, ranging from philanthropic to near-market and market-rate capital. The funds involved also work as a whole, through an interactive and mutually supporting portfolio of assets and value creation that we've known for decades may have positive multiplier impacts across asset classes, communities, and continents. In sum, it is not about activating across a capital continuum, per se, but enabling diverse components of a unified capital community within a larger eco-system market place to resonate and realize their full potential for value creation.

Impact investing includes the entire tool kit of sustainable, responsible, thematic, ESG integration and what has most recently been understood as impact investing in the form of direct investment of capital to create some level of intentional change in our world. The underlying rationale is that all capital carries within it the potential to generate forms of influence, redirection or alterations in the course of the lives of its recipients. Traditionally and in the mainstream, much of this impact influence is incidental or unintended, yet it occurs nevertheless to one degree or another, for good and for ill. Impact investing is the *intentional* deployment of resources across the entire capital continuum wrapped around itself, transcending the dualism of doing good and doing well as it embraces others in the pursuit of various levels of financial performance together with the generation of positive social and environmental value.

Impact investing is, first and foremost, an exploration of the purpose of capital. It is the tip of the fiscal spear in surfacing, defining and challenging 17th century concepts within which our 20th century understanding of financial capitalism and its most pernicious practices are rooted. It seeks to lay the foundation for the emergence of new 21st Century forms of economics and capitalism that shape-shift form under regenerative, stakeholder, fiduciary, blended finance and other banners but which are all part of the same parade of humanity and history. Impact investing is about re-defined, expanded fiduciary duty, active asset ownership, and moving money in new ways toward old yet renewed ends so we may all live more fully and in so doing have a positive impact on our world.

Impact investing is also about mindful money that integrates the power of presence with considered intentionality within capital flows throughout the world. It places resources within new structures, pumping life-affirming blood into new organizations and corporate forms. Impact investing is about pursuing an array of related strategies that promise to optimize *total* performance of financial returns *with* the generation of social and environmental impacts. It is integrated impact, not disconnected from life, but life promoting, life affirming and life creating capital. When understood at this level of purpose and meaning, those who continually question whether or how one may achieve "competitive" or "market rate" returns on impact capital are skating on the surface as opposed to delving into the greater possibilities of how we might optimize the total performance of capital in the fullest sense of the term.

But know that intentionality within impact investing is a tough concept to understand and execute well in that it frequently affirms the duality between one and Other, between have and have not, as opposed to assisting in linking, connecting and weaving our self with the Other. In that process, impact investing brings self and Other toward a new understanding and synthesis, of holism, in a world that is, itself, One.[47] Impact investing is about cultivating an awareness of how capital impacts our society and is an extension of our being, our values and our beliefs with regard to what is and should be.

Many debate the definition of impact, how it should be measured and what forms it takes, leaving others of us to wonder whether it is all worth the efforts made over past decades to explore and address just those questions; efforts now either ignored or forgotten. In philosophy, many argue terms such as 'truth' or 'reality' cannot be defined; yet such concepts are critical to our world. And within the area of science, there are aspects of our universe that remain beyond our understanding, yet we do not doubt the powers of science to describe the inexplicable. In this same way, concepts such as impact, social return on investment (SROI), or blended value may be hard to nail down, but remain central not only to our professional lives but to how we each personally experience the world and its vast realities.

Why should we care about any of this?

We need to explore the underlying frameworks of how we understand the purpose of capital because if we do not, we will find our world increasingly commoditized, monetized and assessed by financial metrics and economic understandings of value alone. With that comes the risk everything will be "up for sale" to the private sector and monied interests will continue to widen income inequality because it is convenient to their market goals. Therefore, in coming years we may move toward greater levels of moral and financial corruption,[48] witnessed domestically in the U.S. by the current administration, but also manifest in other governments, national and local, around the world. "Economists often assume that markets are inert, that they do not affect the goods they exchange. But this is untrue. Markets leave their mark," Michael Sandel has so accurately observed.[49]

Impact investing provides an opportunity to reestablish our understanding of the purpose of capital as being more than simply its efficient management and ongoing reproduction—capital's purpose as making more capital—and reconnect with a deeper understanding of how capital may be used to serve the needs of humanity and planet. Impact investing offers an opportunity for us to move from ignorant to intentional and Mutual Impact.

Impact investing is a sound entry point for our discussion of the purpose of capital in that it is a discovery of how we may best deploy our assets. Financial assets to be sure, but also intellectual assets, social assets, environmental assets, cultural assets and, yes, an even broader portfolio of assets existing beyond our present comprehension. This definition of assets stands outside the realm of current investment practice presently dominated by a mainstream, short term understanding of time, of returns assessed as strictly financial and, of course, our misplaced though popular comprehension of what constitutes value itself.

Impact investing is an exploration of the Other—discussed in detail below—in which one must be engaged if one is to be genuinely successful first in life and only later in the promotion of impact within and through capital markets. It is only in this pursuit and engagement with the Other that we will come to fully understand our Self and, by extension, the goals to which we should apply our resources—financial and personal.

Having only then done so, perhaps we may live up to the name we have bestowed upon our own species, in opposition to all others:

Homo Sapiens,
Which, as the historian Yuval Harari reminds us, means wise man.[50.]

CHAPTER TWO

ON IMPACT:

From Ignorant to Mutual

OUR TRADITIONAL UNDERSTANDING OF THE PURPOSE OF CAPITAL IS TO USE IT AS A TOOL BY WHICH WE HOPE TO INCREASE AND GROW ITS AMOUNT IN OUR PORTFOLIO.

Accordingly, in traditional investing forums we consider how best to generate financial alpha from our active capital investment/management strategies and focus upon tactics to grow our financial capital rather than engage with the extra-financial purpose of capital. As previously discussed, this focus on the financial How as opposed to the greater Why of capital threatens our potential for attaining the more significant and real-life goals of many a family member or fiduciary, much less goals of communities and societies of which we are all a part. This manuscript will address questions of purpose and self, but if we are to understand capital as being about more than money we must first explore our understanding of the use of capital as something higher than its own replication and potential to generate ever greater financial returns. We must examine our understanding of its impact.

IGNORANT IMPACT

When the term impact investing was first gaining traction within investment and philanthropic communities, those who had been advancing responsible and community investing for many years were modestly incensed and more than slightly dismissive. "All capital has an impact!" they would say, "We've been doing this for years...". And they were, of course, correct for all capital does have an impact and these pioneers had indeed spent years pursuing their understanding of positive impact through investment. What the early investor entrants into what is now the field of impact investing were attempting to say, however, was that they sought to draw as direct a line as possible between their investments and the generation of street level, meaningful, intentional impact. And to their mind, the options available to them seemed to lack a level of measureable and engaged impact.

Yes, all capital has impact—but for many, that goal seemed incidental to the management and deployment of their investments. It seemed to be impact generated as a by-product of investing—more a function of screens and values than the pursuit of defined value—even as those who promoted sustainable and responsible investing in those years knew and felt impact to be core to their practice. The reality is that for most investors job creation, tax payment and a broad sense of social value is as far as they go in understanding the impact of their investment practices, something to be trotted out every four years to chants of "Jobs, Not Welfare" and other self-satisfied sentiments. Such an approach might best be thought of as the "What's good for GM is good for America!" approach to impact investing. While good intentions are welcome, for many within mainstream investing, any positive impact of their investments was (and for most—even for many now claiming the mantel of impact—still is) secondary to the pursuit of wealth, profits, and personal gain.

When it comes to the generation of intentional, positive social and environmental impacts, it is our great misfortune we live in a world of flowing ignorance, punctuated by pinnacles of insight, which then fade into a fog of presumed knowledge and awareness before we devolve yet further to new levels of ignorance and begin the process anew. Despite our current rhetoric, we live in a world where most of the positive impact of our capital results as a function of this ignorance—not because of our deliberate and insightful strategy.

We know—and our leading thinkers, philosophers, and scientists have demonstrated in various ways—the difference between self and Other is an illusion. In this and every moment we are all connected. We are united in the simplest of ways as members of humanity, of community or society and our families; yet it is not only these factors but the ultimate nature of the physics of natural experience, of life force and death, which connect us. Despite that truth, we act as if we are individuals, separated, one from another, each on our own path, which is right in one sense yet not Truth in another. We operate throughout our daily lives, shielded behind this veil of ignorance and denial.

These realities make the pursuit of impact within our world challenging at best. We think we know and ultimately must act as if we do, yet in fact we do not—we cannot—for knowing and truth are each iterative, transitory states of experience. Our knowledge of truth stands in opposition to our ignorance, or we would stop knowing and fall short of understanding with any stated certainty, whether defined as static or dynamic. We must act, to do something, even as we know that what we do is not enough, correct or perhaps only situationally the "right thing." Despite all our efforts to be evidence-based, informed by objective analysis and act according to enunciated strategy, in the end, we operate in ignorance of our ultimate outcomes. We want to believe what we do matters, that we may be a positive presence in our world, but we cannot know the long-term impacts of our actions.

Is the life we save through our efforts

- The child lifted out of a war-torn region or decimated local community?
- The provider of a family in need who receives job training?
- The young woman whose game-changing venture receives funding?

Do we know that any of these is the life that will lead us all to a new path or experience that will add its light to the world?

Or is that life we save destined to evolve into a new leader of the alt-right, a latter-day voice of division or perhaps merely a passive supporter of our President's authoritarian tendencies?

We act with passion and conviction and believe what we do is right, correct and moving us collectively forward in the proper direction, yet most often we act with no meaningful consciousness of the lives and realities lived by those we profess to care about, those about whose lives we claim to be committed. Sometimes it is only after the fact when we look back and cringe, it is only after our actions that we can see how incredibly misguided we were—if we are lucky and that is all it was.

More often, we create a rationale for our actions to justify our lives and decisions made or not made. We tell ourselves it is all good in that even if our efforts fall short, we meant well and isn't that the point? As we walk the path of the road paved with our good intentions, isn't it enough that we made a good effort? We don't need to hear from the objects of our charity or track their long-term experience or hold ourselves accountable to them for higher standards of impact for whether intentional or incidental our impact efforts are sound in and of themselves, are they not? No need for humility or self-doubt, given the drive for positive impact is now our life's work. Yes, all is good—it says so in our impact reports, and we are told as much by those admiring seekers of our capital with whom we surround ourselves.

Let's get specific. Let's get personal.

I funded a start-up social enterprise over twenty-five years ago that never attained its potential to scale, yet provided the launching pad for a young man, just out of rehab, who then went on to create his own social venture which today not only operates on a hugely profitable basis but provides transitional employment to scores of others attempting to get back on a path of life and not death. This may be viewed as positive impact despite the marginal success of the enterprise that gave him his start and my own ignorance of his impact over the years.

However, thirty-five years ago I launched a nonprofit that has been very successful, providing meaningful exits from life on the streets to hundreds—at this point, no doubt thousands—of formerly homeless youth who now find their way to better, healthier lives. But it was also the program—*my* program—that failed at least one charismatic teen who then hung himself from a tree in his parents' front yard.

Who else did our efforts at impact fail? Who else died at least in part because of our various and many shortcomings? Do each of these impact outcomes balance themselves off in some grand chart of accounts? We are all ultimately ignorant in our efforts at attaining whatever levels of impact we seek. Yet often, we presume positive impact in the absence of our wanting to pursue knowledge to the contrary. And who could blame us, given this is our life's work, so ours must be a good life, a life well lived, a life of meaning and purpose we have created in the name of the oppressed Other?

While traditional investing and our modern system of financial capitalism are grounded within the perspective of the asset owner or fiduciary, at its core impact investing is not about looking from the inside out—from your own perspective, priorities and plans for your financial goals and objectives, and then to the time worn and predictable investment strategies, tactics and practices you used to believe in. Impact investing is about stepping beyond what you today believe to be true of your world and our society to embrace a holistic, historically aware, catholic, catalytic perspective of our *future* life and its meaning. By extension, we seek to implement new investment practices for asset management and capital deployment with intent that is more transcendent than quarterly, more hopefully transformative than predictable in sets of cash flow projections or SROI spreadsheets.

Impact investing is about the future potential for change in the world, in community, in capital and, finally—if you are lucky—in you.

Impact investing is an entry point to an exploration of the purpose of capital because it begins with our understanding that how we presently think about capital's place and purpose in our world is not adequate nor enough to confront the challenges before us, as a planet and as a people. Impact investing is not simply about aligning one's capital with one's values but rather is a recognition that an exclusively economic understanding of capital and value falls short of both what is and what is needed.

We are required to drill deeper, to operate with greater considerations than the simple econometrics that financial capitalism asks of us. In this way, impact investing moves us along a path from the world we are presented with to evolve beyond what we currently understand as reality, toward something we seek to create in the future. We are called first to adopt a posture of servility, accepting our state of initial ignorance, and only then move on in an effort to expand beyond that ignorance to embrace a sincere and greater appreciation of the many complexities embedded in the value we aspire to create; to quietly and consistently build upon our previous beliefs regarding why we manage our lives and capital as we do or at least have in the past.

We would each be well served, regardless of the type, form, or nature of the impact investment strategy we pursue, to keep this in mind:

We do not know.

We may hope. We may create a host of tools, metrics, definitions and management information systems by which we seek to track our impact in the world. But in the end, all our efforts unfold against this backdrop of pale ignorance. As we move to advance Other Impact, as we hope to participate in Mutual Impact, we would each be well served to seek greater humility in our aspirations and claims.

IN CONSIDERATION OF OTHER IMPACT AND ITS COMPONENTS: BROAD, DEEP AND MUTUAL

Within impact investing, a core concept is that in any given portfolio capital may be deployed across an array of asset classes and through a host of strategies spanning a capital continuum. This continuum ranges from philanthropic to near-market and market rate investments. Other writings explore the practice of portfolio construction within such an approach, so for our purposes here let us simply acknowledge that Total Portfolio Management seeks both the appropriate amount of financial return within any given asset class as well as to optimize the nature and form of impact each type of investment might generate.

Going one step deeper, we may identify a number of themes within impact investing. These themes range from community level (i.e. the construction of affordable housing or provision of lending capital to small businesses traditionally overlooked by mainstream lenders) to population level (i.e. gender lens investing, investment targeting various racial/ethnic groups, investing targeting lower income individuals) or environmental level (for example, conservation easements, land banking, green bonds). Other themes might include health and wellness, education and so on. These various and diverse impact themes one might pursue are at the, let's say, 10,000-foot level while the broadest most nebulous and vague impact one may seek, to "do well and good," is at the 50,000-foot level. In between (let's say at the 30,000-foot level!), rests the notion of Other Impact which in turn has three types of impact: Broad, Deep, and Mutual.[1]

We like to view ourselves as possessing various levels of wealth, from rich to poor, and to think of ourselves as asset owners; however, while one may temporarily own capital, it is not in its essence yours. How do we come to understand the purpose of wealth beyond the needs of its temporal owner and in addition to our superficial understanding of its prioritized preference for self-replication—by which I mean an understanding which states that its purpose is to grow financially for you and that is all?

We might consider the possibility that the purpose of capital is to provide for all things external to your Self so that you may live a more full, free and fulfilled internal life. All aspects of human and environmental degradation devalue the worth of your having lived and at some point, detract from your ability to experience life in its fullest. One might argue that in the final analysis, the value of your wealth is worthless in the absence of you using it in a manner that creates the highest value for all since this will, in time, then revolve back to your self. The purpose of capital is grounded in maintaining a healthy circulation of lifeblood through the body of our community, of which you are indeed a part, but which you do not solely define nor control. All impact is woven within Other Impact.

This understanding of impact will be a theme to which we will continually return. But for now, consider the notion that the purpose of having money may, in the end, have more to do with your managing that wealth on behalf of the Other than on behalf of your Self. And the further out you place your boundary of who and what that

Other is, the greater blended value you may create over the course of your life. Through the more effective management of your assets, the more informed you will be in terms of how best to allocate that capital and the more profound understanding of the total returns you may generate, positioning you to capture the most significant amount of value creation—the greatest overall financial and impact returns— a life might offer.

By extension, when you expand your understanding of the boundary of Self, you could well die wealthier through investing in the Other than you may die by merely seeking to invest for the sole benefit of your Self.

Imagine that...

By way of example, your investing in specific companies, investment vehicles, and strategies in pursuit of economic justice and greater equity, has the potential to support better corporate practices and increased hiring. This investment, in turn, benefits others operating within their cycles of economics which then link back to your finances providing even greater benefit for not only yourself but all market participants. And so the circle turns.

It is that simple.

As Layth Matthews reflects,

"Viewing the world from an egotistical point of view is like limiting your perception to a peephole in a fortress gate. You have made this huge assumption, which you don't realize is so huge. It seems very innocent, but you have made this assumption that you are separate, continuous and defensible or supposed to be. The belief that me and mine are a separate entity legitimizes all the things I might do to support that separate entity. This assumption makes the world a scary place and walls us in. It also reduces altruism to just a stepping-stone or distraction from one's main purpose, which is the perpetuation of 'me.'"[2]

The inverse of this, as we might think of it in its broadest terms, is Other Impact.

FOUNDATIONS OF THE OTHER

Our understanding of "The Other" has evolved over time,[3] just as our appreciation of the role of the Other in our transformation may also develop over the course of our lives. Columbus viewed the Indians as the Other in the sense of an object to be stored "in a naturalist's collection, in which they took their place alongside plants and animals..." whereas for Cortes Indigenous Peoples were viewed as subjects—reduced to the role of "producers of objects, artisans or jugglers whose performances are admired—but such admiration emphasizes rather than erases the distance between them and himself; and the fact that they belong to a series of 'natural curiosities' is not forgotten."[4]

Other Impact focuses upon our relationship specifically to the Other as opposed to impact which is merely a function of reporting outputs, such as the number of jobs created, cost of job creation, cost benefit analysis or other derivative approaches to assessing progress toward interim goals. In the parlance of the nonprofit sector, we think in terms of input, outputs, and outcomes. Other Impact may be deemed as the ultimate outcome, greater than all others.

Other Impact plays out on the three levels of Broad, Deep, and Mutual, but may be easiest for us to initially explore in terms of family:

You have a certain amount of wealth, and you manage it well on traditional, financial terms. How you handle it (the integrity with which you engage in that process) as well as how much of it you decide to leave to your children and the causes you care to support are all original functions of the purpose of capital. They are in that sense simple, initial aspects of Other Impact, the lowest hanging fruit, as it were, that sits just outside your own life and personality, resting in the lives and character you are developing within the family members you love.

And so you begin to operate at this first level of impact by giving funds to family members so they may attend school (primary, secondary and then post-secondary), but in any case, these family members are directly connected with you. Your impact is clear to see throughout the family, and you know where your money is going. Seeing the great effect sound education has on your family, you then attend a graduation ceremony and realize many other children are working hard to attain education and decide to create a scholarship program to help pay the costs of education for those who might otherwise not be able to afford it, expanding beyond your first level of Other Impact. In time, you realize having well-financed, well-staffed schools are also important, and so you invest your philanthropic capital in a variety of schools across the country, getting your name on a few buildings as a result, but also contributing significantly to the infrastructure of these institutions and further expanding the realm of your Other Impact to that of Broad Impact.

This is not a bad thing for one to do with one's wealth. Writing a check to have an effect on the lives of the Other, requires little effort and you receive financial consideration in the form of a tax break every time you contribute to an institution of higher learning.

Still later, you come to embrace the idea that public education is a central, civil right and you fund public policy initiatives focused upon expanding educational opportunities for all while deciding to volunteer some of your off hours in tutoring children at a public school. Over time, you find yourself sharing a part of their lives, questioning your own journey and becoming more fully engaged in the Mutual Impact which enhances your life, the lives of other individuals and the greater life of your community.

Congratulations! You have arrived at the fully impactful life!

Broad Impact is the impact a vaccine initiative has, while Deep Impact is a community program housed within that overall health and wellness public policy and infrastructure initiative. Mutual Impact combines the two with your meaningful engagement in the process, both at a strategic and service delivery level, so that you open yourself up to becoming transformed as much as those you seek to have impact upon.

IN CONTRAST: CHEAP IMPACT

In the 1940s, Dietrich Bonhoeffer, the German Theologian, wrote about the concept of "cheap grace." Cheap grace is the idea one could kind of "show up" as a Christian and be accepted by God's love simply by professing a faith in Jesus Christ. But in his book, *The Cost of Discipleship*,[5] Bonhoeffer explores the idea that we should not settle for cheap grace; rather, we should pursue a deeper understanding of the cost and sacrifice of being a Christian. Following this idea, Bonhoeffer left his academic post in the United States, where he could have remained as an armchair theologian, and returned to Germany in the latter days of World War Two to teach and serve physical witness of his faith to his community. As the Allied Troops were moving through France and approaching Germany, Dietrich Bonhoeffer was first incarcerated and then executed by the Nazis. Just two days after his death, the prison he had been held in was liberated by the Allies.

Dietrich Bonhoeffer lived a life of Mutual Impact that I may only pray I would have the courage to follow. Coming years may offer that opportunity.

Turning the lens from one's personal life to our discussion of investing, within one's portfolio different investment strategies carry various forms and levels of impact. Some would argue public securities have no impact since they are traded on secondary markets and investing in them does not result in direct, street-level impact in the same way that, say, a micro-finance bond note may. But investing in public markets means one may participate in shareholder resolutions, engage management in debates regarding various corporate practices that directly affect employees and communities, and pursue a host of initiatives with the company that may result in meaningful changes in the lives of thousands of employees and scores of communities around the world. It is not that public securities do not have impact; rather it is impact of a certain type and form appropriate to that asset class and strategy of investment. It is Broad Impact.

Today one hears traditional, mainstream investors talk about their core business in health or telecommunications or technology as generating impact because it advances a general level of social or environmental value that would have been created regardless of their investor or managerial intent. This approach is the type of incidental or "cheap impact" generated by, say, Twitter that was used to help Iranian activists organize during their efforts at advancing the Green Revolution a number of years ago. Twitter did create a significant measure of impact via its social networking platform. But the platform also enables folks to tweet about their latest latte or night out; or, by way of another example, for an American leader to promote his oppressive lies and destructive ideas to his base, rallying them in ways that foment violence and anger against other citizens, immigrants, religious groups, journalists, or various manifestations of the Other within our nation. The potentially positive social value generated by Twitter is incidental to the firm's pursuit of its standard business model. It does not intentionally seek to generate, pursue or manage for its potential impact outcomes.

Do electrical access and the installation of cell phone towers create positive impact in our world? Of course! But this is a form of cheap impact that does not challenge the status quo or advance justice or systemic change—it does not seek to change the fundamental nature of our world that in turn demands we act to advance impact to begin with. It may be turned to either promote change or maintain the status quo in an unjust world. Does business have the potential to create positive social impact? Sure! Does it always and is it managed toward that end with a level of intentionality and commitment? Certainly not. The impact potential is present, but not cultivated to optimize the fund or firm's impact possibilities. It is a form of Broad Impact; that does not mean it is lousy impact, only that one should not over promote its sustained value in advancing a more just world. We must adopt a level of modesty when we describe our efforts at promoting cheap impact of this broad type.

The celebration of Carnival is meant to prepare the community for the sacrifices of Lent, yet with the secularization of this festival, it comes to be only a party, a bacchanal moment for a celebration of our individual lives resulting in the drunkenness that comes from consuming our arrogance to excess; in this way, the spirit of the festival is lost on the hordes and diluted by the Crowd. For many of those coming into the practice of impact investing today, it is merely a party, a release wherein investors celebrate the notion they may be blessed to pursue full financial returns and the material benefits thereof, while largely ignoring the broader potential impact of the practice and what mobilizing capital for more than money may truly mean. This type of impact investor will wake up in mornings to come, hung over from the spirits of financial excess and limited reflection, only to find their total returns to be minimal, their full life potential unrealized, all to their loss, certainly, but also to our own.

In contrast, Deep Impact is strategically managed and pursued as a core aspect of the firm, organization or investor's business strategy. It does not happen simply because the firm is in pursuit of economic value creation and happens to create positive social or environmental impact while executing the standard business model. Deep Impact requires a level of awareness, consciousness, and careful execution in its pursuit of impact. It is intentional and meaningful and part of an effort to not simply acknowledge that social and environmental components of value are fully embedded within every pursuit of economic value creation, but is a strategic effort to raise up, nurture and cultivate that element and aspect of value creation which is of benefit to outside stakeholders and communities of interest.

As worthy as those activities may be, we are called to reach down deep into our supply chains and employee relations, to cultivate more nuanced levels of potential impact buried within the firm and within our portfolios, and help them flourish beyond what would generally be required in pursuit of a traditional business plan and standard, benchmarked financial returns. We have before us the opportunity to engage in and cultivate a more profound measure of value through the course of our lives' work and the deployment of our capital in the world. Impact investing is the tool by which we may generate Broad Impact, capture Deep Impact in collaboration with our various stakeholders and through which we may then become more fully, personally engaged at a level of Mutual Impact.

OF MUTUAL IMPACT

Mutual Impact is a connection with and linking of the Self and Other that is sought in the realization of our complete connectivity in Life and in the pursuit of the value we aim to create. It is a form of impact that links us with the Other as it connects us more deeply with our true selves. Mutual Impact is the flow that is in constant motion between who we are, the broader communities (regardless of size) of which we are a part and each of our embeddedness within the ever-larger Life and Eco-System within which we rest with no boundary or division.

"Closing the gap between self and other, between humanity and the world, has to be a central preoccupation for the times in which we now live. Not long ago, we really could avoid each other. Impoverished communities on the far side of the planet with strange, even abhorrent religions and customs could be invisible and ignored. But now they see us all too clearly. They see our extraordinary wealth, our encouragement of values and behaviors that strike at the heart of what they care for most. And we now see them. Our globalized economy brought us so much closer; through global travel, global media, global brands. But that was a physical closeness only. The distance in terms of human understanding and empathy remains breathtakingly vast," says Dominic Houlder, of the London Business School.[6]

Broad Impact has a level of value—it, after all, does create and advance a form of potentially positive impact within the world—but it is distant and unengaged, and so therefore positive and good in the sense that a fighter blind with rage gets lucky and lands a punch or a poor student taking a test gets lucky and selects the correct answer out of multiple choice options, one of five possible answers.

Our goal is not to fall into impact accidentally, but rather to create it in partnership with the Other and our selves as in love, both of which seek to become more than when we began upon this path. We find fulfillment, enlightenment, and impact by design and intent, not by default. And yes, if we must take it by accident, then fine, of course, we shall have it. However, that is not quite the same as discovering impact within our selves and community as a part of our more significant process of becoming. Broad Impact is not the same, nor does it hold the intrinsic value of Deep, or better yet, Mutual Impact.

The Pirke Avot (a Judaic writing, Ethics of Our Fathers) presents forty-eight personality types (called *middot*) as necessary for attaining Torah (by which is meant, a binding to the spiritual force of the Torah). While each of these types is viewed as important,

"…Rav Simha claims that 'carrying the burden of one's fellow' is the goal of all the rest; reaching this goal testifies to the
transformation of one's human nature into a spiritual nature,
transcending even death itself. It is to this transformed infinite
soul, whose infinity is affected by bearing the pain of others,
that the spiritual Torah adheres…This description of the Torah
implies that the relationship between the enclosed self and the
other person bridges the gap between the finite and the infinite,
between each of us and God, by our assuming responsibility one
for another."[7]

Mutual Impact is attained when the separation between Self and
Other dissolves and one sees the integral nature of our relationships
with each other and the Planet, our resources and our ultimate outcome,
our actual destination and full comprehension of what is finally real.
We are all part of the realities we create and are creating.

The value we seek in life is not only the value generated over the
course of our lives that we may track and assess—in Hume's selfish way
relative to what we have done or created—rather Mutual Impact is the
ongoing integration of the value we create through the course of a life as
expressed through our relation to the Other (to those who are the objects
of our impact efforts) as well as the Planet (from which our wealth originates and in which we are rooted), with each of these combining in a
timeless presence of how we understand who we are relative to community, to society, to the Earth and its diverse creatures and energies.

Mutual Impact opens us to global flows of social transformation as
well as natural and human energy.

Mutual Impact connects us with what Spinoza called substance and
others may call God or Spirit.

Mutual Impact is how we are most profoundly called to pursue,
engage and be in the presence of what we seek to realize as the ultimate
purpose of our capital.

CHAPTER THREE

HUMANITY IN CONTEXT OF SELF:

Key Stages of Our Journey

T O PARAPHRASE THE HISTORIAN PETER BROWN, WE MUST, AT ALL COSTS, AVOID THE TEMPTATION TO FORESHORTEN HISTORY.

We tend to seek out the Cliff Notes version of the world, to find a brief Wiki entry that can give us the key points and allow us to move on; to listen to a single talk, read one defining book and believe we understand. During my brief time at Harvard Business School, I gave a faculty seminar in 2001 where I presented the evolution of my thinking from a bifurcated to blended value framework. This led to a spirited discussion with my colleagues, at the end of which one senior professor stated he would have preferred I not outline the evolution of the concepts and ideas upon which I based my thinking but that I should have started with a presentation of the theory of blended value and gone from there. I thought he could not be more wrong because the idea I was presenting was a summary not only of my thinking but that of many others whose ideas I have built upon over the years, which themselves were built upon ideas countless others, himself included, had also advanced.

Not only honoring this work but understanding the flow of thinking from past to future is key to understanding the present context; So, too, with this book.

What we know as a people—what we honestly think we *know*—cannot be summarized in some well-designed PowerPoint deck, presented in a single numeric proof, or communicated within a brief, smoothly produced on-line video. History—the story of how we arrived where we are today and how that experience of life may inform, improve and better position our lives moving forward—is to be experienced at a more visceral level for each of us, what we think and how we act in the world, are a part of that story. The world we inhabit is one of our imagination and vision. It is the world as we see it, experience it, feel it and perceive it around us and within us. That history is made all the richer by linking our imagination and ideas with those who have come before, exploring many of the same notions and concepts we entertain today while pointing us in the proper direction for our inquiries to come. Human beings must avoid the temptation to foreshorten history!

When it comes to our understanding the path we have taken, as a community of humanity and individuals, to understand and advance our comprehension of the purpose of capital, we must play with what is in many ways a complicated set of building blocks:

First, we must reacquaint ourselves with our economic, political and social histories—which in today's world seem too often ignored.

Second, we must outline our intellectual history—which, again, we tend to take for granted. We frequently assume we all share the same set of facts as well as comprehend what those facts mean.

And, finally, we must each have a level of self-reflection adequate to the task before us, that of defining the purpose of capital.

Historians differ concerning how best to slice and dice this journey of exploration and development. Our intellectual history is, in many ways, the story of that discussion and debate of what matters and is significant versus what is just the flotsam and jetsam of our various processes of dead end inquiry. Within all that time, history, and complexity, at the most fundamental level, one could argue there have been only three stages of development over the past 20,000 years:

- The Agricultural Revolution,
- The Industrial Revolution and
- The Great Acceleration (the transition from coal to mixed fossil fuels)[1]

For the purpose of much of our discussion, this may be the best way to understand our journey since our definition of the meaning of capital has evolved in significantly different styles within each of those periods that bring us to the place we stand today. However, in the course of my research, I found the most significant personal resonance with the idea that this process has played itself out over the centuries through what the religious historian Karen Armstrong defines as the following six stages of human history:[2]

1. The Paleolithic Period (20000 to 8000 BCE)
2. The Neolithic Period (8000 to 4000 BCE)
3. The Early Civilizations (4000 to 800 BCE)
4. The Axial Age (800 to 200 BCE)
5. The Post-Axial Period (200 BCE to 1500 CE)
6. The Great Western Transformation (1500 to 2000 CE)

Against that backdrop, a few specific points are worth keeping in mind. As Professor Ashley Dawson says,

"The Neolithic Revolution also generated a fateful metamorphosis in humanity's social organization. Intensive agriculture produced a food surplus, which in turn permitted social differentiation and hierarchy, as elite orders of priests, warriors and rulers emerged as judges of the distribution of that surplus. Much of subsequent human history may be seen as a struggle over the acquisition and distribution of such surplus...The increased importance of warfare led to the rise of military chiefs; initially elected by the populace, these leaders quickly transformed themselves into permanent hereditary rulers of the ancient world."[3]

Second, the other hereditary rulers of the ancient world to evolve—and in some ways, the most important regarding our discussion of the purpose of capital—is the merchant, class which occurred during the Axial Age (800-200BCE). As economies developed and markets emerged, it was the merchant class that in truth controlled the keys to the kingdom and through a shifting set of characters continue to rule that kingdom today. In many ways, it was our economic

development through the vehicle of exploration, war, and domination of discovered cultures, that gave diverse societies throughout the centuries and across entirely different empires, the breathing room to step back and more fully explore cultural and human development.[4]

As the evolutionary economist Richard Nelson of Columbia University states, humans deploy two types of technology that make for our economic development and ability to maintain this "shared language-of-state"; they are physical and social. Physical technologies are the hard tools of steam engines and micro-chips, while social technologies are the mobilization of people to act within the world whether through organizations or with the soft tools we create to function as economic actors.[5]

These two types of technology must coevolve in the same way that impact investing is a social technology innovation that has evolved out of traditional economic theory and financial practice. This was facilitated by innovations within physical technologies, such as cell phones being used to bring micro-finance and banking to outlying villages. In this way, there is a constant interplay between what we may be able to do and what we understand as the meaning and purpose of the tools we control. It is we who choose how to apply the means and toward what end.

Sharpening our focus upon our understanding of the purpose of capital is key to the future not only of our successful impact investing, but to the possible success of our work in social and personal liberation. Not being clear on these points makes for the difference between doing well and good and actually using capital to attain its potential purpose of changing the world and freeing us to be the community, people, and planet we're called to be. It is the difference between having a tool and knowing how to apply that tool in the creation of something truly innovative and revolutionary.

Social technologies will determine what we think and do—what we may be positioned to bring forward in terms of thought together with the physical manifestation of our ideas. It's interesting to note that during the Protestant Reformation, "When Luther went to visit parishes, he took with him one theologian and three lawyers."[6] The state of the church could not be changed through faith and a new vision alone but required new legal norms and practices and laws by which the Reformation could be managed and take root. However, it was not the attorneys, the functionaries of the new rules, who were in charge. They were directed and held accountable in their work by Martin Luther who held clear on his purpose and vision, in the same way, asset owners and financial activists must see clearly the purpose of capital lest we default to our traditional, extractive practices of investing and see our work taken hostage by institutions of finance seeking their own benefit.

Modern, financial capitalism, given its legal and economic infrastructure, will also need a total revisioning and evolution to integrate stakeholder interests and rights as well as formalize new understandings of fiduciary duty, elements of economic structure and other aspects of deploying capital that will require a rewriting of the rules. I am reminded of the work of B-Lab in introducing not merely a set of metrics and evaluation standards for a new type of corporate practice (the B-Corp and IRIS metrics), but also promoting that new legal structure within states across the U.S. and beyond—and in their efforts to create a global community of mutual support to best position entrepreneurs for long-term success. In many ways, they and countless others around the world act as innovators of a new form of capitalist Reformation, challenging and rising against the business and financial orthodoxies of the existing order within the context of financial capitalism as presently practiced and accepted as our faith orthodox, taken as truth by the mainstream.

This process of analyzing what is, proposing an alternative vision or set of options and then promoting those against the established order is, at its core, the process in which we are engaged as we encourage a new understanding of the purpose of capital. And it is a process of evolution that is consistent with those processes which have taken place in the past, for "...(e)volution is typically an interwoven fabric of coevolutionary loops and twists; in surprising ways, our so-called native intelligence depends on both our technology and our numbers."[7] This technology is as previously described, but the process of attaining various turning points in history where the tide shifts and we witness what was accepted as truth turning into the old prayer book as we move to a new set of first principles and practices: this is our challenge, opportunity and calling.

We need to study the broad social history of economics—not simply the history of capitalism and modern financial, Chicago-school economics—if we are to understand the place in which we now find ourselves and, more importantly, see the direction and course we must now set with an evolved appreciation of the social construct we call capital and the practices we now brand impact investing. As,

> ..."(t)he British biologist D'Arcy Thompson (1917) famously said, 'Everything is the way it is because it got that way.' Many of the puzzles (or 'mysteries' or 'paradoxes') of human consciousness evaporate once you ask how they could have arisen—and try to answer the question! I mention that because some people marvel at the question and then 'answer' it by saying, 'It's an impenetrable mystery!' or 'God did it!'"[8]

This is the same mindset as the corporate captains and apologists of traditional finance who argue that any phenomena not accounted for upon the balance sheet or quantifiable through analytics isn't of value.

THE NEXT STAGE OF DEVELOPMENT

The accepted wisdom of this god of finance is one of bifurcation and externalities that social and environmental factors are to be considered separate and apart from economic elements, as defined and determined by the early economists and then later put into formal doctrine by those high priests of the old Chicago School of Economics. That is what we challenge today. This traditional understanding of economics dominates everything in modern life, from our "knowledge" of the rules of business to our social, political and even religious practices.

One may view the task before us as one of transcendent mission and passion, but it fits squarely within the course of our secular history as well. We are drawn to this due to our need to engage in creative responses to our desire to bring needed change and impact to the world, to transform both our condition and that of the Other.

We seek to inaugurate a new age of America—no, of the world—a new connection between and integration of developing and developed or First and Third Worlds.

We seek a new order of global impact economics even as we recognize modern financial capitalism as presently constituted will not be the vehicle to take us where we need to go. Those who dare call themselves impact investors, as we move from fringe to mainstream, must hold onto the historic origins of our revolutionary thought and seek to explode upon the stage of our world, as we collaborate in "blasting open...the continuum of history."[9]

We seek change—not accommodation.

And, of course, and as always, we are not the first.

As the American Philosopher David Roochnik comments:

> "Thales' rational articulation and empirical defense of his conception of the *arche* is such a stunning break with Hesiodic *mythos* that the year 585 (BCE) is as significant as any other in the history of western culture. For the first time human beings attempted to penetrate reality with reason alone. No longer was a Muse needed to supply inspiration. No longer was the heart

of reality indeterminate and mad Eros its driving force. Instead, human reason, unaided by external (and unreliable) assistance, could work hard and figure out what the *arche*, the grounding principle of all things, is, and then take responsibility for giving good reasons why it should be so. Philosophy has begun."[10]

And that initial framing of philosophy was predicated upon an understanding of universal meaning and purpose. As author Grant Maxwell says, Descartes and modern secular philosophy sought to rupture human fascination with divine causation:

"Teleology, the ancient idea that processes tend to develop toward ends or purposes, has generally been denied in modernity in favor of material and efficient causation, which have been enshrined as the only valid causal modes. For most of pre-modernity, from astrology and divination to Judea-Christian, Muslim, and Hindu eschatologies, to various streams of Confucian and Buddhist thought, final causation was usually interpreted as divinely ordained fate...To a great extent, the emergence of the modern mind was a reaction against this pervasive assumption of predestination in its many complex permutations, so that Descartes' claim that the human mind, and not the mind of God, is the only thing that provides evidence of our existence (despite his attempt to reconcile this view with his Catholic faith) was a direct challenge to the hegemony of that mode of thought which located agency primarily outside the human mind."[11]

There are, then, several implications of this process of focusing upon the human mind as the sole source of defining what our world is and what is the nature, if any, of our purpose:

First, this process formalized the movement toward separating our understanding of Self from Other, asserting that anything we cannot understand or define does not indeed exist or is outside the realm of demonstrated reality. This makes it possible for us to have concepts such as 'externalities' wherein we can think aspects of corporate or financial performance which do not appear within our calculus of 'the firm' or how we measure 'cost' do not exist or may, therefore, be assumed to be public costs born by the Commons or government or some vague place we don't have to think about.

Second, by way of extension, this evolution of perspective takes a historic step forward and yet away from our real goal and true quest in that it makes it possible for us to think of social value as a subjective good whereas economic value is taken as objective, measurable, and rational. This topic is explored at length in coming pages.

Third, this grand step forward, this rejection of teleological perspectives and this separation of arche from mythos, leaves unanswered a host of questions concerning deeper meaning, purpose and self. We focus on the mechanics of capital and investing (the how), but do not as a part of that process raise or explore more fundamental questions (either as individual asset owners/investors or on a more everyday basis of family, community or society) concerning the essential nature and purpose of capital (the Why). Within the operating values of modern society (by which I mean latest—not best or most evolved), we feel this is fine as such matters are taken to be questions of individual faith, taste or perspective. Yet, as many become dissatisfied with the answers offered by this modern approach, we must reintegrate considerations of this more profound purpose within how one should responsibly manage capital. *Why* should one manage it—toward what end?—and what extra-financial aspects not appearing in our numeric algorithms and formulas should we then bring to our understanding of the purpose of capital as defined by individuals and refined within the larger crucible of community?

As fellow travelers exploring the impact eco-system, we are each traveling in this way. We are alone on the path, yet linked, influenced by and informing the journeys of others. We are not a crowd of lemmings crossing a windswept moor, but gather along and pass over well-worn byways of social responsibility, sustainability, and impact—routes themselves not new, but paths we have trod since capitalism was first created centuries ago.

That said, there is no going back. Perhaps some may turn around, looking wistfully at the reassuring path behind, but most know there is no putting the genie back in the bottle once the profound questions of meaning and purpose have been engaged. The notion of money's sole purpose being the geometric and exponential expansion of itself to create more and higher and even

ever less connected piles of cash and processes of commerce does not adequately respond to our desires for connection and meaning. Our shared, black holes sucking in the light of the universe are infinite and will never be filled regardless of how much money we pour into them or clever arguments we advance as we gather to seek comfort for our souls during the cold, damp nights of this shared life and individual death.

We need more.

We need some sense of greater comprehension.

We need to know.

BEYOND THE BASICS

In terms of how we interact today across the cultural, class and historical divides created over the many years (most recently, via slavery, colonialist relations between First and Third World, the growing gap between rich and poor, to be sure, but also the ever increasing divide within our own selves as we attain greater material wealth and yet in the process achieve greater distance from that personal value we strive so hard to reach), when it comes to individuals reflecting upon and learning about history, we do most of that work on our own.

We read, learn, and connect the dots between what we thought we knew and what we come to know through creating the space to pause and hear the voices of various generations coming down through time to our minds and evolve our understanding of what we believe to be our today. We understand history in the quietude of our imagination and gathering of those voices through books and exploration of the folds of time that, as pulled back by our effort, come to reveal various and foundational truths regarding who we are, where we've come and the direction in which we're headed.

In silence, we ultimately find comfort and the Comforter or Paraclete. "The Latin word paracleta means 'the one who answers the cry.' This living, billowing silence is needed to be able to hear the cry of the soul, and the cry is needed in order for the Comforter to respond,"[12] Robert Sardello tells us.

In this way, we understand that as part of our journey one needs to define the elements to be unified and then bring those parts into a new wholeness, healing and unity of opposites while keeping awareness of the constituent elements of which that totality exists. It is weaving and blending the triple bottom-line into a new, more powerful and centered universal One that is the blend of value generated out of our energies and efforts, personally, organizationally and within community, which in turn unleashes the full potential of each of its members.

For many who read the philosophers of the Enlightenment, we mistakenly believe the debate was around the *existence* of God when in fact it was focused upon the *nature* of God, whose life was in many ways taken as a given.[13] And the nature of God within the community of our nation's revolutionary founders, was primarily understood to be a belief in a religion of Nature's God,[14] as first professed in Western terms by Thomas Young in 1770. Much is at stake in defining the purpose of capital in how history is read and interpreted. Using our post-modern intellect to underplay the power of God's role in social formation and mores affects our understanding of who we are and how we define how we come to be in this world.

BEYOND THE BEYOND

To continue beyond that edge, within the Judaic tradition it may be said,

> "All human beings are formed with both a *yetzer ha-tov* and a
> *yetzer ha-ra*, an inclination for good and an inclination for evil...
> We are conscious human beings in so far as we have before us

at every single moment, a choice between good and evil. Our humanity is defined by our awareness of this choice and by how we choose to act when faced with this choice…The physical life of all living creatures is sacred. But full consciousness—what we call 'Mussar consciousness'—implies a level of life and maturity beyond the physical. This level of life is defined by our accepting the responsibility of the choice between good and evil that faces us at every moment."[15] (Stone)

We might also reflect upon how that choice of how we manage and rise above the good and evil in each of us is viewed within Buddhist concepts of mindfulness and right living, Christian notions of being in the world and yet not of the world, and so on, across a host of spiritual doctrine. The process by which our predecessors have grounded themselves in these ideas is one of evolving revelation. As the scholar Tzvetan Todorov writes:

"I do not believe that history obeys a system, nor that its so-called laws permit deducing future or even present forms of society; but rather that to become conscious of the relativity (hence the arbitrariness) of any feature of our culture is already to shift it a little, and that history (not the science, but its object) is nothing other than a series of such imperceptible shifts."[16]

The history of our cultures, religions and, overall, our shared experience as humanity is one of the subtle shifts resulting from our search in pursuit of an explanation of Why?

- Why do we exist?
- Why is there injustice in the world?
- Why am I mortal and why can I not see beyond the curtain of death into the final beyond?

It is upon the foundation of our responses to this question of Why? which we then build the various levels of our defining of the How:

- How we act;
- How we understand the nature of value;
- How we approach whether to invest in traditional financial instruments, to invest in and seek out safer "impact" investments or opt to explore the outer boundaries of impact in the Other in pursuit of investing in our selves.

And so we return, for in a reflection of the real circle of life, regardless of our particular response to these timeless questions, our answer to the how in each of them is rooted in our understanding of the Why.

In our conferences, events, and meetings of investment committees, we seldom delve into this deeper exploration of why we are considering the actions we propose and why we manage capital and impact toward what ends and what we believe is the real worth or value of any of it. Many assume it to be a question of trade-offs within our bifurcated understanding of philanthropy versus investing when, if we take the time to more fully consider the problem, we know our efforts (the "how" of what we do) to be rooted more deeply in a set of assumptions of this unexplored Why. But we let the curtain of Reason and what we pretend is objective analysis cloak and quiet our deeper, much more significant, questions and potential inquiry. And, Anderson infers, that is the legacy of our enlightenment:

> "...In Western Europe, the eighteenth-century marks not only the dawn of the age of nationalism but the dusk of religious modes of thought. The century of Enlightenment, of rationalist secularism, brought with it its modern darkness. With the ebbing of religious belief, the suffering which belief in part composed did not disappear. The disintegration of paradise: nothing makes fatality more arbitrary. The absurdity of salvation: nothing makes another style of continuity more necessary. What then was required was a secular transformation of fatality into continuity, contingency into meaning."[17]

Anderson then goes on to make his argument for how this all laid the foundation for the modern imagination of "nation," but in our context of capital, the implication is more individual, more personal.

Our embracing of notions and inquiries related to impact investing is rooted in our desire to align our money with who we are and how we seek to be in the world to say nothing of our desire to manage that capital to transform our world. But we mostly gloss over such discussions in our rapid pursuit of the right fund or investment strategy or new advisor to guide the deployment of our capital—all in dark denial of the fact that to understand the appropriate course of action, we must first dive into our understanding of the purpose of our lives relative to those whom we aim to help.

What appears unappreciated in mainstreaming the practice of impact investing and our excitement about being validated by the big brands of Wall Street investment houses is that impact investing is less a question of changing the world than one of shifting our understanding of self and then only later, society and world. Impact investing is only secondarily a question of how to invest capital or modify our approach to finance; it is first and foremost a matter of refining our personal and community understanding of meaning and purpose. And at its best, it is a dance, an interplay, between the two.

Christopher Budd noted that money fundamentally is a semiotic creation that people agree to share; it has no value qua money:

> "The most important thing about money…is that men [sic] consciously agree to its purpose. Something non-economic is thereby introduced. The Greek word for money means custom, consensus, convention. When men arrive at a consensus they are not involved in economic processes, but in 'rights' processes. Money belongs to the rights life, it enables the rights lore to permeate economics. The question is: to what purpose? Money in itself—a coin, a note, a cheque—in no way determines what is to be done with it. Money is utterly emancipated from the economic processes that give rise to it. What happens with money is up to the user. The past cannot live on in money. Money by its very nature belongs to

the future. The only way of knowing what can happen to money is to observe the use it is put to. Moreover, the use will reveal the intention of the user and thereby reveal the user also."[18]

Before our being able to engage in the process of exchange, in confirming a sense of trust, we must enter that relationship from a place of grounding and personal knowledge of the Self. The author Emily Smith observes that the first piece of human literature, written four thousand years ago, *The Epic of Gilgamesh*, "is a about a hero's quest to figure out how he should live knowing that he will die. And in the centuries since Gilgamesh's tale was first told, the urgency of that quest has not faded. The rise of philosophy, religion, natural science, literature, and even art can be at least partly explained as a response to two questions: What is the meaning of existence? And How can I lead a meaningful life?"[19]

The answers to these questions may be informed by but are not to be found in books of science or finance or from the public journey of others, our much-celebrated fund managers, conference panelists, innovators, and keynoters—among whose number I must reluctantly include myself. Instead, "the study of logic, though healthy for the mind, offers meager food for the soul. Sir Thomas Moore once said that he 'might as soon obtain bodily nourishment by milking a he-goat into a sieve as spiritual nourishment by reading the schoolmen."[20] And it would seem today we are beset by masses of schoolmen, jostling to come forward and justify their pasts, competing to lead us into our future.

In contrast to the dim light of the quick-witted thought leader, there are many lights off to the side of us, lights cast by those boats we sense sailing near yet not so close to our own. While we may take some bitter comfort in their presence, those are not the lights that will guide us. The lights that will give us the perspective we seek and direction we intuit are those lights that sparkle above and beyond our present world. Those are the celestial lights we may raise our heads to see on our own, yet have the potential to view together and by which we will sail most true.

PART TWO

REFLECTIONS ON HOW WE SHAPED THE PRESENT CHARACTER OF CAPITAL

CHAPTER FOUR

BOOKENDS OF HISTORY:

The Axial Age,
The Anthropocene, and Art

A CENTRAL QUESTION IN MY INQUIRY HAS REVOLVED IN ONE FORM OR ANOTHER AROUND SEPARATION AND DUALISM; NAMELY, HOW IS IT THAT WE HAVE COME TO VIEW OURSELVES AS SEPARATE FROM EACH OTHER, THE OTHER, NATURE AND IN SOME WAYS, SEPARATE FROM OUR EXPERIENCE OF LIFE ITSELF?

I first came to this inquiry as founding director of a venture philanthropy fund in the 90's, the performance of which we assessed on social and financial bases, which is how I was brought to the realization that our traditional approach to understanding value creation was premised upon a split between social/environmental and economic elements—a bifurcated value proposition—as opposed to what seemed self-evident to be the natural and more compelling order of our world, what, in 2000, I called a Blended Value Proposition. Since that time I've been curious about and have explored how it is we came to accept this notion of bifurcated value and under what terms we might unify it.

This is key in that within our understanding of this question lies our future ability to think more holistically, to work collaboratively, to make more compelling decisions regarding our relationship with the Earth, to manage organizations and capital with an eye toward the creation of economic, social and environmental value, and, again, to advance what I've referred to as Blended Value. If we do not understand how we came to operate in a world of parts, how might we ever come to live in the world on a more sustainable, holistic basis? An inner reflection, then, becomes an external inquiry seeking to comprehend something of how we first came to think of our selves as being separated from all else in our world.

THE AXIAL AGE AND ITS IMPLICATIONS

As discussed in the previous section, economic development and, before that, cognitive development played roles in making our continuing process of separation and individuation possible. While it is true this separation—known as dualism—took a significant step forward with the Age of the Enlightenment, that was not the first time we became aware of and grappled with the implications of our bifurcated self. While many and diverse people and cultures have navigated this divide, one of the more significant concepts I came upon in my reading was that of the Axial Age (800-200BCE)—a time in human history where over a period of centuries in diverse places around the world, ideas, understandings, and beliefs simultaneously emerged regarding who we are and our relation to the gods and Planet. In an authentic sense, during the Axial Age is the first time where, collectively, the idea of We became supplanted by that of I.

It is important to acknowledge the entire concept of an Axial Age is much debated within certain scholarly circles, with many questions being raised concerning whether such a period occurred and if so, during what specific dates it took place, who its central actors were, its real significance and so on.[1] This rich discussion stands well beyond our ability to explore fully herein.[2] I intend to reflect on the basic concepts and ideas of the Axial Age as they relate to our understanding of the evolution of thinking regarding dualism, purpose and what is. I will then briefly discuss the other end of the historical continuum, The Anthropocene. I do this to have greater appreciation of where all this has brought us, as well as how we might evolve in addressing today's problems by transcending this experience of dualism in pursuit of our rediscovery of an integrative understanding of capital and value along with the many implications of such a rediscovery.

This becomes central for those investing for multiple returns and for those who seek to change the world through the deployment and effective management of capital. Why? Because our understanding of the origins and implications of bifurcation is key to our future advancement of a framework within which to consider the idea of value as integrative or blended. This is, in turn, critical to our ability to affirm a new definition of the purpose of capital and its deployment in pursuit of transformative impact in our world. But first and foremost, if we are to understand these various factors and issues, we must know how we came to be separated in the first place.

Before outlining the essential elements of the Axial Age, it is important we appreciate the context within which the Age emerged. The period immediately before the Axial Age was one of increasing urbanization. For the first time, people in multiple places across the known world began to leave their tribes, settlements, and countryside to gather in cities. As those cities became more organized and ruled by new social orders, the place and role of the gods came to be questioned, creating a "spiritual vacuum," leaving many uncertain regarding their world as they then knew it.[3] This, in turn, laid the groundwork for sages and prophets to promote new understandings of religion and meaning. It was at this time, separately and in different regions of the world, four religious/philosophical systems emerged:

- Confucianism and Taoism in China;
- Buddhism and Hinduism in India;
- Monotheism in the Middle East and
- Greek rationalism in southern Europe.[4]

It was also during this time new market economies developed in many regions. These markets and their emerging material and capital flows were then connected by the new power actors of the merchant class, who increasingly challenged the authority of the kings and priests.[5] People questioned the reality and causation of human suffering and violence. They sought new ways to think about the world and position themselves within it, just as they found new ways to understand how not only to survive, but to thrive in this new, evolved social and economic order, while at the same time others sought to adhere to existing beliefs. It was a period of reassessment and reflection; one of new ideas and evolved beliefs confronting those of the past.

It is fascinating to note that during this same period, in the late 6th century BCE, there had been a sense of spiritual malaise in the Ganges region of India where many had concluded the religious practices of the ancestors were not adequate to the new day. One may imagine a similar sense of dis-ease permeating throughout much of the known world. The religious historian Karen Armstrong writes:

> "This malaise was not confined to the subcontinent, but afflicted people in several far-flung regions of the civilized world. An increasing number had come to feel that spiritual practices of their ancestors no longer worked for them, and an impressive array of prophetic and philosophical geniuses made supreme efforts to find a solution. Some historians call this period (which extended from about 800 to 200 B.C.E.) the 'Axial Age' because it proved pivotal to humanity. The ethos forged during this era has continued to nourish men and women to the present day. Gotama would become one of the most important and most typical of the luminaries of the Axial Age, alongside the great Hebrew prophets of the eighth, seventh and sixth centuries; Confucius and Lao Tzu, who reformed the religious traditions of China in the sixth and fifth centuries; the six-century Iranian sage Zoroaster; and Socrates and Plato (c.427-327), who urged the Greeks to question even those truths which appeared to be self-evident. People who participated in this great transformation were convinced that they were on the brink of a new era and that nothing would ever be the same again. The Axial Age marks the beginning of humanity as we now know it."[6]

The significance of the Axial Age is its promise to be the first moment when new conceptions of the transcendent were advanced, where not only could one go beyond the human world or cosmos, but in doing so be able to take a perspective separate from the traditional and act as a critic of the norm. It is in this way the Axial Age seeded the first time in history where the Self emerged separate and apart from either the gods or tribe and society. The fact this appears to have simultaneously occurred within hundreds of years, across multiple cultures and contexts, resulting in potential weakening of links to single, mainstream cultures in favor of belief systems that cut across culture and time is extraordinary. As one of the leading scholars of the Axial Age commented, this represented a powerful shift away from practices of "feeding the gods" toward an understanding of human virtue, goodness, and salvation, as positively supported by the gods.[7]

As such, the Axial Age is vital in that it represents a significant break from previous cultural structures and operating practices. "The Axial Age might be considered the first period that germinated the seeds of later full-blown Theoretic cultures, such as those currently governing the developing world..." as opposed to Mythic styles of "cognitive governance." Mythic cultures have characteristics such as Narrative, Authority-based, Slow/Deep, Highly Emotive and so on; whereas Theoretic cultures characterize social phenomena by such qualities as Analytic, Evidence-based, Fast/Shallow, Less Emotive, and so on."[8] This is how we frame a transition from *mythos* to *logos*[9] which is important on several levels:

First, on a cross cultural and (regarding the world as it was known at that time) global level it represents the shared experience and natural outcome of what Harari terms the Cognitive Revolution which resulted in the development of brains first capable of thought and then actually engaging in the thinking that defines who we are as individuated beings separate and apart from gods and community.[10]

Second, in many ways it could be viewed as a precursor to the mind/body dualism of Descartes and the material/spiritual division that has shaped much of our current thinking regarding the nature of reality and, therefore, economics and impact investing as operating on an "impact first/finance first" basis or, more traditionally, a "make money and give it away" understanding of wealth and value creation versus philanthropy and acts of charity. The notion one may separate the social from the material should be viewed as having its cultural and institutional roots in the Axial Age. Indeed, these constructs have their origins in a time of the ancients, over two millennia ago.

Third, this is not to say this process saw the dominance of Theoretic over Mythic, as both frames operate within our world and minds today as they have for centuries. What is important to note is that "the Axial Age might be regarded as the time when humanity went through a major evolutionary step in self-monitoring and supervision that can be described as metacognition. This capacity is an abstract form of self-awareness, a feature of mind that is essential for planning action and for conscious self-regulation..."[11] This period made possible the social, legal and financial organizational structures created over the many centuries to follow.

The Axial Age saw, for the first time, the rise of the concept of the individual and the Self and, as the theologian and philosopher Mark Muesse observes, "was the time when people began to experience themselves as separate, autonomous individuals—as selves. With this developing sense of selfhood came a greater consciousness of the human being as a moral agent, one who is accountable and responsible for his or her actions...Humans have not always been 'selves.'...During this era, the purpose of religion shifted from what John Hicks calls 'cosmic maintenance' to 'personal transformation.'"[12] In this way our understanding of personal responsibility and the potential for salvation went from something our tribe advanced collectively to something we were each accountable for and in control of.

And yet at the same time, the philosophies and religions that emerged during this period also advanced an understanding of the Self's *responsibility* to Other:

> "If there is anything on which one could say the Axial Age religions seemed to agree, it may be this point: that an unbridled sense of self leads to devastating consequences for the individual,

society, and the world. And although they proposed many different ways of understanding and addressing this concern, the response of the axial sages seems equally unanimous: practice self-awareness and compassion,"[13] continues Muesse.

While development of an awareness of the Self and the subsequent realization that we are not at the mercy of the gods made us free to pursue our visions and create our societies, it also had the inverse effect of separating us from each other and the Earth. If the gods did not need us to engage with them in bringing the seasons to pass, we are freed from the earth itself, to go our way, but perhaps, more importantly, to *have* our way with the planet, its precious resources, and creatures. This period laid the foundation for the idea that an individual could possess parts of the planet or its resources.

Many individuals have found this separation artificial and not reflective of who we are or how, as conscious beings, we want to exist in and experience the world. We might submit one of the most pressing agendas for our future is for us to re-engage with the earth and cosmos to find our way forward through our present 'post-modern malaise.'[14] While this gift of the Axial Age—this hunger for meaning—is what gave us knowledge of self and insight into the Other, it was also the gift that drew us out of the Garden and into a world of risk, divisive returns and separation from what ultimately is. We have sought to return to that Garden ever since.

FROM AXIAL TO ANTHRO

If the Axial Age was the beginning of history as we've come to know it, one might think of the Anthropocene as its end, as a time when humanity will destroy the very Earth that gave us life and generations upon generations of human experience. I first came on the term, Anthropocene, several years ago and wondered what it meant. While my personal interests lay more in the area of earth sciences, my professional journey took me toward sociology and community work, so when I first came across the word, it wasn't immediately apparent to me what, exactly, the term referred to: "The word Anthropocene is descended from the

Greek 'anthropos', meaning either 'man' or 'human.'[15]...The name suits it because human societies exert a novel and distinctive degree of sway in the physical world..."[16]

Historians date the start of the Anthropocene to the Industrial Revolution (1760 to 1840). It was in 1781, that James Watt invented the steam engine, allowing us to move power from place to place, to run it all night and to do so consistently,[17] so many would probably place the start of the period at that point. Others argue the time when humanity was first able to impact the Earth goes back well before that, perhaps 5000 years to a time when methane levels rose as tied to a massive increase in rice cultivation in Asia, and so marking a significant change in our relationship with nature.[18] But then again, it was "(i)n 1945 there occurred the Great Acceleration of the Anthropocene, marked by a huge data spike in the graph of human involvement in Earth systems."[19] It might therefore initially appear that there is a wide range of dates (3,000BCE to 1945CE) one might consider as the start of the Period.

This issue of time is an essential question. Those who would have the date placed earlier tend to be of a conservative, humanist bent. An earlier date "smooths" the timeline, making humanity's impact on the Earth less abrupt, less brutal and more a part of our natural evolution as but one actor in Earth's systemic devolution, making the argument that we have an equal, though not deterministic, place in the world. Those of the progressive/radical bent would argue for a later date, the mid-1940s, in order to directly tie the Anthropocene to climate change and the rise of modern day, financial capitalism, which presently serves as fuel for our ever increasing and rapid destruction of the planet. I suppose this must mean that Moderate-Dems and Conservatives of the Pre-Trump type, were they to consider the question, might settle on the late 18th century date as the preferred start of the Anthropocene.[20]

To be clear, the Anthropocene and global climate change are two separate topics. However, with that in mind, I don't know that this is a tricky discussion to have as it would seem those climate scientists who've considered the whole of the research are clear as to the direction it points whereas other scientists with less focus on the topic might perhaps still draw different conclusions. It is my understanding many of those few scientists who have participated in signing dissenting opinions don't have areas of expertise within this climate debate, but I might have just picked that up somewhere. Regardless, as Bob Dylan observed, I don't suppose one needs a weatherman to tell which way the wind blows.

ON TIME AND
A PERSONAL ANTHROPOCENE

When I was a boy, we had a cabin near a wilderness area high in the Colorado Rockies. In the winter, in fits of boredom and reckless, adolescent self-amusement, I could stand on the deck and drop our dog over the side. She would plummet ten or fifteen feet, down and away, to settle into a thick, white snow bank, only to explode out seconds later, swimming through an ocean of cold, bright powder. Back then, there were periods when we would have cold snaps, sending the temperature plunging to minus twenty or even thirty degrees below zero for days at a time. More recently, in the very same area where our current home looks across to the hill my family's cabin was on nearly fifty years ago, you're lucky to get just a few days each winter down to twenty degrees below zero. As a consequence, over recent decades the pine beetle larvae survived the warming winters quite well, meaning they would then come forth in their masses in the early spring and devour the trees in our region and elsewhere throughout the American West, leaving acre upon acre of copper-colored standing dead wood in their wake. I've no test or evidence to present you, but it sure as hell feels like we've done something to the thermostat settings of our natural home.

And what happened to the Pika? Those little, gerbil-like rodents that would stand up on their hind legs, offering a piercing squeak at my parents and me as we passed by, hiking to Stone Lake, up the Roaring Fork drainage, transitioning from 8,500 feet to somewhere over 11,000 feet, moving from lakeside to high alpine? They seem to be pretty much gone at this point, reliant upon a habitat that over the years has moved up the sides of the scree fields, to the ridge line and then...where? The old slogan of The Mountain Gazette, now defunct due to the wonders of new and what we're told is "social" media, used to be "When in Doubt, go Higher!" but what do you do when there is no above?

I have good friends who state, "We can have a difference of opinion on climate change," despite the fact that today in the same area of Colorado, while we get snow and it is still enough to play in, it is nothing like when I was a boy and it would pile up, foot upon foot, in sub-zero temperatures. And down on the Front Range one may now go through an entire season of Winter without ever once pulling out a snow shovel, which I find shocking and incredible in the wake of the enormous snowstorms and closed schools of my younger years. If we would just pause in our listening to the pundits' distorted diatribes to sincerely see and hear the Earth, there would be no debate. And besides, I miss the Pika greeting us on our walks above tree line.

In reflecting upon my youth, now nearing sixty, it strikes me that consideration of the Anthropocene also makes one ponder the concept of time in a different light. In the American West, where water is life, the time periods where they began documenting rainfall amounts which became the basis upon which we calculate average rain fall and

expected water flows of the Colorado River as it runs by our home, we now know took place during a period of decades that were the wettest on record. But at that time we didn't have the perspective of research that framed the rain in centuries as opposed to decades, so we didn't know dry from wet. The politics of water is such, however, that we can't pause the conversation for even one moment to consider this new information or allow it to expand our perspective; and, therefore, folks still think in terms of "first use" and "water right seniority" as opposed to either the needs of the Earth and aquifers or human versus natural rights.

Our understanding of time and resources is all just the ebb and flow of humankind's politics and power, both of which it seems will be blown away in the wake of larger trends now on the move. Ask the ancestral Pueblos who inhabited Mesa Verde in Colorado from 600 to 1300CE[21]—but then mysteriously abandoned their life, leaving their cliff dwellings and fields atop the plateau. We're not sure, but best estimates are they left due to a turn of drought that would not withdraw, driving them from the area. Or perhaps others came across their land, seeking new territory away from their own droughts, and beat them in battle (though there is less sign of that).

There was a time in 1854 when an explorer such as Captain George Johnson could have a steamer built in Baltimore, shipped to San Francisco, have it reassembled there, sail it down the Baja Peninsula and then sail it up the Sea of Cortez, into the Colorado River's estuary and get all the way to Yuma. But today, the water starts to peter out just over the U.S. border and then dries up completely, miles from the beautiful Cortez. Either way, over the centuries water in the West, remains our lifeblood, and that blood is seeping, seeping away due to our impact upon the Planet, its weather and all that stands in between or upon each.

I read a host of interesting books on the topic of the Anthropocene, but perhaps my favorite was by Jeremy Davies. And I think, all in all, one must confess as Davies does, that

> "...The world is seen as characteristically full of devious chains of cause and effect; of intricate braids that link economics to ocean currents and ecosystems to plate tectonics; and of what

climatologists call "teleconnections," far-distant perturbations that prove to be coupled by hidden bonds—although here tele-connections can take the form of trade routes and cash flows as well as seesaws in atmospheric pressure."[22]

Such connections draw your mind to a longer term perspective and understanding of our world; a perspective of Deep Time, which may be understood as being "...by analogy with 'deep space,' the abyss of time that stretches back from a few thousand years ago to the beginnings of the earth...'[23] ...and more than anything else, the Anthropocene is a way of thinking with deep time."[24]

I'm good with that, since (as discussed elsewhere in this manuscript) taking the long term, multi-century perspective within which one may place our current thinking and experiences is perhaps the only way to approach an effort to understand not only the role and purpose of capital but our role in the world and personal meaning as well. I believe understanding where we are and are heading takes the perspective of glacial time rather than the digital time of 24-hour news cycles that influence so much of our thinking and outlook today. In contrast to that, Davies continues,

"...To understand the current environmental crisis, you have to think about very long ago. From year to year, and from decade to decade, the world of early twenty-first century is undergoing changes that can be grasped only by switching to timescales of tens of thousands or even millions of years. Facts that politicians and pressure groups are prone to argue about, to assign blame for, and to promise their electorates or their memberships to ameliorate—contemporary political facts, in other words—need to be explained by referring to eras long before any such thing as politics even existed. Climate change, biodiversity loss, chemical pollution, and so on have made journalists talking to the public invoke geological time spans as casually as if they were paleon-tologists engaged in conversation with glaciologists."[25]

When impact investors speak with traditional investors about investing for the long term, our frames of time must also be radically extended, from daily and quarterly to multi-decanal and generational. It is not enough to say that as fiduciaries we have a greater responsibility to consider long-term factors in our investment policy statements and the guidance we offer our managers. Preferably, we must require, demand and hold ourselves and our managers accountable for bringing a *truly* long-term perspective to our investing.

This is a perspective beyond board meetings; we're called to consideration of the movement of Time, not cash flows, and of Deep Time at that. Thinking in Deep Time does not mean humanity's place on the earth, being but a blink of the eye, is somehow an aberration or separate from the movement of Earth's geological and biological histories. But within that web of Deep Time, within these interlocking ecosystems of which we're a part and which we now increasingly influence, drive and seek, through our great infatuation with our discoveries, to direct, we still think we can do something to alter the current course of events. We are each called to this task.

The Anthropocene has been presented and portrayed as being fundamentally universalist and technocratic, meaning humanity is presented in an undifferentiated manner, and the only way out of our predicament will be through the salvation offered by experts. Davies sees that how we approach our analysis of the Anthropocene is a political act in that by framing solutions as the purview of scientists and experts we remove the role of our citizens and representatives from participating in both analysis and the development of proposed solutions. He goes on to say,

> "...Struggles involving both human and nonhuman lives, from the patenting of rice genes in America to the seizure by gunmen of South Korean ships fishing illegally off Somalia, are equally political. And no less political than either of these are struggles involving geophysical forces, from earthquakes triggered by groundwater extraction in Spain to the effects of pollution on the Indian monsoon...The birth of the Anthropocene is a many-sided disruption and reconfiguration of innumerable

relationships within the earth system…To understand the Anthropocene means widening the focus of sociopolitical critique and working toward *an analysis of the power relations between geophysical actors, both human and non-human.*"[26] (Emphasis in the original).

In the context of impact investing and those seeking to understand the current and future purpose of capital, this observation becomes key. How do we bring the power of markets and economics to advancing solutions to our current situation when much of that traditional capitalist framework places humanity at the center of the equation and does not consider the needs and interests of all peoples and species much less inert materials of our planet? After all, anthropos means "man" but also implies "not-animal"[27] and in this way, we are actors upon and actors within a more massive, geologic, politicial, and biological drama now playing out around the world and within a great number of diverse and diminishing ecosystems.

As Jason Moore concludes,

"The threatened plentitude of Life asks that we view timeworn stories of human ascent with the deep suspicion they deserve, seen through the self-serving ontology of the world recorded as 'resources,' 'natural capital' and 'ecological services' and question what it is we are salvaging in desiring to sustain the human enterprise. For there is no 'human enterprise' worth defending on a planet leveled and revamped to serve the human enterprise."[28]

Moore goes on to promote the idea that this whole conversation is misguided in that it is not the broad movement of humanity that is at fault in our Earth's destruction as much as the system, the mechanism, of our economics—specifically, our system of global financial capitalism—that is advancing our environmental collapse and so, therefore, a more appropriate name for this period is not Anthropocene, but "Capitalpocene."[29]

When I first read his analysis—and despite having since read a sound critique of his position[30]—what he was saying rang true for me. I've long felt that what has been lacking in so much of our current discussion regarding impact investing and our approach to understanding the nature and purpose of capital has been an informed critique of capitalism itself—and by informed, I mean informed by a perspective not grounded within capitalism and all its inherent assumptions, but rather something that sought to look from the outside in as opposed to beginning with our cultural framework regarding capital and capitalism as its jumping off point. What is needed is a new way of understanding economics, earth and our global human community—a new paradigm—the development of which has taken center stage for a number of organizations and actors.

THE CREATION AND PRACTICE OF A NEW CAPITAL PARADIGM[31]

During the spring I like to start the day by clearing my head with a morning hike on the Doe Creek Trail near our home. This one morning broke with a heavy mist from a night's light rain. I was on the trail by six, moving rapidly through an initial stand of woods, up to a low ridgeline that runs through an area of timber fall, which left mountain ranges exposed to both the West and East; sharp, clear and snow covered in the bright morning light. In that moment, I felt I could actually see the eco-system, alive, vibrant and verdant. I felt aware and knowledgeable of the woods, its inhabitants and how it all somehow "fit" as a single, unified system.

Minutes later, coming down off the ridge, through the lower woods and into the meadow below, I splashed through puddles of water on the trail, left from melting spring snow and the night's rain, as I moved out of the woods and into the opening of tall grass and skinny Aspen. I heard but could not see what I took to be deer weaving their way through the thick woods to my left as I sunk to my ankles in frigid, rich, meadow mud, dead grasses wrapping my feet, frogs squawking on either side of me, birds bombing through the air, snagging the first bugs, the mist still blocking my view over the top of the grasses. But I was deep in it, cold, lost in the muck and mire of my thoughts crisscrossing the sensations of the world and ecosystem I was visiting—layers of dirt, fluids, flora and animals, intertwined, thriving and alive.

In this moment it struck me that while one might be intellectually aware and know a certain truth, one cannot actually know a truth in the absence of experiencing that reality with the multiplicity of senses, of knowing and being. One may stand on a ridgeline, dry and with great perspective, yet it is below one, in the muck and mire, where a deeper appreciation of reality is cultivated.

Within our community of mission directed capital (in which I would include foundations, impact funds and other such actors) over this past year there have been various discussions regarding the importance of a new economic if not life paradigm to frame our understanding of our world. There are those who would say our sole focus should be upon envisioning and enunciating that paradigm, that, within impact investing, anything less is simply living deal-to-deal or not relevant to the larger and compelling agenda we must pursue toward reinvention of the very systems which have brought our world to the point of social and environmental breakdown.

Others seem more focused upon operating at a level of strategy and tactic, believing the larger Whys and links between various parts of the whole will reveal themselves in the course of our doing the work as we stride through the muck and mud of the meadow. These folks share papers on perceived best practice, focus on discussions of metrics and evaluation of the work in which they are engaged and follow a path of doing the work to discover a way to better understand the work. And that is all for the good—we need to think differently about the work *and* do the work differently.

What seems curious is the degree to which we often neglect to remember we are called to and must engage in both. As Karl Marx said, philosophers have only interpreted the world in various ways; the point, however, is to change it. And, as Milton Friedman said, concentrated power is not rendered harmless by the good intentions of those who create it. The time has indeed come when we must revisit the underlying assumptions regarding our most recent neoliberal economic order, but we will evolve that new vision not simply by reflecting upon the elements of a potentially new paradigm or executing our capital deployment strategies in the absence of that broader paradigm shift, but rather by engaging in a continued process of our doing both—of engaging in *collaborative praxis*; our thoughts being informed by experience, which then leads to more enlightened thoughts and perspective, bringing us to yet better execution and on and on. It is our action that addresses Marx's interest in changing the world while our focus on justice positions us to respond to Friedman and our larger community's concerns regarding the dangers of an ever-greater concentration of wealth and power within increasingly smaller segments of our societies around the world.

Traditional philanthropists not mobilizing their total portfolios for impact and being absent from the community of philanthropists deploying growing percentages of their portfolios in intentional impact strategies, remove their institutions from the potential experience of learning through practice what many others seek to intuit through research and reflection. And, while I don't know the degrees to which every foundation engaging in mission aligned and impact investing does so, impact investors must also step back from their work to refine and promote new paradigms of economics, eco-systems and societies. Two sides of the same coin, yet each limited in its ability to realize full, blended value potential.

By viewing these as distinct perspectives and approaches—those that "do" versus those that "envision new paradigms"—our community is simply affirming a dualistic framework for understanding what is at heart a single inquiry. In doing so we promote the illusion of separation that in this context would have us believe thought and action are not intrinsically intertwined. It is as if we are promoting the notion we should think with half our brains or box with one arm tied behind our backs, when if history shows us anything it is that our potential future success rests in our shared experience *and* common knowledge evolving within an integrated, holistic approach to understanding what we should do, why we should do it and how we might create new conceptual *and* practice frameworks to assist us in advancing the societies and world we seek. We must both hike the ridge and wallow in the mud of the spring meadow if we are to truly find our way out of the woods.

I would suggest we might be better served by engaging in fewer of these debates regarding which approach is best and spend more of our time in deeper, common and truly open dialogue combined with humble personal reflection. We must each be in and of the process of change we long to create. By pursuing this path of integrated inquiry, we may, in the end, actually find the mutual enlightenment we seek.

Two additional points are worth our common consideration:

First, I'd remind us that as we raise our eyes to envision a new economic future, it is critical all members of our community be present and engaged in that exploration—not simply leading academics, foundation executives and impact investors, but those stakeholders we seek to ensure benefit from these deliberations and their economic innovations. Foxworth, Burton, Fund for Shared Insight and a host of others have already framed aspects of this important point. There are no doubt many others whose voices we've not as yet heard who are waiting to engage in a more meaningful way as we move further into this exploration of the future of economics and finance, doing so from the perspective of those communities and individuals presently shut out from access to capital and opportunity.

Second, and as ever, it must also be acknowledged this is not a new discussion; others have been engaging in the exploration of this new paradigm for many years. As I argue in these pages, our exploration of how we think about the purpose of capital is, in fact, an inquiry central to humanity's journey over millennium. More recently, there most certainly have been discussions regarding impact investing and systems change and beyond that, a large number of organizations have been actively engaged in promoting the new paradigm to which we all now aspire (perhaps some of which have received philanthropic investments from the same foundations advancing this present conversation). This group includes The Capital Institute, The New Economics Foundation, The New Economy Coalition, Transform Finance, A Whole Person Economy, The Schumacher Center for New Economics, The Buckminster Fuller Institute, The Natural Capital Project, Regenerative Economy Fund and no doubt many others too numerous to list here.

In truth, a great many in our community have concluded what Larry Kramer, President of the William and Flora Hewlett Foundation, rightfully observes, one of the most critical challenges we face today is that of enunciating a new, global/local paradigm to guide the management of our species' approach to economics since today that approach determines not only our own future but that of the Earth itself. Finally, of course, we may also benefit from the ideas and lessons of those areas of academic inquiry known as Social Economy and Social Economics, which have growing bodies of academic research and reflection we may draw upon.

The many foundations, governmental, corporate, community agents and other actors interested in advancing new paradigms to guide the future of finance and economics would benefit from the experience of actually investing in the creation of new financial practices just as those that invest in new financial innovations will benefit from deeper reflection and philosophical inquiry to better see the links and connections between capital deployment and our potential to more profoundly comprehend what we take to be the fundamental nature and purpose of the capital we deploy. Friedman, Keynes, Hayek and their various followers came to new understandings of capital markets and policies not by virtue of attending briefings and conferences alone, but through reflecting upon the lessons learned from the application of their ideas and concepts in practice within real world capital markets and societies.

Our community will be best positioned to advance new ideas and thinking—new paradigms—if those ideas and thinking are grounded in the evolving and innovative investment practices of impact investing and whatever becomes of the future of finance and global economics.

It is all one journey of which we are all a part.

But now with the broad adoption of impact investing by mainstream finance, what has felt most absent has been any reflection upon this new paradigm or discussion of the critical role to be played by those promoting regenerative capitalism, circular economics and other, related visions of our future economic system—a critique and promotion not heard coming from the large private equity funds, wealth management and advisory firms or other mainstream adopters of impact, sustainable and responsible investing practice.

Capitalism as currently practiced is not the issue alone, for as Timothy Morton observes, "…Capitalpocene misses the mark. Capital and capitalism are symptoms of the problem, not its direct causes. If the cause were capitalism, then Soviet and Chinese carbon emissions would have added nothing to global warming."[32] All of which brings us back to the work of those organizations leading our efforts to construct a new capital paradigm.

Along those lines, one of the last books I read at this stage of my process was by Ian Angus. He is a real innovator and socio-political critic whose two books are excellent, but who also offers a more than scathing critique of Jason Moore's work. Yet, in reading his piece and recalling the many debates I've been enmeshed in over the years regarding the "right" definition of impact investing and social entrepreneurship, the "best" way to think about metrics, the "right" terms and metrics we should be using and other minutiae of our field, all reminded me that the back and forth regarding the right way to go, the right way to think about our future work—much less, the right way to think about our future, period—has within it the seeds of our demise.

My concern is that in light of our chatty nature and love of discussion, we could well find ourselves spending massive amounts of time verbally rearranging the chairs on the proverbial Titanic as opposed to working together to build a new ship. We may well be confusing a good discussion at Davos or SOCAP or period of shared reflection at a conference retreat with our engaging in some form of actual change or transformation—much less transcendence of our current thinking and state of being.

To be clear, I have certainly been a part of the movement of those seeking new ways to think about and deploy capital and community in pursuit of the creation of a better world, a sustainable planet, and a regenerative economic system capable of supporting our societies as well as our natural eco-systems. And I have contributed my fair share of passionate and well received conference keynotes with obligatory cute asides—as well as adding some books, articles, and papers to our field's archives.

Yet, I must still conclude, we are avoiding a large part of the problem by presuming we can turn back the tide of destruction we've unleashed on the Earth with the same rationalistic, data-dependent, analytic frames that have brought us here. After all, it was the hubris of Man that has brought us to this point. I say that explicitly, since while many in the First World have benefitted, the vast majority of our destruction has been directed and executed by the white male of the species. And I believe it to be a point of no return, ultimate accounting and comeuppance in which we will all share but that will lay the most significant burden upon the poor and the young who at this stage have only inklings of what their fate will be long after we pass.

BEING PRESENT IN THE CREATION OF THE NEW PARADIGM

All in all, these are a heavy set of reflections to entertain...I was therefore oddly relieved to find a considerable degree of solace in a somewhat unexpected place:

Art

Toward the end of my research, courtesy of the only magazine about the West worth reading (*The High Country News*), I came on the work of the Dark Mountain Project. DMP is a collaboration of artists, mainly writers but I believe others as well, who are shaping a response to the present ecocide and adopting a posture that rather than fight what is, we need to transcend it, to get a new perspective on it and call it out for what it is. The article, by Brian Calvert, titled *How to Face the Ecocide*, is an excellent reflection on the opportunity we have for reconnecting ourselves to our processes by integrating our art with advocacy, our act of presence with a pursuit of justice. This is what we're called to do, *how* we're called to be, in the face of the current global ecocide. We are called to a form of Buddhist action to respond not only to the Age of the Anthropocene but to heal our selves, our community, and the Earth we share with all living things. While I'm not a formal, card-carrying member of the Dark Mountain Project, I like the work and process in which they are engaged. Their new collection of writings, entitled *Walking on Lava: Selected Works for Uncivilized Times*, is excellent. It offers a path forward for us all.

And then, last summer, while exploring the most Northwest corner of Norway, out on the edge of an archipelago of islands jutting into the Atlantic at but one end of the world (so far out, that the village is actually called *Aa*, which is the final letter of the Norwegian alphabet and means "end"), I came on a book in a gallery on an island at this end of land, which caught my eye. The book is, *Living Earth: Field Notes from the Dark Ecology Project, 2014-2016*. It details a set of art installations and events executed in the farthest reaches of Northern Norway which sought to engage a diverse community of artists, area residents, policy makers, writers, business executives and so on in a set of intentional, artistic experiences and dialogues concerning the Earth, humanity's impact upon the Planet and our expression of self in the context of community and ecological destruction.

Both these initiatives are, I imagine, a part of a broader movement (I say "I imagine" since every time I discover something that is new to me, I find it to be part of something more substantial and greater than I was initially aware, like Newton and gravity, its existence a surprise to me, but not the Universe) that seeks to explore the relation of self, community and Planet, not from the perspective of economics or science but rather from our shared experience and more significant process of Being and Becoming.

All of which puts me of a mind to say we are now, instead of at the end of history, potentially at the beginning of a new history. The shifts that occurred during the Axial Age are of note not just regarding how we came to where we are today, but also in reflecting on our current times and future possibilities. One must consider whether, in fact, we are not due for a New Axial Age, to move us forward in a transformative manner and better position us to address the profound challenges now before us. Some of that is already underway across the world, in multiple cultural contexts, as new technologies connect ever higher numbers of the world's citizens to share analysis, tell stories and join together in the face of the global social and environmental destruction we have ourselves created.

This is similar in some ways to the push within physics to discover the Theory of Everything, which is interesting in its own right. However, within the context of capital and impact investing, one is reminded of a host of initiatives, whether those of the arts community seeking a more in-depth exploration of how we are called to be in the face of the Anthropocene, to that of those promoting Regenerative Economics to the recently created investor network and advisory group, Jubilee, to the practices of Total Portfolio Management and a host of other capital actions we may take. In each and all of these, various actors are exploring how to integrate self, Other and Earth in new ways within a meta-framework of not only capital management and deployment, but our understanding of self in the context of community and value creation.

Just as during the original Axial Age centuries ago, current efforts to engage these questions are evolving out of a diverse set of regions and communities across the globe. The original Axial Age gave rise to four significant religious and philosophical traditions. Today's communities, coming together in person and virtually, hold the potential to integrate our scientific knowledge with our shared wisdom to position us to take the great leap across the chasm dividing us from each other and a more promising future.

Together we must work to divine the true purpose of capital within a more comprehensive understanding of the nature and definition of the multiple returns we seek to generate over the course of our individual lives, as well as the lives of our fellow beings and Earth itself.

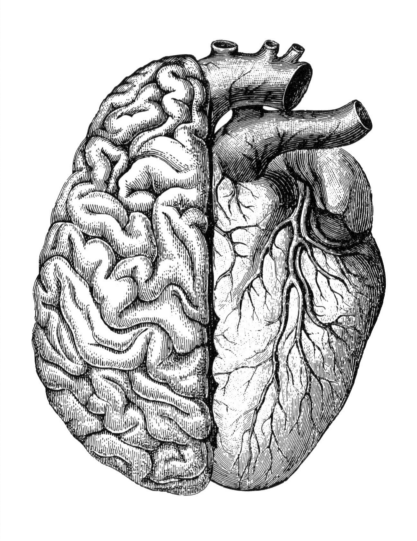

CHAPTER FIVE

VALUE LIBERATION FROM THE TRAP OF DUALISM

I BELIEVE VALUE TO BE TRAPPED BETWEEN THE UNDER-STANDINGS OF OUR PRESENT AND THE POSSIBILITIES YET TO COME.

As is true of many of the aspects of capital explored in this book, value lives simultaneously, first within the world as we know and understand it and later within the Universe of what we are learning, coming to see and in the process of creating. It is a moth, held between the light of what is known and the darker light of another experience of knowledge, beyond what is toward what is becoming. In its essence, value is whole and integrative, a blend of elements we've come to think as consisting of what is the social, environmental and economic in our and other worlds.

From the very start of civilization, economic and social components of value have been considered concurrently. During the pre-Axial Age, sacred and secular, holy and profane, were not sharply distinguished. There was no separate domain of life that could be identified as 'religious.'[1] It was just life, and we lived more fully connected and integrated with both God and Nature. As Historian Arnold Toynbee observed, "The way of life that was bequeathed to primitive Man [sic] by his pre-human ancestors was monolithic. His religious life was part and parcel of this total social life. The religious and the secular side of life were not separable or even distinguishable from each other at this stage. Each of Man's activities was religious and political and economic and artistic simultaneously."[2] And originally, even—or perhaps, especially— agriculture was initially as much a religious as an economic act.[3]

The divide began to emerge in many diverse communities as a result of many different developments. The separation of Self from God and Other was described by the First Philosopher, Thales. Roochnik states this Pre-Socratic, Ionian philosopher (600 BCE) believed in the concept of an *arche*,

> "...a first principle that is the origin of, and so responsible for, all beings. It persists: it does not come into being nor does it cease to be. It is not itself a being nor does it participate in Becoming. Instead, it is that which is most real and enduring: it is Being or Nature. It is the unifying principle of all reality...Thales distinguished Being and beings, between the one enduring principle that is most real, and all the many little beings in the world that are here today and gone tomorrow...Being and beings are inextricably related, precisely because the former is the arche, and thus the origin of the latter. To reformulate this point: Thales was an ontological dualist who divided reality into two categories, Being and Becoming."[4]

And so the divide—*our* divide—is conceived and advanced from this point forward.

Thales is viewed as the first philosopher since he was the first to use reason alone to frame his argument of Being as opposed to relying upon myth and the gods to do so. However, the critical challenge or even crisis of how this dualism was framed is that once having done so, we must then learn how to bring Being and Becoming back together.[5] But later, as Christianity emerged, this initial dualism continued to be promoted. Within the Old Testament of the Hebrews, God is woven in and through Nature, but in the New Testament, God's place with nature is exchanged for God's place dominating over Nature—a role he then gives to Humanity.

As the sustainability strategist and visionary Giles Hutchins writes:

> "Up to the late sixteenth and early seventeenth century, Catholicism, natural philosophy and ancient Hermetic traditions blended with Neo-Platonism, paganism and Aristotelian-Scholastic traditions to allow for vestiges of the ancient belief in the divine immanence of Nature to exist alongside a transcendent God. The natural world was viewed as exhibiting a World Soul, or *anima mundi*. Yet Europe was then in a time of great upheaval. Plagues and famines as well as the Thirty Years War (1618-48) followed on from the break-up of the Church through the Reformation. The rise of Protestantism, rationalism and empiricism started to alter the worldview of Nature as divine towards a view that God was divorced from nature (Nature then became nature with a small 'n', de-spirited, de-animated, without World Soul)."[6]

It was in this context then, that on November 10, 1619, Rene Descartes[7] had a dream in which he conceived of the universe as a clock leading to his rejecting the idea of Nature as living in favor of the concept of nature as inert, mechanical and without spirit.[8] By the 1650s, the notion of "value-free" science was "founded upon the materialistic notion of a de-spirited mechanistic worldview."[9] And over the centuries we have built upon this division between the rational states to continue a process of sub-division, specialization and spaces divided, both physically and socially. Or as Hutchins writes, "This dualistic outlook is not so much the product of the rational as the abuse of the rational—due to a mechanism of abstract separation imposed on reality—and reason itself may be called upon to question and correct it."[10]

Thus over the past four centuries we have evolved a world in which we must today exhort people to bring their "whole selves" to work as we see the evolution of a generation of Millennials seeking to engage in profit with purpose and integrate more of their life parts of personal and professional with social and environmental value creation; while the Boomers find they have in some ways created lives of success but not value, many turning in their final years to the pursuit of deeper meaning and purpose whether in regard to what they buy, how they live or what they think as they look back upon their lives and try to understand it all.

Descartes' position was that there are only two types of entities in our world: Minds and Bodies. Humans are special since we alone can think and operate with free will, whereas bodies operate within set parameters and laws of nature. This understanding of reality was unique for the 17th Century, with philosophers arguing this insight established peace between the forces of religion and those of science, which at that time was focused upon defining a host of "physical" or "body" questions.

While Descartes certainly believed in the importance of separating out and appreciating the parts to two elements of mind and body, his perspective on these as two separate components have been overstated in our popular understanding of Descartes' framework. As the historian Matthew Stewart points out, there is good reason to believe, writing during the Spanish Inquisition and a period of numerous religious purges, part of Descartes' motivation was to separate science from religion to free himself from the possibility of being subject to the punishment of the Inquisition. If he could present science and religion as two separate and distinct parts, then scientists could engage in exploration of the natural world without fear of intrusion from the inquisitors.[11] Picking up this same point, Stewart observes:

"By isolating the mind from the physical world, the philosopher ensured that many of the central doctrines of orthodoxy—immortality of the soul, the freedom of the will, and, in general, the 'special' status of humankind—were rendered immune to any possible contravention by the scientific investigation of the physical world. Conversely, the complete self-sufficiency of the machine-like material world guaranteed that physical science could proceed without fear of contradiction from revealed religion."[12]

This perspective, nevertheless, allowed a number of questions to remain (if you're sleeping and not thinking, do you exist?).

Spinoza rejected this notion of bifurcated being, however, stating the mind is not exempt from natural laws: "Man is a part of Nature and must follow its laws, and this alone is true worship."[13] His challenge became that of explaining how two such different things (Mind and Body) could be manifest in a single way; a question he answered by stating they were simply two aspects of the same thing, what he called substance. Specifically, Spinoza says,

> "Mental decision on the one hand, and the appetite and physical state of the body on the other, are simultaneous in nature; or rather, they are one and the same thing which, when considered under the attribute of Thought and explicated through Thought, we call decision, and when considered under the attribute of Extension and deduced from the laws of motion-and-rest, we call a physical state."[14]

There are a host of implications, therefore, to this perspective (for example, that while 'free' humanity exercises that freedom within the limits of Nature, or that the notion of 'will' becomes eliminated), but fundamentally he proposes that mind and body are one with Nature. Curiously, as the historian Yuval Noah Harari submits, from a neurological point of view the notion of Mind or Spirit are merely the biological and chemical manifestations of synapses firing within the brain and so, from the perspective of modern science, Spinoza is correct and, together with the Ancients, should be viewed as a father of blended value!

Despite Descartes' dualistic approach to the world, he also affirmed these two parts were inexorably intertwined—a point that seems lost in today's discussions of dualism, of doing well or good, of the material corporation and the spiritual presence of the individuals of whom it is constituted. Descartes said:

> "I am not merely present in my body as a sailor is present in a ship, but...am very closely joined and, as it were, intermingled

with it...[15] ...we "experience within ourselves certain...things which must not be referred either to the mind alone or to the body alone..."...these arise..."from the close and intimate union of our mind with the body."[16]

Despite this sentiment, the notion of a mind/body split, of a profound presence of dualism in our world, came to be established in the Western mind and evolved to become what Terrence Deacon called "the Cartesian wound that severed mind from body at the birth of modern science."[17] The irony is for over a century now a large number of scientists and philosophers have operated under the belief that there is no mind/body split and the concept of dualism is false, yet the damage had been done.

Moving backward from the period of the Enlightenment to that of the great Roman Empire, consideration of social, spiritual, and political attitudes flowed through each other. Many Romans feared the shakes and tremors rocking their society in the fourth century. The Republic had been initially founded by those who were viewed as living in a state of "heroic poverty"[18] and one important consideration in the impending demise of the Empire (together with the belief the gods were angry with Constantine's conversion to Christianity!) was thought to be the corrupting influence of wealth together with the crushing accumulation of money by the top ten percent of the population, which some have referred to as the "fortunate decile"[19] who lived a life of lavish excess while 90% of the balance of the Roman populace lived a life of scarcity and uncertainty.

It was the new rich (those called out by Ammiannus), living at the feasting tables within their ancient versions of McMansions and barreling down Roman roads in their Lexus chariots, who threatened the very soul and survival of Roman society. One can hear chants of "We are the 99%" drifting down the cold canyons of an ancient Wall Street, the clattering noise of their massive horses and outsized arrogance nearly drowning the vows to "Make Rome Great Again!" and various other words shouted by commoners in the street, longing to return to the days of order, a specific knowledge of the cosmos and the rule of law, all under the watchful, if slightly unsteady, gaze of an aging, straw-haired Caesar.

THE INTEGRATION OF VALUE AND VALUES

Moving from historic to modern empires, while we are used to the notion the word *values* speaks to the good in humanity, and our discussions regarding economics and *value* often take off from that starting place, we should not neglect there are a variety of benefits and ways in which our values then weave into, through, and define our understanding of economic value.

The relation between our knowledge of what is good for the state (as opposed to society) and how we then create economic order and processes to advance the interests of the state intertwine with our understanding of individual economic benefit and how we approach the operation of supposedly objective capital and other markets. This is value understood as economics that advances and serves the interests of the state because it is assumed state interests are the same as those of society (as reflected in the previously cited phrase, *What is good for GM is good for America!*). This is an understanding of the value of capital and enterprise that has been with us since the establishment of the first joint stock corporation in the early 1600s.

> "By the time a twelve-year truce (between the Spanish and Dutch) was signed with Spain in 1608, the VOC (United Dutch Chartered East India Company) had made more money from capturing enemy vessels than from trade. One major investor, the Mennonite Pieter Lijntjens, was so dismayed by the Company's warlike conduct that he withdrew from the Company in 1605. Another early director, Isaac le Maire, resigned in protest at what he regarded as the mismanagement[20] of the Company's affairs."[21]

Thus from the very beginning of capitalism, with the creation of what has been called, "perhaps the single greatest Dutch invention of all"[22] which is to say, the jointly held stock company, we see the integration of economic with political (an extension, then, of social) interests.

We cannot make war without trade, nor trade without war.

So said Jan Pieterszoon Coen, who became the first governor-general of the Dutch East Indies and led the effort to drive the British, Spanish and Portuguese out of the region to corner the market and turn a profit for his firm, the VOC.[23] And this is the insight shared by those who railed against another, more modern Army going to war for ancient oil and against our entering into an exchange of blood and treasure for the black gold of the Middle East. We appear to have lost our touch of the Midas as the lives of our warriors turn to sand and blow away with the winds of what we had hoped to be a moist Sirocco, but which we only too late discover as the winds of the latest Levanter, winds carrying the dry, chaffing sands of the East within which we hear the distant, heart-broken howls of modern day Moors, buried beneath time as their cries play in a warm breeze, lost amongst the dunes.

This link between State, private capital, and social interests is reflected in warfare and the use of it to gain an advantage over other actors in the world. History is replete with example after example of State action to protect private gain and commerce over State action to advance the broader, social interest of the majority of those laboring under its weight. The story of this tale is best told by religious historian Karen Armstrong in her *Fields of Blood: Religion and the History of Violence* but is also explored by Niall Ferguson and other economic historians who sometimes seem to make the point yet fail to make the connections we ultimately seek. If we can promote our better nature within our financial markets in the same way we allow our animal instincts and political interests to drive our economic practices, we could more intentionally integrate our values and beliefs for the betterment of humanity. We should be able to attain the pinnacle of doing well and good, should we not? And we should then have the potential to move even further to blend the One with the Other.

Historically, states and markets have always operated in a supportive relationship with each other[24] and such is true of impact investing markets as well. Research conducted by Cathy Clark, Ben Thornley, and I found a significant number of the early, leading impact investing funds were seeded, either directly or indirectly, with public capital.[25] Over time as those funds developed track records of success, private equity came to complement the initial investments of public funds and support from public entities seeking to use markets and enterprise to drive social change and impact. Though they are often loath to admit it, in a genuine sense, all those who today are investing for market rate returns through impact investing strategies owe both a metaphorical and real financial debt to those who went before, investing public and philanthropic capital in early, inefficient markets—buying down risk, as it were—which then made it possible for commercial, market-rate capital investors to later "do well and do good."

The specific ways in which companies and markets manifest our social and other beliefs ebb and flow—as does our understanding of their value to us in maintaining a stable society. Adam Smith argued joint stock companies were a disaster, writing that "The directors of such companies...being the managers of other people's money than of their own, it cannot well be expected that they should watch over it with the same anxious vigilance with which the partners in a private company frequently watch over their own...Negligence and profusion, therefore, must always prevail, more or less, in the management of the affairs of such a company."[26]

In that context, Smith was speaking of the question of financial agency—of who speaks for the owner of capital and monitors its deployment, he speaks of who and what is the nature of true fiduciary duty—which at its core is a form of social obligation and responsibility, defined narrowly and with sole interest for the shareholder. In this way, the first order of social responsibility of the fiduciary is to steward not only the wealth but the uses to which wealth is applied.

As a moral philosopher, this Founder of Capitalism might have come into conflict with many of his future followers, who view themselves as modern experts in business and finance and have argued against the idea companies should be thought of in any way as having a social obligation to their investors and society. They have argued the social aspect of the firm is an assessment best made by the individual and not grounded in societal assumptions or expectations. Milton Friedman was especially active in promoting his views against any need for corporate social responsibility. As he famously stated (Okay—maybe not broadly famous in the sense of celebrity, but undoubtedly renowned within a particular group of those committed to shareholder primacy who hung on his every word, as well as those others focused upon promoting the social obligations and opportunities of business who were confused and befuddled by the thought a company could be viewed as operating within a vacuum, removed from the social context where it most obviously *did* play out its existence!); my apologies for the digression—to both those who believed in shareholder primacy and those who believed corporations have obligations to shareholders and stakeholders, Friedman cried out with all form of conviction and little doubt, dare we say humility:

> "There is one and only one social responsibility of business—to use its resources and engage in activities designed to increase its profits so long as it stays within the rules of the game, which his to say, engages in open and free competition without deception or fraud.' Corporate executives who purported to strive toward some higher goal were not only cheating their shareholders but 'undermining the basis of free society."[27]

Frederick Hayek, in his *Road to Serfdom*, also argues against those who would use economics and corporate management as vehicles for advancing social justice,[28] while others who come later make the counter argument that in favor of business promoting social value, based upon Hayek's own words and understanding of the proper role of economics in our lives.[29]

While there are no doubt those who would still argue in line with dead economists and members of ancient academic empires, times change. Today, we see greater truths than we were able to previously intuit and what was once questioned is now apparent to a growing minority within the ranks of business leaders, even those still clinging to notions of shareholder primacy. Recently we've witnessed such mainstream financiers as Larry Fink, Paul Tudor Jones and Jeremy Grantham all speak of the need for expanded understandings of the role of corporations and investors in stewarding social and environmental aspects of business—but we will see in time the degree to which their words have real impact for themselves or others.[30]

In the future, new generations of leaders will increasingly take as a given this idea capital and corporations must advance profit with purpose. And the glacial defenses of the old corporate guard will continue to drop with a roaring crash as they plunge into the ever-warming oceans that surround them, exploding like calves off the crumbling face of an Arctic glacier. What is accepted as the right way to think shifts and evolves, as it was most certainly meant to do.

We, therefore, may rightly herald the potential of the firm to advance social value as a core component of its overall value proposition as a social and legal entity active in our world. It is not a question as to whether or not a company *should* advance social value via its impact through the management of its business model, but rather *how* it will best seek to do so. The days of our operating within a traditional, bifurcation of nonprofit versus for-profit, good versus evil, impact first versus finance first dualistic frame of the purpose of capital are surely dead and past, left behind us in a burial ground of other ideas and practices once handy, now historic. Just as all capital has an impact, either positive or negative, all companies create social impacts in the course of their work, either positive or negative. The issue is one of whether, to what degree and in what ways corporate leaders will act to intentionally manage the social components of their value proposition in complement to their environmental and economic elements to optimize their full, blended value potential. While mainstream investors and corporate executives have made pronouncements, the jury remains in recess and we shall see if current word and future deed advance as one.

This issue is not a function of morals or normative values as much as an evolved understanding of value itself as consisting of social, economic and environmental components waiting to be found and liberated

like forgotten treasure in the depths
of the ocean, that rests, quietly, waiting to be discovered.

Fiduciaries, whether corporate
or financial, in fulfillment of their
duties, must act to optimize value
on an integrated, holistic basis even
if those managing the firms in which
they invest might plead ignorance or
an inability to control aspects of firm
performance traditionally believed
to be external to the firm's interests.
Those who do not advance over this hill will run the risk of leaving
value on the table as well as under appreciating a host of factors standing
outside our traditional calculus of risk and return which does not consider off balance sheet components of social and environmental risk and
opportunity. Over the long term, such factors have shown themselves
to be material to the firm, effecting the company's potential for market
performance and the generation of financial return. Increasingly, we see
how firms not moving to take such off-balance sheet risk into account
carry legal, operational and market liabilities that will, in time, affect
their ability to thrive within fully global and hyper competitive markets
across the world.

Risk and return have been the dual considerations of business as
usual, but in a world of global climate change, pandemics, water depletion and a host of other risks traditionally thought of as beyond the
domain of the firm, business as *unusual* is increasingly the order of the
day. We now understand that to thrive in such an environment, corporate and fiduciary leadership must operate with consideration not merely
of risk and return, but risk, return and impact.

By extension, we must no longer assume companies and markets can operate in the absence of values and morality, because they
are part and parcel of our world just as those in their employ and
those viewed as owners of capital are part of our world. Components
of value coalesce within a single, integrated vehicle of value and its

creation, affirms the economist, Wayne Visser. There is no commercial versus social just as there is no individual outside of community or species outside of ecosystem. As Michael Hardt and Antonio Negri have argued, "...economics, if it is to be a science, has to return to something closer to the ancient Greek meaning of the term and take *all of social life* into consideration."[31] In this way, we understand value to be liberated from the split restraints of its supposed dualism and seen in its natural state as whole, unified and integrative; as a blend of its parts and potentialities.

The moral philosopher, Adam Smith, wrote, the merchant need have no interest in social good ("...by directing that industry in such a manner as its produce may be of the greatest value, he intends only his gain...he is in this, as in many other cases, led by an invisible hand to promote an end that was no part of his intention."[32]) and, as Joan Robinson in turn wrote, Smith gave us 'the ideology to end ideologies, for it...abolished the moral problem. It is only necessary for each to act egotistically for the good of all to be attained."[33]

Whereas some in traditional finance will still argue any consideration of the social aspect of value creation is forcing an unnatural requirement upon economic analysis and business practice, or that removing certain companies from a portfolio will limit the investible universe to the point of restricting investment manager practice as well as investor financial returns, in point of fact what we are calling for is an opening of the investment aperture in order to include *greater* consideration of a *larger* number of factors material to the maximization of value within firm and society.

Impact investing is not reductive, but additive to the traditional practices of finance. It does not limit the ability of individuals to act in their own self-interest, but steps back to view individual and firm self-interest as resting within the broader context of stakeholders, community, markets and planet in order to define a greater universe of value and possibility. Such impact investing practices add to the quiver of the investor, strengthening her set of tools and instruments with which to analyze and reflect upon any given investment opportunity or market. Such an approach to understanding what matters within our value equations inevitably moves us closer toward realization of full, true and sustained blended value as such an approach simply seeks to acknowledge and place within our algorithm that which we already intuitively and naturally know must be a part of the new calculus of capital.

Values within markets are there and active—whether in the promotion of war or peace, in response to panic or greed. We need to recognize investments and markets are dynamic and living flows, whether of capital or energy, requiring ongoing monitoring and modification just as one actively manages a portfolio or companies within traditional investment practice. Such practices are the same as before—protecting and advancing shareholder interest—but understanding such interest stops not at the boundary of the self but of the surrounding Other and that by operating within such a frame both self and Other are made all the wealthier, the relative interests of each advanced and promoted for the greater good of all, human and non-human.

ON THE IMPACT TAO, THE OTHER AND LIMITATION OF WORDS

We need understand, there is no bifurcation of the components of value. Value and values are in motion, changing not in their essence but in terms of how they manifest and, in this way, may be challenging for some to call out, to name. This is as it should be. That which can be named cannot be the Tao,[34] and the Judeao-Christian God Yahweh is a name one may not speak—yet we know how to worship that which we cannot see or name, whether in financial or spiritual realities. We then chant this liturgy of the Church of the New Capital, we know how to call for and embrace the tangible and intangible elements active in our world. Impact investing speaks directly to this new calling within finance, to optimize those elements of value and value creation that are subject to our analysis and those that are not in the pursuit of capturing the total value and impact opportunity before us.

How we describe and promote values (or at another level, *value*) is the real challenge in that, once one puts metrics and words around any effort to describe and define value(s), one is immediately aware of the limitations of language to explain what is in many ways ephemeral and intangible yet still extant. The seeping Cartesian wound with which we have come to live is not to be understood merely in terms of how we view the split between the material and the spiritual, but also in terms of how we came to understand notions of logic, rationality, faith, and wisdom; it determined how we came to appreciate our connection in time and with truth for touching the moment means touching truth.

The long-term impact of dualism has been to underscore and place a bold mark beneath those elements of identity and consciousness that serve to separate us from the Other as opposed to those that move us toward a deeper appreciation of our connections, one to another or self with local community and greater humanity. This split between self and Other gave license for Hobbes—and much later, Richard Dawkins—to make the argument that humanity is, at its core, motivated solely by attaining benefits for each individual as opposed to the common good or gods. And to argue further, within this bifurcated frame even gestures of good will have selfish motivations. David Hume, in contrast, felt the whole discussion of whether humanity was fundamentally good or bad to be misplaced, noting there is "some particle of the dove kneaded into our frame, along with the elements of the wolf and serpent."[35]

And while our motivations are truly integrative of positive and potentially negative elements, what is interesting to observe is how modern American political rhetoric and perspective have turned the two

parts upon each other, thus promoting a new perspective that positions the investor and capitalist as selfless servant of the common good and those who are not a part of the new economic order, the low-income, homeless or destitute, as shiftless "takers" from the good work and benefits of the economic winners. As the theologeon Joerg Rieger says,

> "Mainline economic theory holds that all relationships, with the exception of family relationships, are governed by the self-interest of independent individuals…Such self-interest is often sanctioned religiously as an inevitable expression of fallen human nature or human sin. At the same time, this self-interest never becomes a real problem because it is redeemed by the activity of the market. The market magically transforms self-interest into the common good. Assmann and Hinkelammert find the 'dogmatic core of a new orthodoxy' here according to which self-interest is transformed from being the private vice of those who hold economic power into a public virtue….An odd reversal results from this assessment: those who pursue their now self-interest, even if they command large amounts of capital and wield quasi imperial power, are now seen as humble servants, while those who have no power in this system are seen as conceited, jealous and perhaps even arrogant."[36]

The trick, then, is to manage ourselves and our processes in a manner that first balances and then integrates these seemingly separate aspects of the self and society in a consistent and considered manner. We must guard against the potential of "doing well and doing good" to become simply another opportunity for those in control and power (for those who own society's economic resources) to do well yet again and in so doing end up doing even better for themselves, their immediate relations and their peers.

Finally, while we tend to think of subject/object dualism as a Western notion, in point of fact, many Western philosophers, beginning with the Pre-Socratic, Greek philosopher Plotinus, have spoken eloquently against the idea that a dualistic approach to thinking and life is the route to go. Among them are Spinoza, Schelling, Hegel, Schopenhauer, Bergson and Whitehead.[37] And as author Charles Eisenstein reflects,

> "Separation is not an ultimate reality, but a human projection, an ideology, a story…It is a story of the separation of the human realm from the natural, in which the former expands and the latter is turned progressively into resources, goods, property, and, ultimately, money."[38]

Speaking of this is challenging since words themselves are tools of dualism and division. As Ralph Waldo Emerson explains when discussing words, 'They cannot cover the dimensions of what is truth. They break, chop, and impoverish it."[39] Yet, words are the basis upon which we build our collective self in the form of communities and society. They form the narrative that weaves our history together with our present and projects us into the future by shaping and defining a common identity.

These ideas are all relevant to each of us in a variety of ways, however in the context of our discussion of the purpose of capital, as impact investors reflect on the nature of our story, of our narration that both distinguishes us from a history of financial practices while at the same time tying us to a possible financial future yet to be created, it is this emerging narrative within which we must root ourselves. Traditional finance is the Old World territory, the land of the past, while the current tensions between traditional finance and our understanding of the purpose of capital are set out upon new frontiers of thought and how we might understand economics, moving from 17th Century frameworks to future century visions of capital—who owns it, who has the right to use it, how we define its complex value, components of worth and so on. Capital and our understanding of it is a narration created and promoted by those who increasingly understand the old story of the colonial state has not served us well. The old approach must fall to the wayside as a new narrative, a new story of the purpose of capital, comes to the fore. In this way, we are shaping and promoting a new culture of capital.

As we think about the cultural aspects of finance and the world within which it operates, impact investing is the 'them' standing in opposition to the 'us' of traditional finance. The multiple returns sought by impact investors (social and environmental to be sure, but also new considerations such as non-extractive investment practices or new ways to understand the fundamental purpose of capital or even our definition of profits) calls into question the singular, historic understanding and definition of traditional finance with regard to our measure of value creation, profit and economics, creating what are potential conflicts between traditional and impact investors concerning not simply worldview and vision but of culture and fundamental values. For these reasons while structures and concepts (the how) are important for us to consider and understand, our focus should be upon more nuanced properties and ideas (the Why), which is what links the parts to the greater whole within which we all exist.

OF SILOS, WELLS AND WALLS

Against this backdrop of structure versus property, we must also acknowledge separation of self from Other, a reduction from the cosmic to the microscopic, is not altogether negative. Such separations allow us to define components and elements, to explore links between parts and whole, and to understand where various disciplines connect and transcend the silos from within which they sit, potentially reaching out to that larger whole. All living things must operate with a boundary in one form or another. This gives us and other living beings the ability to take in elements and the ability to push elements out into the world. That is life.[40]

At the community level, this boundary setting is what made civilization itself possible:

> "...Because of the city wall (as portrayed in the Epic of Gilgamesh), people in the city can devote themselves to things other than worrying about their own safety, and they can continue to specialize more deeply. The permanence of a city surrounded by a wall brings [sic] is also noticeable. Human life in the city gains a new dimension and suddenly it seems more natural to take up issues going beyond the life span of an

individual...The wall around the city of Uruk is, among other things, a symbol of internal distancing from nature, a symbol of revolts against submission to laws that do not come under the control of man and that man can at most discover and use to his benefit,"[41] Sedlacek says.

Operating within walls and silos allows focus, specialization and development of unique skill sets. Identity comes to be shaped within those same walls, value is defined with reference to the wall and all that is held within it, and one's sense of purpose, possibility, and future is framed by the boundaries defined by the wall. This functions well in the short run as one seeks to focus and create but is limiting in the long run as one ultimately must evolve to transcend the wall and its definition, its frame of reality. This is the challenge of everything from inter-faith dialogue to non-partisan policy initiatives to race relations and inter-disciplinary academic work. It is an insight I fell into in the late 90s and which laid the foundation for my exploration of blended value as well as my academic research that led to the publication of the Blended Value Map in 2003. Silos hurt, hinder and help but we must seek to work at the crosscuts of the silos and not be bound by their walls.

The central point is this:

The silo allows us to focus and attain expertise yet then becomes the well shaft that traps us below the surface of the earth.

Well shafts allow us to see a portion of the sky but not its complete horizon or possibilities beyond the limited diameter from which we peer upward. The Earth and its natural geography, then, are perhaps our first experiences of boundaries and silos, in that they define our sense of location and place, they become where we are from and have historically defined our prospects and future. We quickly embrace this sense of place professionally, within whatever area of focus we bring to our work and in so doing over a career lose the ability to naturally play across space and time, trading that ability for an artificial sense of grounding, certainty, and competence. If we are to succeed, if we are to capture the potential impact opportunity before us, we must rediscover our peripheral vision, recapturing our original ability to live not just outside the box, but simultaneously see, think and feel beyond the box of our present circumstance. We may then more fully experience who we are and our very being.

But this geographic grounding, this place that defines culture and people, soon manifests solely at the social, not geographic level. We come to be determined less by the logic of the land and professional silo of a field than by the history of human interaction, politics and social forces that push and pull across regional geography and natural, physical space; the physical comes to stand in opposition to the cultural as we experience a new form of dualism:

> "...Unless one is looking for it, one rarely sees in maps these transactions of political-economic and cultural power. This is because maps offer us cooked representations of raw data. In their cooked form maps seem to objectively chart territories— whether these are economic territories or spatial territories. Mapping offers a way of seeing that appears fractal, realistic and proportional. However, mapping is a representational process that distorts through selectivity and omission, emphasis and combination, exaggeration and simplification. While conventionally we think about mapping from a geographer's perspective, we might also speak of mapping from a cultural studies perspective. Capital not only produces flows of goods and monies but also flows of signs. Capital has been pressing into new spaces for about three centuries. At each new stage of expansion, there is a cultural dimension as well—and this is the matter of the representation of Capital in its landscapes."[42] (Goldman and Papson)

It is in this way the concept of the 'imagined community' moves, on the one hand, to create new forms of separation and isolation while, on the other, defining new forms of potential connection and community.

A Cha'an Buddhist saying states, "Reality is right before you, and yet you are apt to translate it into a world of names and forms."[43] We place limits on reality by operating as if our names and forms are the end goal and object of our actions. We forget that, as the Semanticist Alfred

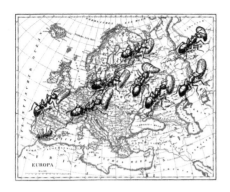

Korzybski wrote in 1933, "The map is not the territory, the word is not the thing."[44]

By placing limits on how we understand our world, we operate within a defined space, we live within our inability to rise above our dualism. This bifurcation inhibits our full, blended value creation potential to see the whole or operate concerning more than one insight or truth at a time. Language limits our understanding of what is by putting restrictions on what is observed or sensed—or what our senses observe.

We must pause in our seemingly endless efforts to measure, define, frame new strategies and embrace new definitions to let go, step back and re-conceptualize the task before us within a broad, new framework of comprehension, knowledge, wisdom, and awareness. We must seek to go either deeper below or rise higher above our dualism as presented if we are to be still, fully present and with that which is the complex and natural substance of our life and living. It is out of this substance we will find the true nature of value, being, and the purpose of capital in our lives and world.

At a recent gathering of Upstart Co-Lab consisting of foundation executives and asset owners interested in financing the future of culture and the arts, I began by telling them I had no talk, no 10-step Power-Point deck to walk them through and put them on their way to financial enlightenment, for if we did not first stop to recognize we need to think differently and reframe the conversation, then any supposed solution or tool would be flawed or misapplied. As a way of grounding us in the possibilities as opposed to the prisons of our present understanding of capital's—and our own—potential, I asked them to sit comfortably, clear their minds and imagine the following:

Picture yourself away from the city, far away from
its bright lights, noise and rushing activity.

You are deep in the countryside,
sitting in the living room of a
quaint, old farmhouse, surrounded
by fields of grass and the night. The
lights are on, and you look around
you, taking in the furniture, the rug,

seeing the floor lamps and fireplace, glancing through the window
to see the railings of the porch wrapping around the house…

The house and room you now inhabit are how we think about
traditional economics, finance, and philanthropy. It is defined
and bathed in the bright light of what we think we should
see; there are marked and understood corners to the room; you
feel secure in the room, but aware of the darkness outside that
surrounds the house and is layered upon the fields beyond.

You rise and turn off the lights of the living room. You now see a new,
soft light from a crescent moon, casting a warm glow into the house
and the room you occupy. In this dark light, you turn, pass through
the door to the outside, walking out onto the porch where you see a
flurry of moths, now as uncertain as you about where to go. You
pass down the short steps and into the field that surrounds the house.
You lay down in the long grass, stretch out your arms and legs and
look deeply into the night sky. You see your favorite constellation.

The moon and stars are what you know. They are bright, casting
light down to you. You know their light falls across a spectrum and
depending upon the color of the light you see, you can tell whether
you're looking at a star or a planet or perhaps something else. You
take in both the light of the stars and the darkness between them.

Until relatively recently, we thought this space between the stars and
planets was simply dark space. We thought it to be nothing. We could
not measure it, and therefore it did not exist in our understanding
as anything other than the cold, dark space we thought it to be.

More recently, we have discovered this empty space consists of what we now call dark matter. We have only just begun to measure it and to understand it is there. We are only just beginning to appreciate the reality that dark matter is the connecting fascia of space and time. It is what links and connects the stars we previously thought we knew to be the reality of the universe, but what we now see is just the beginning of our coming to understand space, time and the Universe. It is less a question of our beginning to understand the Grand Answers of Humanity than our being open to an emerging awareness as we are coming to discern more deeply the Grand Questions which draw us forward.

In the context of Blended Value and Impact Investing, the stars are traditional finance and investing: measureable and laid out into constellations we know. Dark Matter is those aspects of value and creation we may intuit and are beginning to assess, but which are fundamentally the intangible nature of human existence. Dark Matter is what we are coming to understand as Mutual Impact, the Creative Economy, Restorative Justice, Sustainable Economics, Blended Value, and, ultimately, our understanding of the purpose of capital.

You rise to look about you, seeing the full expanse of stars, trees and field through which you now pass as you head back to the farmhouse. Mounting the stairs, you see a large moth trapped between the outer screen door and the inner door of glass. Opening the screen door and passing through, back into your home, you see the large moth fly off, into the night, up into the stars and reflect upon how you have liberated the value you'd previously held between two worlds.

You re-enter the now dark house, lit by moons, stars and matter, and sit in what others might think a dark room.

You see and now are the light.

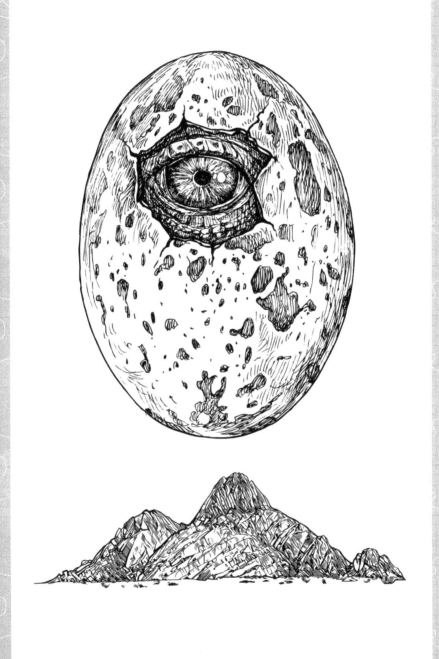

CHAPTER SIX

NATURE IS NOT
THE OTHER

I'M SITTING AT MY WRITING TABLE IN OUR SMALL HYTTE LOCATED IN THE CENTER OF NORWAY, NEAR THE HIGH-EST POINT OFF THE TRAIN TRACK THAT CONNECTS THE FJORDS OF THE WEST WITH THE ISLANDS OF THE EAST AND BERGEN WITH OSLO.

Looking through the open window, a cold breeze comes down off the long, transverse mountain called 'Hallingskarven' (which translates as ridge or 'crust') that now sits in the dark, pre-dawn gloaming, patch-es of snow on its top set off against black rock that will later be revealed as covered with a tundra-like moss and olive-green brush growing low to the ground.

About a three-hour hike above us, inside the boundary of what is now a national nature reserve, tucked up against the cliffs, sits Tver-gastein (which we translate as 'Cross the Stones'), the hytte of Arne Naess, the Norwegian who framed the philosophy of deep ecology. Within deep ecology, the Earth, with its interlocking systems, ancient spirits, and primal forces, is viewed as dominant to humanity's 'civ-ilization' and over countless centuries superior even to our capital released to strip its resources. We've skied and hiked in the shadow of Tvergastein for years. Today, for the first time, we will head up to the cabin itself; sitting at its door, listening for the thoughts of the old man who used to inhabit the cottage and left tall shelves stacked with short jars of local herbs, samples of plants, dirt, and a host of other items giving witness not only to a life lived, but a life of material simplicity and personal reflection. He is said to have been a smart and funny, but irritable fellow as is true of many who touch truths not perceived by others.

Our relation to the Earth has always been one of tension, sometimes living lightly upon its surface, other times shaping its contour to meet our needs for food and water, and still other times cutting sharp wounds in the ground, ripping off mountain tops, filling in ravines and rivers with earthen, rock debris, doing whatever we thought necessary to meet our temporal desires. It is a relation that has given birth to religious conviction and more recent philosophies such as deep ecology, as well as provided the resources to fuel civilizations, ancient and modern. It is a relationship that has served as the canvas upon which we express our understanding of how we are connected—and disconnected—from the land upon which we walk.

In her essay, *Art at the End of the World*, the academic Heidi Julavits reflects on the Land Art created by Robert Smithson, who explored humanity's relation to Earth in his work before he was killed in a plane crash at the age of 35. Julavits writes about the experience of traveling to view 'Reverse Jetty,' an installation Smithson created on the Great Salt Lake. She discusses how her children respond to the experience of being out in the vastness of the American West and how Smithson wrote about the connections between our interior and exterior landscapes, and their interaction as a form of dialectic.

Her piece reminded me of a time I found myself on the vast plains of eastern Montana, parked on a rise, looking out over miles and miles of flat land with not a soul in sight. I remember the weight of that expanse and how I climbed back into the car, shuddering and in search of a reassurance to be found in the company of others, even if only the company of another vehicle spotted ahead on the road as it lay stretched out, cutting through the ranch land before me.

In part, Naess' and Smithson's ideas show how we experience the Earth as separate from ourselves. They address the tragedy of humans acting upon the Earth, to shape and mold it as we feel called to do; we enter our relationship with the Earth as the ultimate Other upon which we walk and move to deconstruct according to our will. In this way, we express our separation from self and Other; through the destruction of the Earth from which we feel ourselves to be distinct despite our being integral with it, our rising from and being shaped by its forces and resources, our interior landscape connected with exterior landscape.

While we think of ourselves as dominant over it, the Other acts upon us—shaping how we live, dress, experience life and come to survive in our brief existence. We interact with it, having various impacts upon it just as it impacts us. Traditional historians tell the story of our lives and civilizations, but most often separate and apart from the planet upon which that story plays out. One of the best books I've read was Arnold Toynbee's opus, *Mankind, and Mother Earth: A Narrative History of the World.*[1] Toynbee presents history not merely as the unfolding of human experience over the span of centuries rolling out over thousands of years, but as that history unfolding against the dramatic backdrop of geography, place, and environment, all within that few mile boundary of the biosphere which envelops our Planet and us with it.

The nature of our relationship with Earth and Self becomes a grand metaphor for and reality of how we each interact with and are affected by the financial capital we've unleashed and that flows across the Planet, shaping communities, individuals, and societies as well as the Earth itself, just as that capital is in turn formed by us as we move to structure it in various ways toward various ends. How we understand our relation to money and our connection to the Earth has significant impact on how we evolve and develop. Those who endeavor to go more deeply into this relationship with the Other as Earth and capital as a modern expression of our separations have opportunities to experience a profound sense of being, of who we are. Those who opt not to go deeper into this relationship experience little more than the mainstream view; the starting place for each of us on our walk through this life.

It is this aspect of the dynamic between the biosphere and our shared identity that was explored by Robert Smithson and Arne Naess. It is this aspect of our relation to capital which offers impact investors an opportunity to engage more deeply not just with the investments they make, but with our own selves, our sense of identity and being which, if we let it, may be profoundly altered through how we connect with our capital, our structures, and application of it, as well as the communities it flows through and geographies it influences. We tend to hide, however, from the implications and connections of our capital to Earth, society and Self. As Michael Parenti writing in *Against Empire*, says "The essence of capitalism is to turn nature into commodities and commodities into capital. The live green earth is transformed into dead gold bricks, with luxury items for the few and toxic slag heaps for the many."[2]

As the field of impact investing scales, as more investment product is created and offered through anonymized global markets potentially linking investors' capital with a host of investible opportunities in communities and eco-systems across the Planet, we run the risk of continuing, despite our efforts, to be disconnected from our money. While impact investing offers the prospect to more deeply connect with the Other through our capital with community and planet, we now risk losing that opportunity. The power of impact investing is not simply our ability to deploy that capital in alignment with our values or as a vehicle to potentially advance positive value creation across the globe, but in our potential to, through our capital, link more deeply to and within that same world—natural and social—as a means of exploring on a more intimate basis who we are, what we are becoming and how we ultimately want to be present in our world. This opportunity is one of Mutual Impact experienced on environmental as well as social terms.

And yet as we seek to understand this world and our relationship to it, our initial inclination within the Western tradition is continually to set ourselves off and apart from it. As Giles Hutchins describes it in his excellent offering, *The Illusion of Separation*:

"The anthropologist-philosopher Gregory Bateson viewed Darwin's theory of evolution as fundamentally flawed because it is based on the organisms as the unit of evolution rather than the organism *and* its relationship with its environment. This definition of the organism as separate from its environment Bateson saw as a basic flaw which corrupts the thinking that flows from it, as for him relationships are paramount to the organism's health, viability and evolution. He viewed comparing one species against another or versus its environment in a struggle for survival as inherently wrong. He felt that it is what pits humanity against Nature and provides for our prevalent worldview of survival through competition, in what he viewed as 'an ecology of bad ideas', breeding parasitic humans, purely self-centered and destructive of their host environment. This flawed worldview serves, in turn, to deeply acculturate us to the notion of 'self' and 'species' as distinct and separate from our environment. This separation of content from context—which encourages a perceived separation of humans from Nature— creates a disharmonious way of living with our environment where we foolishly seek to subversively control it, bizarrely blaming it for our disharmony."[3]

Bateson's critique of Darwin's framing of the species as isolated within an ecosystem points us toward our critique of Friedman, Hayek, and countless traditional business people and financiers who would argue we must view the modern firm as responsible solely for its own functioning and the generation of financial returns to shareholders. Such advocates of the corporation as individual would have us believe the firm has no social obligation and the primacy of shareholder value should rule absolute over all other stakeholders, financial or otherwise.

The firm does not operate in isolation from the communities, markets, and societies—from its eco-systems—that give it life. It does not create its value solely as a function of its management and operations but rather as an outcome of how it operates in the world, takes resources out of the world and is advanced through the policies, values, and energy offered it from that world. A central premise of many impact investors is that the management of companies and those who invest in them must consider a host of long term, off-balance sheet factors that will impact the firm's operations over time. From the perspectives of many asset managers operating within a sustainable investment framework, such managers need not always offer the "right" answer to the challenges of water depletion, health pandemics, global climate change and so on, but must take such factors into account in their development and execution of business strategy. The fundamental health and wellness of the firm is interwoven with the long-term health and wellness of its employees, communities and various non-financial stakeholders.

ON NATURAL POLITICS

In the cultural and historic context of the United States, we've moved through various forms of relationship to the natural environment, but the relation of nature to politics—the social expression of our reductionist tendencies—has always been central. Frederick Jackson Turner, active in the early 1890s, proposed the "Frontier Thesis" which said our initial run of democracy was enabled by our ability always to move on to the next frontier, with little consideration of long term consequences. The open wilderness and "free land" served as a safety valve, allowing "malcontents and ambitious" Americans to find new land in which to explore and expand. While true of our early years, with the closing of the American Frontier, he called for a conservation and managerial approach to the natural environment to ensure a new type of democracy and land management flourished.

Turner's words echoed Hegel who, writing in the early 1800s, had argued the United States would not fully develop until we ran out of land and "Americans had to turn and face one another" on deeply political and social terms.[4] In this way, our relation with the Earth as Other and our engagement with each other takes the form of a 'Dialectical' connection, a term which comes from the Greek *dialegesthai*, 'to converse.'[5] Whether we know or acknowledge it, we are engaged in a conversation with our self through the vehicle of the Earth as Other and via our connection with other humans. We each come to that conversation with our own set of values, perspectives, and comprehension of the nature of that relationship and prospect of growing more aware of the social, ecological and economic web of which we are a part. It is within that web, as we each seek to situate ourselves, where we must 'turn to face one another.' Clearly, this is our current challenge and one we have yet to surmount.

Originally, there was an understood link between the political vision of the United States and the place of Nature within the process of realizing our national vision. "…Never far from its heart was an idea about nature itself: that it was made to collaborate in human progress, as we were made to develop it for our needs."[6] It was understood to be there for us, to be used by us, as we built this nation. We operated largely within the framework of other Westerners who had come before, if not within the framework of those First Nations and Indigenous Peoples whose land we occupied.

For the most part, we did not stop to question or challenge our assumptions…

"Unquestioned beliefs are the real authorities of any culture. A central unquestioned belief of this culture is that humans are superior to and separate from everyone else. Human supremacism is part of the foundation of much of this culture's religion, science, economics, philosophy, epistemology and so on….Until this supremacism is questioned and dismantled, the self-perceived entitlement that flows from this supremacism guarantees that every attempt to stop this culture from killing the planet will fail, in great measure because these attempts will be informed and limited by this supremacism, and thus will at best be easy to slightly mitigate harm, with the primary point being to make certain to never in any way question or otherwise endanger the supremacism or entitlement,"[7] as Derrick Jensen, author and environmentalist, states.

For the Tukano Tribe of Colombia, "…the problem of game resources will eventually depend on the confrontation between outside pressures and shamanic authority [which governs hunting practices and other aspects of their relation to the ecosystem] and there can be little doubt about the outcome and the consequences. One Indian said to me, 'When people lose their respect for animals, they soon will lose everything else.'[8]

Or, as Jensen went on to observe:

> "We believe we are superior to all other life forms on the planet, and yet we are in many ways blind to our own sickness. The 'mirror-test' is used to assess the degree and level of self-awareness of animals, but if we hold that mirror up to our own face to assess our true awareness, how do we fare?

> 'Ah,' the human supremacists insist, 'we understand that the tiger is aware of its hunger, but is the tiger aware that it is aware of its hunger?'

> That is the question.

> To which I ask, are the human supremacists aware of their own hunger? Are they aware of the violation imperative that drives this culture?

> Are they aware that they've indentured themselves to authoritarian technics and that they are no longer fully human, that they are, to use the Buddhist term, hungry ghosts: undead and unloving spirits of the greedy, 'who, as punishment for their mortal vices, have been cursed with an insatiable hunger?'[9]

THE OTHER IN THE WOODS
OF THE ROCKIES

Together with a friend, in the dead of winter, I skied into a Colorado wilderness area where no mechanical conveyance is permitted and was surprised to find myself following snowmobile tracks. As we progressed through an open tunnel of tall trees sagging with the weight of recent snows, we began seeing moose tracks and scat, deep bowls in the snow where they had slept and had been at rest, followed by tracks of five

or six moose, scattering and moving in and out of the trees, onto the trail, off into the trees again, clearly running away from motorized sleds through knee deep and ice cold, powdery snow.

When we came upon the snowmobilers, who were ice fishermen looking for easy access to the lake, I asked if they knew they were in violation of the regulations and that this was a "no machine" area. They shrugged and said,

"Sorry, we didn't know that..."

to which I said,

"It's like hunting regulations—it is your responsibility *to know* and if you don't, that is no excuse; if a Ranger comes along, you'll receive a steep fine...".

They mistakenly took my warning as kind comment and effort to protect them from a fine and went on to describe how the moose had been startled, with one approaching the lead sled and attempting to kick it. They hooted and laughed at how close they'd come to getting moose stomped—yet with no acknowledgement or reflection on how distant they were from the animals in the midst of their deep encounter; they were unaware of the life energy they'd encountered as well as unaware of the shallowness with which they had entered the woods and its various lives.

Those men, wrapped in their stained, insulated brown Carhartts and warmed with their tawny liquor would have failed the 'mirror-test.'

Here's the thing: these were not "bad" or evil men. While I did not know these guys personally, they are my friends and neighbors who live in a different reality, with different insights and perspectives from my own. We differ in our path and the light we see, but if we're lucky we may engage and connect and walk with each other—though they would no doubt jeer were they to read those words. We simply operate in different understandings of value and consciousness—but I think we have the promise of connecting in other ways and an obligation to seek to do so, to see how these parts might fit into a better, more promising whole, as opposed to simply remaining separate and in tension.

The encounter brings to mind another friend of mine here in Grand County who tells the tale of his hunt last year. He is an avid outdoorsman who prepares well and takes in packhorses with supplies as he enters the deeper forests, up North of us in a region called "The Troublesome," where he will stay for days on end. On this occasion, he had tracked a bull elk for many hours, moving slowly and deliberately through the trees and brush, until he came to a point of confusion, thinking he'd lost the track. Sitting with his back against a tree, taking a moment to regroup, he suddenly caught a scent of musk. He turned to glimpse a flash of brown against the black of the dark wood and then, there, just before him, the bull took one step and turned…exposing a small portion of himself through the undergrowth uphill from where he sat. My friend knew a flick of his safety would send the bull crashing off and away through the brush—he was, in essence, too close to take the shot. A different type of hunter might have taken the chance and tried to quickly click off the safety to go for a kill through the trees and brush—not clear but possible—but my friend found himself locked in the moment, connected, not simply near the bull, but *with* the bull, the two of them, engaged with each and the Other there in the wilderness. In an encounter of seconds, there was a connection broken only by the animal's slow turn and deliberate retreat up, deeper, and now back to the beyond.

NATURAL AWARENESS IN OUR JOURNEY

Spiritual ignorance is not a lack of knowledge, but rather something we all share in the form of "…the deep-seated belief that if only we had more of what we like and less of what we don't like, then we'd be happy, forever. It also consists in a kind of vagueness about the things that really matter."[10] More of what we like, by which we might say, more of what we determine to be of value.

Over the centuries, this notion of human primacy over Nature—of our determining what is of value and what value is worth— did not go unchallenged. For example, as Lynn White points out, Saint Francis of Assisi, in the 13th Century, tried to undermine the Christian anthropocentric worldview, grounded within an understanding of that "Great Chain of Being:"

> "Francis tried to depose man from his monarchy over creation and set up a democracy of all God's creatures. The greatest spiritual revolutionary in Western history, Saint Francis, proposed what he thought was an alternative Christian view of nature and man's relation to it: he tried to substitute the idea of the equality of all creatures, including man, for the idea of man's limitless rule over creation. He failed...".[11]

Others leaned forward to pick up and carry that torch:

> "Drawing from Plato's Republic, Jean-Jacques Rousseau lamented the corruption of nature in humanity he believed was induced by property, agriculture, technology and commerce. Like Sir Thomas Moore in Utopia, Rousseau was critical of existing mores and values and sought a design to reconstruct society. In his *Discourses* he challenged the belief that better technologies, material wealth and knowledge would lead to the improvement of humanity and morality. Large commercial centers, he warned, were bad for the human spirit. He prescribed instead the formation of cooperative agrarian communities,"[12] observed the environmental author Mark Dowie.

He continues:

> "With the exception of a few small bands of utopians who settled briefly in the Midwest, European settlers and early Americans did not heed Rousseau. Most preferred the ruminations of scientists like Francis Bacon and Isaac Newton who, along with Enlightenment philosophers Rene Descartes, David Hume, and John Locke, created a world view that desacralized nature and

provided ideological fuel for the industrial revolution. Bacon
referred to nature as 'a common harlot' that he hoped mankind
would 'conquer and subdue...and shake to her foundations.'
Descartes invoked Bacon in his defense of vivisection: animals,
he said, were 'soulless automata' whose screams under torture
were 'the mere clatter of gears and mechanisms.' To Newton the
world was a clock, wound by God: 'The entrepreneur, merchant,
industrialist scientist [were] God's counterparts, the skilled
technicians that used the same mechanical laws and principles
that operated in the universe to assemble the stuff of nature
and set in motion the industrial production of the modern age.'
Locke created the anti-ecological creed that justified the commercial exploitation of natural resources: 'Land that is left wholly to nature,' he wrote, 'is called, indeed, what it is, waste.'"[13]

Other civilizations coming before the supposed great Enlightenment opted to revise their understanding of our connection to Nature
rather than operate within a philosophy that viewed us as part of that
great web. For example, the Romans in the early centuries of their
society "regarded the Mediterranean landscape as the sacred space
of nature deities such as Apollo, god of the sun, Ceres, goddess of
agriculture, and Neptune, god of freshwater and the sea. As Rome
expanded, however, these religious beliefs became largely empty rituals, disconnected from natural processes," according to Dawson. As
the empire grew, eventually Roman attitudes shifted markedly, "to
justify this carnage [of hundreds of thousands of animals killed in
the Coliseum and other entertainment centers across the Empire] of
wildlife....During the high days of the empire, Stoic and Epicure-
an philosophies that legitimated the status-driven debauchery of the
Roman upper class prevailed."[14]

We continue to create philosophies and ideologies not to raise us as
a people above our place in the world, but to place us above the world
itself, to justify and advance our basest instincts of anger and destruction. Such a link between who we are and our justification of being
lives entirely on today as those representing our shadow self roll back

limitations on our current industrial practices, opening vast stretches of wilderness to drilling, mining and other forms of landscape mutilation.

Going back further still from the day of the Romans, while the Pre-Socratic philosophers viewed humanity as an integral part of the Earth and beyond that, the Cosmos, Aristotle laid the foundation for the formalization of our conceptual and philosophical separation of self from Nature which Naess would seek to bridge two millennia later:

> "Aristotle rejected the Pre-Socratic ideas of an infinite universe, cosmological and biological evolution and heliocentrism. He proposed an Earth-centered finite universe wherein humans instead, by their rationality, were differentiated from and seen as superior to, animals and plants. Aristotle promoted the hierarchical concept of the "Great Chain of Being," in which Nature *made* plants for the use of animals and animals were *made* for the sake of humans."[15]

As my favorite Buddhist writer and poet, Gary Snyder, reflects:

> "It seems that a short way back in the history of occidental ideas there was a fork in the trail. The line of thought that is signified by the names of Descartes, Newton and Hobbes (saying that life in a primary society is 'nasty, brutish and short'—all of them city dwellers) was a profound rejection of the organic world. For a reproductive universe, they substituted a model of sterile mechanism and an economy of 'production.'…Most of humanity—foragers, peasants, or artisans—has always taken the other fork. That is to say, they have understood the play of the real world, with all its suffering, not in simple terms of 'nature red in tooth and claw' but through the celebration of the gift-exchange quality of our give and take. 'What a big potlatch we are all members of!!' To acknowledge that each of us at the table will eventually be a part of the meal is not just being 'realistic.' It is allowing the sacred to enter and accepting the sacramental aspect of our shaky temporary personal being."[16]

Accordingly, as our assumptions regarding the purpose served by science evolved, we continued to shape our conceptual frameworks in justification of our material goals and ambitions. "Before the scientific revolution of Galileo, Descartes, Bacon and Newton, the goals of science were wisdom, understanding of the natural order and living in harmony with that order. Since the seventeenth century, the goal of science has been knowledge that can be used to control, manipulate and exploit nature."[17] (Sessions)

And, of course, as Toynbee said: "It is not possible to worship anything that one has mastered; and, therefore, when Man became aware that he had established his ascendancy over Nature, he subordinated the worship of conquered Nature to the worship of the collective human power that had given him his victory."[18]

In contrast to these developments, others call for a return to our commitment to science as the pursuit of wisdom. Arne Naess, in describing this connection in the context of his understanding of the need for a philosophy of deep ecology, writes that

> "...ecology as a science does not ask what kind of a society would be the best for maintaining a particular ecosystem—that is considered a question for value theory, for politics, for ethics. As long as ecologists keep narrowly to their science, they do not ask such questions...The emergence of human ecological consciousness is a philosophically important idea: a life form has developed on Earth which is capable of understanding and appreciating its relations with all other life forms and to the Earth as a whole."[19]

As is true in our modern debates regarding conservation of nature and our supposed right to develop the Earth to meet our own material needs and manufactured desires, our 'victory' over the natural world came early on in our human development and has served to keep us from the pursuit of a more wisdom-based approach to understanding our world. According to Toynbee:

"Man [sic] gained a decisive ascendancy over Nature in the Neo-lithic Age, with the invention of ground stone tools, agriculture, the domestication of animals, pottery-making, and spinning and weaving. But he seems not to have become conscious of the mastery of Nature that he had already achieved till he had won the first triumphs of organized collective human action on the grand scale. An advance in social organization—not a further advance in technology—was the new achievement that enabled the Sumerians to reclaim the swamps of the lower Tigris-Eu-phrates valley and the Egyptians to reclaim the swamps of the lower Nile valley. When these former wildernesses had been drained and irrigated by a massive organized human effort, they yielded a surplus of production over and above the day-to-day requirements of bare subsistence. This surplus was a new factor in human history. It made civilization possible, and the creators and beneficiaries of civilization then took to worship-ing their now collective power. In this power of theirs they rightly saw the agency that had brought about this astonishing social revolution, but they were wrong—and disastrously wrong, as it turned out—in drawing the conclusion that human power was God."[20]

Despite this ill-fated conclusion, we continue to fall victim to our own hubris, as we plod onward in our effort to disaggregate the sacred from the profane. Professor Armstrong says:

"Today we separate the religious from the secular. This would have been incomprehensible to the Paleolithic hunters, for whom nothing was profane. Everything they saw or experienced was transparent to its counterpart in the divine world. Anything, however lowly, could embody the sacred. Everything they did was a sacrament that put them in touch with the gods. The most ordinary actions were ceremonies that enable mortal being to participate in the timeless world of 'everywhere.'…[21]…Mythol-ogy was not about theology, in the modern sense, but about human experience. People thought that gods, humans, animals and nature were inextricably bound up together, subject to the same laws, and composed of the same divine substance."[22]

Initially, this same divine substance made itself known to us—but again, over the course of our time we have sought to separate it out from its parts and ourselves. "Before they began to worship a number of deities, people in many parts of the world acknowledged only one Supreme God, who had created the world and governed human affairs from afar. Nearly every pantheon has its Sky God. Anthropologists have also found Him among such tribal peoples as the Pygmies, the Australians, and the Fuegians. He is the First Cause of all things and Ruler of heaven and earth."[23] (Armstrong)

It is fascinating to note that this is, in many ways, the same concept as the Pre-Socratic *arche* (from which the word anarchy, 'ana'-*arche* —or denying of substance—is taken) and which later is described by Spinoza—and much later, Naess—and other 18th Century philosophers as the essence of being, namely, 'substance.'

In the Neolithic Period, which saw the origins of farming and agriculture, there were many rituals conducted that focused upon the idea the earth needed to be replenished and renewed if it were to give back season after season, if the core *substance* of the planet was to continue to be able to operate in its fullness. Two principles were embedded in these practices. First, was the idea that you had to give something if you wanted something in return. One could not only take. And second, was the idea that everything was of a whole and connected. "The sacred was not felt to be a metaphysical reality, beyond the natural world. It could only be encountered in the earth and its products, which were themselves sacred. Gods, human beings, animals, and plants all shared the same nature, and could, therefore, invigorate and replenish one another,"[24] according to Armstrong.

The product and outcome of our modern experience of separation is a sense of apathy, of suffering of the Self, a suffering we carry throughout our world but are loath to call out and name. It requires we look more deeply into our troubles than we are comfortable with or care to do.

OUR INTEGRATION WITH NATURE

Most of us operate in denial of the huge and profoundly negative impacts we have on other sentient beings on this Earth. Our assumption is we are the only conscious beings and all others reside lower on the Chain of Being from us and are therefore subservient to us and our needs. We need this assumption if we are to feel in any way positive about our lives and the value we think we create over the course of our time on Earth. What Hutchins and Loy each explore as the Illusion of Separation and the dualism that many religions are structured to overcome help us become more aware of our separation from self and Other and, in the end, the Godhead.

In many societies we operate separate from not only the lives of other human beings, but also separate from animals in our factory farms, testing labs and stomachs. We must do this if we are to continue our consumption of everything from dogs to whales, to pigs, cows and fish. As we see the increasingly rapid development of Global Climate Change, the effects of our stripping the Earth of her mantle and our dispersal of pesticides into her oceans, we also become increasingly conscious that, as Toynbee said, "Man, the child of Mother Earth, would not be able to survive the crime of matricide if he were to commit it. The penalty for this would be self-annihilation."[25]

Where, then, are we to turn in our effort to manage the suffering we create within our Selves and which we visit upon other creatures,

all as a result of our separation from Nature? We turn back to that which has helped facilitate our divorce in the first place, namely our talent for creating new technologies to manage our relationship with each other and through which we mediate our relation to the Earth. But this can create additional, unforeseen challenges in that "Modernity once more with feeling' solutions to global warming—bioengineering, geoengineering, and other forms of...*happy nihilism*—reduce things to bland substances that can be manipulated at will without regard to unintended consequences,"[26] says Morton. (Emphasis in the original).

Much as we try to protect ourselves from the effects of our actions, as our negative impacts become all the more significant and clear, we also become ever aware that, as Bruno Latour states, our destruction of the Earth "demands more of us than simply embracing technology and innovation; it requires a perspective that 'sees the process of human development as neither liberation from Nature nor as a fall from it, but rather as a process of becoming ever-more attached to, and intimate with, a panoply of nonhuman natures."[27]

We may then need to evolve a new understanding of what it means to be an environmentalist or for that matter, social entrepreneur, for we must ask whether we may save humanity in the absence of ensuring such efforts also promote our saving the Earth upon which we live? We must pursue a unified approach that finds a place for our grand technologies but at the same time repositions us within a set of newly reconstituted relations within the larger ecosystems of which we are a part. Perhaps it is now time to advance a reconstituted form of environmentalism *and* entrepreneurship that embraces who we are as well as our relations with other sentient beings and this planet. What we require is a vision of "Fourth-wave environmentalism"[28] which assesses any strategy or solution within the broader context of eco-system and world as well as human communities of interest.[29] This is the future of business as practiced by growing numbers of entrepreneurs, supported around the world through a variety of thriving networks.

It is less through new applications of technology or capital that we will discern our path forward, than by reengagement with our true nature as humans, a reconnection with our place as beings capable of linking our consciousness with our understanding of place, self, and Nature. Our attainment of technological prowess and financial innovation does not come as a bolt out of the blue, but as an extension and evolution of our deeper Selves which lie dormant in these days of change, technological transformation, and spiritual repression.

> "Though Man's [sic] technology has been by far the most successful of his achievements hitherto, it is not the essence of humanity, and is not even the feature of human nature that is the most crucial for mankind's existence, survival and well-being. These more important features of human nature cannot appear directly in the archaeological record, since they are not material but are spiritual. At the most, archaeology can bear witness to the existence of these spiritual characteristics of human nature indirectly, inasmuch as we can assume that, if these had not been present, Man [sic] could never have created the culture of which his tools are material evidence. This material evidence is trustworthy as far as it goes, but it informs us directly only about one part of human life, and this a part that is not the most vital."[30] (Toynbee)

The most vital part of our existence is our awareness of who we are and are becoming, of our links to a past worth rediscovering and bringing forward as we find our ever renewing place here on Earth, *with* Earth, in a new way of being in and of the World.

For, as we must deeply know, Nature is not the Other.

CHAPTER SEVEN

ON TRUTH:

The Rediscovery of Experience as Evidence

T HE DEEPEST PARTS OF THE UNIVERSE, LIFE ON EARTH, AND OUR SELVES ARE NOT CREATED AS MUCH AS DISCOVERED.

They exist, in point of fact, and it is only we who are playing a form of cosmic catch up to understand what truth is and how the truth comes to be manifest for us. Our sense of truth differs in various ways, at multiple times. This is so not only within the course of our human history but in our individual development. We speak of how various actors over the centuries have made discoveries that have moved our world and our awareness forward on some path of what we've understood as progress. Columbus discovered America. Newton discovered gravity. Einstein discovered the nature of relativity. Our society, our lives, the truth; each lay before us, waiting to be found—not created by us, not proven by us and not by the result of our brilliance or efforts alone. The truth is there, waiting. And on the other side of Truth lies Wisdom, there, just beyond our sight. The intrinsic nature of reality—outside our current definitions and understanding—sits ahead of and around us all.

At some level, my interest in truth and in my obligation to realize purpose came in my youth when I thought I did know the answer (or at least some semblance of answers) that unfolded for me from my teens through twenties and onward. At each stage, I knew what was right and what we were called to do. I knew what I thought to be true. This conviction in my beliefs and analysis of our world and field is what gave me the confidence to promote my ideas and those of my colleagues concerning social entrepreneurship, venture philanthropy and impact investing—ideas which in their origin were sharply differentiated from the popular truth as then known but which now seem obvious and commonplace. I assumed as I aged I would simply augment and affirm these various belief systems as they played themselves out over the course of my life.

What I found instead was that with each decade—and especially when I hit my late-fifties and looked back over the growing span of my life—I felt a sense not of not knowing as such, but instead of being able to rise above my various specific frameworks and ideologies to see the linkages and connections across the whole. I became able to link various aspects and elements of knowledge with a deeper understanding of the process of an evolving truth concerning not only what was right in the world but our ability to trace seemingly distinct evolutions of our shared process of moving more deeply within this flowing truth. I felt an emergent empathy with who I was at each stage of my life and what I knew to be truth within that stage of my development but also saw each step as part of the larger whole of who I was, am today and am in the process of becoming.

Naturally, this empathy was not merely self-directed. This empathy with the various people who I have been then became transposed onto my neighbors, colleagues and others I encounter (personally or from a distance), who I could now see and appreciate at a level of understanding and more profound comprehension than I had had in previous periods of my life.

When I was in my twenties, I read a lot of writings that reflected upon religious and philosophical truths and felt I had a sound framework for understanding the world. Over time I drifted away from that base by simple virtue of living that much longer in the world and working to advance my answers within it. As I came through my late fifties, I felt I'd drifted away from the human knowledge and connections that had grounded me earlier in life and decided to re-connect with our centuries long pursuit of truth. In this way, I wanted to understand not so much what I thought, but rather what we, as a people and multiple tribes of peoples, have considered truth over the centuries. I sought to position myself more deeply within the force of that collective knowledge as we now grapple with variations on the challenges of wealth as well as the meaning and purpose of capital—much less, life.

When we consider the nature of debates in the United States regarding social policy, science, economics, racial justice and so on, it is obvious we've stripped out consideration of so much concerning our understanding of truth which cannot, as mathematicians would say, be demonstrated by a proof. As a result of the Age of Enlightenment, Hutchins says,

> "…(t)ruth was no longer a dynamic unfolding found through
> a participatory experiential embodiment of Nature, it became
> a static truth defined by dissecting an object from its lived-in
> context and analyzing it through experiments supported by
> mathematical logic; this is referred to as the 'objectification' of
> science. By its nature, this objectification is abstract because
> things are taken out of their lived-in context, defined through
> abstract logic and examined through repeatable experiments in
> controlled abstract environments."[1]

Despite our understanding of the limitations and reservations of an evidence-based approach to social programs, philanthropic practice or any number of efforts at moving from investing or philanthropy as an art to a science, we find our efforts fall well short and continue to with the passing of each year. Yes, we may learn more and prove more to our selves; yet we do not necessarily truly *know* more or approach our work with any higher level of humility, wisdom or insight.

Within the discipline of Philosophy, the tension between empiricism and rationalism is at play, the one informing and improving the understanding of the other until we come to a newer, more productive and more in-depth knowledge of the truth, of what is known perhaps somewhere in between the two. Even a casual review of the popular literature of impact investing or strategic philanthropy or any number of related fields leaves one with a sense that much of what is explored and celebrated as the new and insightful is, in short, not. Rather it is derivative, self-referential and affirming of what we neglect to acknowledge is what we already accept as truth—or variations thereof, set to a favorite score and hummed by the masses as we all march merrily along.

These tensions between what we can prove and what we must take as result of Kierkegaard's Leap of Faith, are in fact how we find our way toward deeper and evolved understandings of the quiet and still truth in our world, today, as we experience that understanding of what is in the end and with greater finality, right. The tensions and seeming contradictions within cultures (liberty versus equality, do well or do good, material versus spiritual, yin versus yang) are not a drawback, but instead are crucial to our intellectual and natural development. The tensions between knowledge and faith are two parts of a more profoundly glorious whole. "Such contradictions are an inseparable part of every human culture. In fact, they are culture's engines, responsible for the creativity and dynamism of our species. Just as when two clashing musical notes played together to force a piece of music forward, so discord in our thoughts, ideas and values compel us to think, re-evaluate and criticize. Consistency is the playground of dull minds," says Harari.[2]

Economics, finance, environmentalism, social justice and so on, each operate within their own, diverse set of truths. At the same time, the truths of each of these disciplines become more sharply defined in contrast to a larger world of the mysterious and unknown, bounded and kept at bay by what we profess to "know" within each silo. We then define what is outside our truth as what we call unknown. It is the interplay between the defined and the undefined wherein we discover reality and it is in between this interplay of the known and the believed wherein lies the temporal truth with which we guide our way through a process of what we call progress.

Between not only con-
flicting perspectives within
society but those conflicts as
they arise out of the individual attitude coming into touch
with other, multiple, social
views shows our own still and
humbling truth continues to
evolve and grow. The artist
Anais Nin said, "The personal
life deeply lived always expands into truths beyond itself,"[3] and in this
way as we go deeper in our journey to find what we might consider
being true we inevitably interact and are presented with the opportunity
to integrate with the truths found by others, moving toward a connection with the Other that is beyond our self. Discovery of reality is, then,
a process and pathway more than an end goal and single answer, insight
or calculation. As one sits with, much less participates in, what pass-
es for debate within our world of social capital, impact investing and
sustainable finance, it is hard not to be left with a sense we are mostly
missing the point. Perhaps there is a more real understanding of what
this all represents that we lose in our celebration of quantitative analysis
and what we take to be rational thought, reflection and accepted truth.

As our understanding of truth evolves—and we can place our experiences and lessons in the context of a trajectory of our having lived—we
reach a stage where we want to share those lessons with others. We seek
to prevent other's needless repetition of our errors and feel connected
to the overall perceived progression of human history writ small in the
course of our lives.

And yet, do we then move into another stage where we realize each
of us is on our journey, exploring our path as we move forward?

Are not our particular lessons and wisdom of use to those who come
behind us or walk to our side?

Maybe not.

Is this the meaning of the Taoist saying, "Open mouth, First mistake" in that while we may openly and sincerely offer our knowledge

and perspective, the truth of our experience is not the truth others will experience, others who must learn and evolve in their way? Sometimes, is the strongest connection we may maintain with others—with *the* Other—that of a calm, quiet silence; a compassionate, contemplative presence?[4] *Be still and know the Truth, that I am God,*[5] but know that God is Nature, substance, and nothing. How can you tell that to someone and trust she or he will understand? Truth evolves and looks different to different folks, depending on where they are in their journey and evolution. As a character in *The Alchemist* says, "When you possess great treasures within you and try to tell others of them, seldom are you believed."[6]

TRUTH AS A PROCESS OF VALUE DISCOVERY

In his review[7] of Grant Maxwell's book, *The Dynamics of Transformation,*[8] Cassano talks about Maxwell's notion of 'partial truths' and his proposal of an integrative approach to understanding and world views. I think of Blended Value as being part of this integrative nature of truth, of what is real and what we seek to create over the course of our lives. For years in my talks on Blended Value, I've used the metaphor of light, by which I mean the ultimate value we seek to create (the truth we seek to advance via our lives, our investment of resources and how we manage organizations) is a beam of light, cast through a crystal, which then splits the truth into respective colors of that light spectrum, each color containing an element of truth and being true for those who view it, yet not being in and of itself, Truth. The challenge is to remain aware of the various parts which constitute truth—in the context of this manuscript, what we understand to be the elements of the nature of value and purpose of capital—while at the same time focusing upon the ultimate, integrated view of value and truth as being a blend, a composite of elements which in the aggregate constitute transcendent reality and the final cost of Life. For, as Richard Rohr states, "There is really only one mystery, one truth, one suffering, one love, one life, and it is just showing itself in different forms."[9]

Along this spectrum, there is only a small segment of light that is visible to our naked eye (that of colors), yet we would not, in this time, deny the existence of the other rays across the spectrum which are invisible to our eye (that of x-rays, gamma rays and so on). They exist and are no less accurate for the fact of our being blind to them. Various actors see different forms of truth and value that we may or may not ourselves see. The magic trick in which we must engage is to connect with others, to connect both across our own time and back in time, in order to explore what is the full spectrum of truth and understanding. Standing at the intersects of past and present, of our own experience and the experience of humanity, we may then act to construct a reality that embraces the whole of us as individuals, of our common experience of civilizations and our connection with the Other. We each come to hold a part, yet we are each only part of, this larger Truth.

As I think of those I've known who spend their lives sitting in front of multiple computer screens, scrolling digits and data, engaged in maintaining the flows of capital within the bowels of finance, yet think- ing they sat at its heart, I reflect upon the words of Hannah Arendt. She wrote of those who enter "the maelstrom of an unending process of expansion, he will, as it were, cease to be what he was and obey the laws of the process, identify himself with anonymous forces that he is supposed to serve in order to keep the whole process in motion, he will think of himself as mere function, and eventually consider such func- tionality, such an incarnation of the dynamic trend, his highest possible achievement."[10] Our partial truths are crushed and conformed as we try to live our lives, day by day, number by number, until our world's revela- tions come to be defined accordingly within the predefined boundaries of modern, financial capitalism, which is for many, our present truth.

In contrast, consider the words of Louis Menand in this regard, concerning the evolving truth of justice:

"For the friends of the status quo have no greater claim to the principles of justice and fairness than its enemies do. And if the enemies can muster sufficient support, the presumption of rightness will slide over to their side of the scale. In 1850 the abolitionists seemed to most Northerners, dangerous subversives.

Less than fifteen years later, they were patriots. There is no one way that life must be."[11]

Unsurprisingly, in the process of advancing one truth against another, conflicts emerge and must be anticipated. Maxwell says:

"It may not be too much to claim that every revolution that has occurred in the history of thought has met with great resistance from the current established orthodoxy. The old order has always had decades, if not centuries, to elaborate its point of view, to fill volumes with justifications and explanation, to critique modes of thought that seem contrary to its deepest beliefs. Consequently, it seems likely that every revolution in thought that has occurred in the history of the world, whether on individual or collective scales, has required an act of will, a leap of faith outside the established modes into unmapped realms of cognizance."[12]

In this same vein, Sir Richard Francis Burton, the Victorian explorer, in his poem, *The Kasidah*,[13] spoke of the shattered mirror, with each shard of glass reflecting an aspect of truth and yet none reflecting truth itself. He believed the most profound mistake we make is to assume a single shard reflects the whole.

The historian Yuval Noah Harari then goes a step further to ask:

"How do you cause people to believe in an imagined order such as Christianity, democracy or capitalism? First, you never admit that the order is imagined. You always insist that the order sustaining society is an objective reality created by the great gods or by the laws of nature. People are unequal, not because Hammurabi said so, but because Enlil and Marduk decreed it. People are equal not because Thomas Jefferson said so, but because God created them that way. Free markets are the best economic system, not because Adam Smith said so, but because these are the immutable laws of nature."[14]

While the religious historian Karen Armstrong writes:

"Mythology and science both extend the scope of human beings. Like science and technology, mythology…is not about opting out of this world, but about enabling us to live more intensely within it…[15]…Since the eighteenth century, we have developed a scientific view of history; we are concerned above all with what actually happened. But in the pre-modern world, when people wrote about the past they were more concerned with what an event had meant. A myth was an event which, in some sense, happened once, but which also happened all the time. Because of our strictly chronological view of history, we have no word for such an occurrence. But mythology is an art form that points beyond history to what is timeless in human existence, helping us to get beyond the chaotic flux of random events, and glimpse the core of reality."[16]

As we reflect upon the purpose of capital, we seek to live in a place of animated analysis wherein we tell stories of impact and cultural value creation which we then attempt to prove and demonstrate to our skeptical self and public.

In the end, perhaps it is Charles Lyell who is correct. A geologist whose three-volume work *Principles of Geology* helped shape Charles Darwin's thinking, Lyell was attacked by "Scriptural Geologists" as an atheist, but he would claim that there are merely two forms of truth: Religion and Science.[17] In this way, the reality we pursue should not be one of evidence-based versus experiential and intuitive. Rather, we should seek truth through evidence informed by experience and the wisdom of prior generations who we must keep with us, alive and advancing, in the form of their writings, reflections, and cultures which we make live as we bring them into our world today.

MODERN HIERARCHIES OF TRUTH

Truth has always been challenging to discern, yet especially it seems in this day and age. One person's fair and balanced is another's fake news.

Beyond a difference of opinion concerning what is true or false, we do not seem able even to agree upon the underlying facts of the day, facts that used to be the foundation upon which we would approach discussions of truth and exchange our understandings of what is real. Ours is a time wherein debates are not merely differences of opinion, but of life, meaning and identity; as such one may be left feeling threatened, enraged or seeking recourse.

While that is the case today, our human history is littered with previous periods where the pursuit of truth has both advanced and reversed our world as its inhabitants have evolved. One could say history, rather than a litany of power exchange and culture clash, has been an endless conflict between competing understandings of Truth. Over that history, our knowledge and definition of truth have, of course, also evolved. The preamble of the Declaration of Independence states, *We hold these truths to be self-evident, that all men are created equal, that they are endowed by their Creator with certain unalienable Rights, that among these are Life, Liberty and the pursuit of Happiness.* People have spent well over two hundred years discussing, debating, and arguing the truth of what those words mean with an awareness that when they were drafted they were

thought not to apply to African Americans, Women, Native Americans, and countless others. What truth did those words hold for those communities? What truth do they hold today? The truth, it would seem, is malleable, taking shape out of the pressures we apply to it during our personal and collective exploration of the questions put before us in the period of our particular life and time.

There was another time in the Western world when the truth was understood to be absolute, a single definition flowing from God to Pope and then to the King and his courts. There was to be no debate regarding what was considered correct. There was understood to be only one truth, that of God and him through the Holy Roman Catholic Church. This concept would meet with resistance from those with differing perspectives. The Great Chain of Being, a type of *scala naturae* (ladder or stairway of nature)[18] showed this link between God and Man that connects us all, with truth flowing through various hierarchies, each representing a closer relationship to purity and truth as manifest in and by God. Derrick Jensen describes it as

> "...a hierarchy of perfection, with God at the top, then angels, then kings, then priests, then men, then women, then mammals, then birds, and so on, through plants, then precious gems, then other rocks, then sand. It's a profoundly body-hating notion, as, according to those who articulated the hierarchy, those at the top—the perfect—are pure spirit; and those at the bottom—the imperfect, the corrupt—are pure matter, pure body. Then both men and women lived in a battleground of spirit and body, with men tending to be put more in the box representing mind/spirit/better/perfected, and women tending to be put more in the box representing body/life/death/corruption/imperfection."[19]

This notion of hierarchy resonated not only in the periods of early Western cultural history, but is carried down in modified form today, the difference being we have placed the individual in the role of God. Jensen goes on to say,

"...Part of the hesitation of so many people to acknowledge that everyone else is alive and everyone else is sentient is that they are fearful of living in a world that is nearly infinitely complex, and nearly infinitely morally complex. It's much more convenient to live in a world where you base your morality on a clearly defined hierarchy, with you at the top. To interact with a machine is less complex and less morally complex than to interact with a community."[20]

Some view the individual at the top of our Chain of Being as subservient to one more layer of authority, namely, The Market. As Joerg Rieger describes it,

"The problem is not secularization—as it is often assumed—but a kind of hidden religiosity that promotes the worship of gods of the free market...such trust in the function of the market as a coordinating private initiate and self-interest for the common good can only be considered faith in a providential deity. The work of this deity is presupposed to such a degree and with such confidence, it seems that it never even needs to be named...it is the belief in the invisible hand of the market that is held both by Keynesians and their rivals, the followers of the Chicago School of Economics, as well as many other economists. This belief in the invisible hand of the market might be considered as the element that makes the mainline economics mainline, just like a common belief in "God at the top" is what makes mainline theology mainline—no matter whether it shapes up in liberal or conservative forms."[21]

The concept of the Great Chain of Being, then, is passed on from mediaeval times to today, with the simple replacement of "God at the top" with "The Individual and Free Markets at the top." What is interesting to note in this exploration of understanding truth is that when we talk about religion and economics, we most often discuss how our religious faith should influence our economics, yet we seldom consider how our understanding of economics affects our knowledge of truth, faith, God, and religion.

Rieger continues:

> "(M)oney increasingly creates its reality. One example how this happens in the realm of the economy itself is the creation of a bubble, where the values of stocks, for instance, are less and less tied to actual performance…If we perceive the flow of money as a top-down phenomenon, trickling down from those who have most to those who have little, is it surprising that our most common images of God are top-down images? Or, if we understand the flow of money in terms of the image of the rising tide that lifts all boats, is it surprising that we perceive people at the economic top to be closer to God and that, when we care about less fortunate others, our idea is to 'lift them up' so that they will move closer to the top?"[22]

As the son and grandson of Presbyterian ministers, I find it interesting to note that from a Christian perspective, both social and religious hierarchies should be viewed from the "outside in" or "bottom-up" position. Jesus Christ is quite clear on this point (See Matthew 4:8-10, 23:11 or 20:16). Jesus's actions demonstrate that even if one embraces an approach to Christian witness in the form of how one's capital should be structured and deployed that is more grounded in notions of servant leadership one cannot escape Jesus's critique of power and the injustices that come from our society's massive wealth aggregation.[23] For Christians who seek to pursue investment practices and faith that fit with their theological ones, this becomes a significant, if not critical, issue. Christ would not have us lead from the front, but from the rear just as we are not meant to stand above the Other, but to serve its interests.

Finally, Rieger continues in this vein by saying that:

> "For Christianity, it is the incarnation of God in the construction worker Jesus Christ, born in a stable rather than a palace, in the company of service workers who tended other people's sheep

(Luke 2:1-20), which turns things upside down. The typical
religiosity that goes from the greatest to the least comes to a halt
here and is turned around. This has implications for our images
of God and ultimately for the Godself. If this Jesus was really
God—'of the same substance' with God, as the Nicene Creed
states—there must be something to God's substance that is
overlooked by mainstream religion."[24]

Christian truth may well be one that is fundamentally at odds with
secular truth, much less the reality of mainstream finance with its competitive benchmarks and notions of Alpha and Beta (meaning superior
returns and market risk) as opposed to Alpha and Omega (meaning
the Beginning and End) as reference to the circle of life's continuous
beginning and rolling conclusion. It is the notion of our collective truth
and purpose—not that of the corporate overlords whose myth of the
consumer's shortcomings and purposelessness we daily buy.

TRUTH AS THE
CORPORATIZATION OF MYTH

Our understanding of the role and place of capital in the world is mostly
defined, controlled, and promoted by—when considered concerning the
world's population—a relatively small handful of corporate actors and
agents who direct through a variety of media how we understand what
truth is. They make us complicit in affirming, endorsing, and operating
within the social knowledge they promote, whether through legacy or
new media channels. It is, on the one hand, fascinating, and on the
other, deeply disturbing to reflect upon the reality that the "One Percent" and their agents control and dominate all manner of capital flows
and, by extension, the myths of corporate practice and economic order
within which we pursue our professions and live our lives.

Harari says,

"Any large-scale human cooperation—whether a modern state,
a medieval church, an ancient city or an archaic tribe—is
rooted in common myths that exist only in people's collective

imagination...People easily understand that 'primitives' cement their social order by believing in ghosts and spirits and gathering each full moon to dance together around the campfire. What we fail to appreciate is that our modern institutions function on exactly that same basis. Take for example the world of business corporations. Modern business people and lawyers are, in fact, powerful sorcerers. The principal difference between them and tribal shamans is that modern lawyers tell far stranger tales."[25]

This interplay of mutually reinforcing beliefs between asset owners, corporate organizations, science and government is not new. The professor of literature Edward Said observes that:

"In India...by the 1930s, 'a mere 4,000 British civil servants assisted by 60,000 soldiers and 90,000 civilians (businessmen and clergy for the most part) had billeted themselves upon a country of 300 million persons.'...The will, self-confidence and arrogance necessary to maintain such a state of affairs can only be guessed at...For the enterprise of empire depends upon the *idea* of *having an empire*...Perhaps its ultimate causes, with those of war, are to be found less in tangible material wants than in the uneasy tensions of societies distorted by class division, with their reflections in distorted ideas in men's minds."[26]

The overarching system of modern financial capitalism, with its institutions not merely of finance but marketing, communications, and media provides us with the social constructs within which we create and define our reality through the creation of a broad infrastructure in support of propagating the corporate message as myth:

"Corporate ads offer a vehicle for producing a legitimating mythology of global corporate capitalism. While each particular corporation tells stories to valorize itself, when these stories are put together they tell a de-historicized story about Capital in a world that has become laterally arrayed…In this mythology, Capital seeks not power or even excessive profits, but rather the greater good; Capital does not stand in relation to society, it appears as society via the imagery of a network of markets integrated by telecommunications and cool new technologies. In this mythology, Capital does not discriminate by gender or race or age, nor does it discriminate spatially or geographically—all spaces are equally abstract: the urban, the suburban, the natural are all within reach."[27] (Goldman/Papson)

And

"Like a giant shadow, modern science and technology have blotted out all other forms of human knowledge and inquiry. Most important, the hegemony of modern science, based always on the paradigm of mathematical physics, has obliterated the possibility of gaining knowledge of the 'meaning' of human life itself. For this 'meaning' requires natural or ordinary language, and resists mathematical or scientific articulation."[28] (Roochnik)

It is within that reality where we surrender our agency and individual sovereignty to the modern day equivalent of the 4000 civil servants, consisting not of British but rather a global Wall Street of operators and insiders who direct the flows of wealth from here to there, invisibly wrapping the earth and our own understanding of the purpose of capital within multiple layers of opaque wealth transfers, in the process smothering the planet and our knowledge of the meaning and ultimate goal of our lives.

Consider this critique of an Oracle commercial that makes use of Buddhist symbols to promote its vision of reality:

"Traditional Eastern religious signifiers (the temple, the red chair, and the Buddhist monk) have been appropriated to signify the transcendence of Alienated Mind made possible by Oracle software. This utopian sophistry conceives a problematic equivalence between knowledge attained via reflection and meditation and that attainted through an Internet connection. Indeed, Oracle collapses information and knowledge together as if they are identical. Yet the velocity and volume of information flows made possible by networks (the Internet) might just as easily be a force that fragments knowledge, substituting an emphasis on surfaces over depth."[29]

This is an example of what Raymond Williams was getting at when he stated that culture supports the expansion of empire through its creation of "structures of feeling" that enable economic exploitation to operate"[30] and the observation that "...During the 1890s, the business of empire, once an adventurous and often individualistic enterprise, had become the empire of business."[31] Naturally, in that day just as in our own, there were tensions between those who sought to advance the forces of imperialism and those who would act against its march.

As we reflect upon the implications of major private equity firms and wealth management groups now entering the field of impact investing our concern should be less focused upon the creation of one more billion-dollar fund and hundreds more staff now structuring new impact investment offerings for retail distribution than the all too real threat of corporate marketing and communication teams taking over the impact narrative. We should be more concerned with Wall Street's framing of the impact story and an inclination not to tell a tale of the pursuit of justice and distributed freedoms, but of rationalizing the mindset and practices of modern financial capitalism toward an end not of impact and equity but corporate complacency and commerce as managed by the great but not necessarily the good. Just as history is written by the victors, the story of impact is at risk of becoming one of UN-SDG rainbow washing (to borrow a phrase from the academic, Wayne Visser) and myths of lives transformed through finance, when in the end our stories must be told not by those with the resources to "buy the mic," but by the voiceless and sung by a chorus of the oppressed.

The salvation from this fate of capital and transnational corporations (as the vessels of capital) controlling our stories and myth may then be the "wisdom of the crowds" as manifest on YouTube, wherein individuals can present alternative visions of the world and then the crowd votes with regard to what has value, resonates, tells "the truth" of our perspectives and authentic experience of life. Before we become overly excited about social media's ability to be directed by users and their content, we need only reflect upon Facebook's relation with Cambridge Analytica combined with the truth that what is delivered to you on Facebook, Twitter, and other platforms is determined by corporate algorithms and not who you choose to follow.

We then end up with either pictures of puppies and kittens, or flash in the pan videos like the one about the head of that guerrilla army in Africa that got all that traction several years ago—and then disappeared as the crowd grew bored with the coarse reality of life in war-torn parts of Africa and the challenges of pursuing real, sustained change, turning its attention instead back to…

…yet more kittens.

THE EMERGING TRUTH OF OUR IMPACT EXPERIENCE AS EVIDENCE

Decades before the denizens of Wall Street deigned to address the notion of capital creating community and companies advancing Blended Value, there were the extended family lending pools of the American-Cambodian population, raising funds to invest in each other's ventures, seeding a Happy Donut here and a restaurant there. Before having the notion one might do good and well there were those of modest wealth who funded other's education and ventures, the "friends, families and fools" who seeded the garage-based enterprise and Uncle Albert's grand idea.

While this activity went on for centuries, in our recent history, before there were impact funds, there were the Community Action Programs of the early 1960s, lending to small, local enterprises and promoting community development, not community development as affordable housing alone, but a vision of community with a big "C"— community as housing and gardens and advocacy and education and potluck dinners in neighbors' backyards and spilling off front porches into block parties. This was the excellent impact experience—the connection of self with Other—that I had in my teens while serving as a Volunteer in Mission, working with low-income kids in Denver's Five Points neighborhood long before it was discovered by today's well paid tech laborers and a new generation of urban pioneers displacing an older generation of long time residents.

In advance of sustainable ETFs and environmental REITs, there were Mennonites and Sisters, investing in alignment with their God, integrating the mandates of theology and real humanity with mammon and finance. Before the current popularity of today's impact investment robo-platforms, there were socially responsible investor visionaries and those working in the shadows of the fringes of finance, managing capital for more than money. The seeds were all there; the green shoots being nurtured. Before there was Wall Street Impact there was Main Street Community Impact and the Other side of the tracks; before the money came, there was a vision of something else, of an alternative route beyond the understood truths of traditional financial capitalism and paper trading.

Building upon a natural human inclination to put capital toward some higher purpose, to use it toward some greater end, came the settlement house initiatives of the early 20th Century, training immigrants, mobilizing local money into lending circles and integrating a social agenda with an economic engine of independence and opportunity. Decades later, with the introduction of the Affordable Housing Tax Credit in 1986, the community economic development organizations of the 60s evolved into the affordable housing development organizations of the 80s and 90s—which then left behind much of what had been known regarding how to lend to community businesses, much less operate them[32]—yet that knowledge, that truth and drive—and, yes, a good number of those community-based lending pools themselves, remained, deep in community. They lived on, perhaps less of a presence than before, but they did not completely dissolve away.

In the mid to late 80s, a new generation of disgruntled and wayward social workers began operating ventures aimed at creating profit for nonprofits and employment for the unemployable. While told if one tried to manage a business for social good, one was most likely to have a failed company and no positive social success (also referred to as "no business and no good"), they did not know what they did not know—or rather, they knew something else, something more, something different. They lived within an alternative truth, seeing value in those society undervalues and finding worth in the worthless.

These social entrepreneurs launched small businesses—bakeries, screen printing shops, restaurants, moving companies, cafes and landscaping enterprises—providing transitional and supported employment to those building their way back to employability and self support. They created, managed and invested in vehicles others could ride into the mainstream, carrying forward those the market had expelled, bringing people back into work and self-respect.

Had these community-based entrepreneurs of the 80s and early 90s listened to the truths of the experts within either business *or* the nonprofit sector, they would not have achieved the tremendous initial failures nor future success that came with perseverance and experimentation. They discovered new truths and built new knowledge, a pool of shared learning and experience that rolled into what later happened to be called social entrepreneurship, mission driven companies, purpose driven ventures, impact investing, and more.

The first post-Sixties book on the topic was *The Nonprofit Entrepreneur*, written by Ed Skloot and published in 1987. And throughout the 1990s, a number of us made investments in documenting our work and sharing our lessons.[33] These came out of the experience—out of *our* experience, together—not the observations or reflections of the academics to come years later, or the critics and pundits of philanthropy, or the peddlers of recycled expertise in the guise of management consultation. Our knowledge came first and foremost in those early years from thoughtful activists who put capital and the unemployable to work, people before profit, and only later pen to paper to capture what it was we had learned out of our street-level experience, how we could do better and what the real possibilities and true—not perceived—risks were.

We lived that different truth.

These folks found the traditional ideology of the social sector *and* traditional finance had failed. The routine fundraising, ass kissing, and bootlicking politicking had fallen short of what we'd been taught in the street and seen in our communities, what we'd taught each other or had hoped or were told was possible either in a life or in a neighborhood. And yet the magic of the market had also left our people behind, shackled with the shame of addictions and domestic abuse and illiteracy, lacking the skills and support needed to be successful in a changing world that rolled on by and over them. They had little if any power and the promised power of the Internet remained a promise and nothing more; something they'd heard was evolving on the other side of the 101, over on the Peninsula, just down in the Valley but a world away.

As the field of social enterprise developed (and to be honest, at that point it was more like a garden than a field!), they then found, just over that garden wall, another community; one of for-profit, mission driven folks, launching Ben & Jerry's, Seventh Generation, Patagonia, and The Body Shop, among others. They found *real* business folks using real investment money to start for-profit companies, companies with concern for the return of capital to investors and the creation of community in the world.

And then *those* folks looked around and realized there was a world of wealth looking to invest but seeking to draw as straight a line as possible between their dollars and community level impact. Many of these people had lives, interests, and experiences outside the United States and initially looked elsewhere to identify opportunities in micro-finance and enterprise creation. Social entrepreneurship and financial innovation were thriving in emerging markets where one had to innovate and collaborate or die. One had to learn how best to leverage local, community capital of diverse and many forms or be crushed by established financial capital and its market movements. Entrepreneurship was found to be alive and well in these communities; small and sometimes struggling against corruption and global aid efforts, but with beating heart and fluttering wing.

Some years later, many U.S.-based impact investors turned back to what I considered U.S. domestic emerging market opportunities, bringing with them connections in the U.K. and Europe of C.I.C.s and European-based SRI funds. These relatively new asset owners then "discovered" community banking, rural and "second tier city" investing, screened investment funds, community lenders and various public and private investment strategies that sought to integrate consideration of social and environmental factors into their approaches to wealth management.

In those early days, just like the American West, one needed a guide, a trapper who'd been up into the hills and knew the mountain ranges that lay beyond. Today, for better and worse, one may go on line and if both lucky and discerning discover a world of mission-motivated wealth and investment opportunities, but in the early days, explorers had to draft their own maps and chart their own course. It was a little wild and reckless, but it was free and open country offering new areas to explore and peaks to climb. In the face of today's mass of financial Homesteaders pouring over previously defined borders and boundaries, I find I miss those early, frontier days. It was the West before the Astors, Morgans and Rockefellers organized it, invested in it and profited from it. It was the West of innovation and change, but also of danger and professional risks beyond those we carry today.

THE EVOLUTION OF KNOWLEDGE
TO PERSONAL TRUTH

The knowledge of this embryonic community, what we *knew* to be true, did not initially come from books and journals or even conferences for we did not seek nor would we accept what experts claimed as truth; our knowledge came out of an evolving community of experience we built together in those early years, gathering new friends to share tentative lessons (not best practice, but rather *promising* practice!) and experience, while our old friends from before went on to make their money in business or took paths into government, philanthropy or consulting.

The great Russian philosopher Alexander Herzen wrote in 1844 in his seminal work, *Letters*, that philosophy was worthless absent action in the form of applied and physical science. In our own time, what we came to believe was shaped by what we came to understand—the rationalist

married to the idealist. Our knowledge grew from what we saw form-
ing out of our initial efforts, what we were trying to create in our communities. And that knowledge base was an integration of thought and
vision informed by action, which then created better thought. We did
not know it then, but we were living out the realities of Herzen's "empiricism with speculation"[34] in a manner we today are at risk of losing as
growing numbers seek the security and perceived sanctuary of reams of
numbers, analyses, and faux facts with which we may comfort ourselves
in the face of any perceived impact and financial risk or uncertainty.

Ruiz and Mills say,

> "The truth needs to be experienced. Humans have the need to
> describe, to explain, to express what we perceive, but when we
> experience the truth, there are no words to describe it. Who-
> ever claims, 'This is the truth' is lying without even knowing
> it. We can perceive truth with our feelings, but as soon as we
> try to describe it with words, we distort it, and it's no longer
> the truth. It's our story! It's a projection based on reality that
> is only true for us, but still we try to put our experience into
> words, and this is something wonderful, really. It's the greatest
> art of every human."[35]

We have learned a great deal about how to *do* impact investing, but
at a more profound level what we have found is that successful execution
may have as much to do with changing the world as with changing our
own good selves. We live within a story we have created as a society and
as individuals moving through our lives, brought to a reality defined in
terms of capital, justice, impact, metrics, equity of various types and so
on, all of which we use to tell others who we are, what we believe and
what is right. The challenge is we pretend much of our story is focused
upon others, when in fact our story is actually mainly about our selves;
how we perceive our truth, our understanding of our own and our community's history, our purpose and so on.

We tend to focus upon the folks we seek to have impact upon and
to influence in order to have them gain greater alignment with who we

are and how we understand our own place in this reality. But, as Ruiz observed, "the problem is not with the secondary characters in our story. What we see in them is just a projection of what we believe, and that's a secondary problem. Our main problem is with the main character of the story. If we don't like our story, it's because we don't like what we believe about the main character. There is only one way to change our story, and that is by changing what we believe about ourselves."[36] In this way, what we believe regarding the purpose of capital is in the end less a function of distorted corporate myth making or peer group pressures than our own fundamental, in some ways, broken experience and myth lived large, somewhat warped, yes, that is correct, but still vibrant in the global public square.

We must move from what we currently believe we know with regard to the purpose and structure of capital into a space of what is temporarily unknown or yet to be fully defined. Grant Maxwell observes what is required to take this leap into the unknown:

> "...(O)ne must engage in an act of will to move beyond the seemingly fundamental premises that make the opposition appear irreconcilable. For instance, it has generally been supposed in modernity that one must either believe that the nonmaterial, spiritual world is primary, as was generally the case in pre-modernity, or that the world is simply a vast and inherently meaningless agglomeration of material particles. However the integrative method invites one intentionally to adopt a new and deeper premise: that both of these views, roughly definable as idealism and materialism (often correlated to but not always identical with, religion and science), are not mutually exclusive propositions, but partially true modes of thought applicable in their respective domains of validity."[37]

We come to blend our understanding of our two parts—the quantitative and qualitative, the ability to do well and good, and so on—to affirm we know questions of meaning and purpose of capital can not be considered separate and apart from those of how we then seek to structure and deploy capital. It is all part of the whole, of understanding and practice moving toward impact investing as the bridge between what we have understood as finance versus philanthropy toward a synthesized, integrative approach to wealth management and capital allocation, now manifest as Total Portfolio Management and Portfolio Activation.

It is a question of first sensing the outline of a blended value reality and then moving to understand its implications for how we think about the management not only of wealth but of organizations and, indeed, our lives. As the theologian and founder of the Center for Action and Contemplation, Richard Rohr, says, "This is another access point: knowing by union, an intuitive grasp of wholeness, a truth beyond words, beyond any need or capacity to prove anything right or wrong. This is a contemplative stance toward life, our solid place to stand from and which to move."[38]

OUR FUTURE TRUTH

The roots of our coming social prosperity are set into the soil of rot and entropy. Just as trees fall, die and become part of a new eco-system for new organisms which carry the old within them, organizations, companies and our very selves must also falter, shift and stumble if there are to be new opportunities, new growth and new, sustained organisms moving the wheel of life forward.[39]

Impact investing grew, in part, due to its ability to identify and interest in exploring areas of market failure, stagnation and turmoil; the known and unknown—places mainstream investors viewed as too risky, uncertain or dangerous to invest; places where "the market" as traditionally understood had failed. In the early days of BRAC in Bangladesh the notion of lending circles and practice of directing debt capital to extremely low-income women were viewed as a potential violation of fiduciary duty—yet in later years, mainstream, commercial lenders came to view micro-finance, green bond offerings, Social Impact Bonds and other, related impact investment vehicles as a way to invest in non-correlated assets, to engage in diversified risk management.

We are today suddenly members of a class of respectable asset owners, advisors and managers, those of us who in days past were the real

barbarians, rallying outside the gates of Wall Street, speaking foreign
tongues and promoting ancient dreams in what were for us natural ways
and what was, for mainstream finance, the babble of the insane infidel
coming over the walls of the Street. Who would have guessed Black-
Rock would come to own the domain "impact investing" and trillions
of dollars would be managed on the basis of sustainable, responsible and
impact strategies?

Boy, if my mom were alive to see this now...

But doing this first began with someone seeing a new truth and
believing it might be realized. This belief represented a leap of faith,
which had to be taken by those at the tip of the fiscal spear, those on the
front end who thought they knew the market and possibilities and were
willing to see beyond what traditional, mainstream investors misunder-
stood and wrongly perceived as unmanageable risk.

Over coming decades, as the field of impact investing evolves and
continues to aggregate knowledge, it will formalize, with larger bodies of history and the insights that may be taken from that experience.
There will be new data sets and emerging track records and growing
numbers of those who think themselves "real" investors with Wall
Street experience who will continue to enter the field, telling us what is
possible and what is not; what opportunities are there and what is but
vague mirage. They will need to listen before they may hear.

Newcomer academics will continue to mobilize, defining their
hypotheses and case studies and reams of big data they believe will
reveal the truth like swirling tea leaves settling at the bottom of a clay
cup, gathering in a delicate pile of objective truth as understood by
those who stand separate and apart from our reality, measuring and
judging, spawning others who will then create new advisory firms out of
which they may resell us the knowledge they believe they have received
through their many interviews and extended, studied and, in the end,
distant observations; knowledge they have not yet fully discerned much
less wisdom they have heard in their hearts.

And at some future point in our coming times yet another generation of financial and entrepreneurial activists will come along, a
new crew of community capital collaborators, who will look over the

boundary of the high rock walls dividing what will then be our current practice from their generation's future prospects. This new generation will peer up that wall built by their elders with their salaryman experts and fund managers. This new generation will scramble up to play on a high line, balancing between what is accepted as reality and what is viewed as financial folly. They will balance on the line between two possibilities, traipsing along the top, scaring their elders and bringing new practices to bear upon old challenges elders like me have given up on.

It is in only this way the circle of progress has ever turned and it is in only this way the spiral of knowledge will rotate into the future as it has rotated out of the past. A new truth will slowly emerge, rooted in that past and flowing to our future; a truth to be accepted, embraced, rejected and ultimately itself renewed yet again as the circle turns upon itself to reveal its own self to coming generations of fiscal activists discovering for themselves what they will decide to embrace as the true purpose of capital, a new generation's experience of that capital's purpose and understanding of the meaning of money.

As it was in the past, it will be yet again.

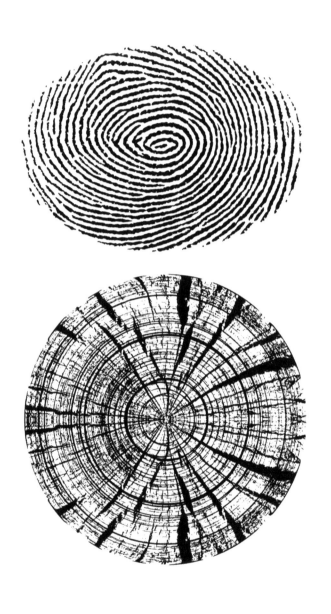

CHAPTER EIGHT

DEMYSTIFYING TIME AND MONEY

O N THE ONE HAND, TIME IS PERSONAL, SUBJECTIVE, AND EXPERIENTIAL. ONE LIVES IN THE WORLD ACCORDING TO ONE'S OWN PERCEPTIONS AND OUR TIME MOVING THROUGH THAT LIFE. WHEN ONE IS YOUNG, TIME CRAWLS, PASSING SLOWLY IN ENDLESS, TICKING MINUTES:

"Are we there yet?"

"I'm four and a half now, but I'm almost five!"

"I can't wait to grow up so I can do that!"

Yet as we age and find the years lying down behind us, time sprints toward a dark finish:

"I can't believe how fast that vacation went...
She only first learned to swim, what, two years ago?"

"When did I slide into my late fifties?
Son, when did *you* get so old?"

"My joints have started to ache,
my friends have started to die
and my favorite musicians now look like my pudgy peers and
older brother…"

The aging uncle at that family event—when was it? Twenty years
ago? Could it be forty years?—is long gone. You now arrive at Thanks-
giving to discover you've taken his place and are that uncle of your
past—only you are your nephew's present, sitting there in a comfortable chair, drink in hand, straining to capture bits of conversation you
find you really don't care that much about and—when you're completely
honest with yourself—about which you understand less and less. You
think to yourself:

Would you *want* a self-driving car? You *like* to drive…Why stream
someone *else's* music, set by some algorithm that brings more of what
you already know when you can explore entirely new sounds by reading
reviews and reflections of artists and others you respect? Besides, you
like having your music collection and have always regretted turning your
vinyl in for digital…what a mistake that was!

It is true: your life negates those that have gone before, just as those
to come will, in essence, be the negation of your own. For them to live,
you must die, your ideas must be shown to be false and those of the new
generation, true.

Beneath a twinge of something approaching transient jealousy,
when you're quiet, alone and entirely on your own a subtle awareness
rises like a large swell on the open sea. You slowly realize (but do not
fully accept) that your current ambitions have moved to a more rooted
place. You don't necessarily settle as much as come to agree that this
is indeed *your* life and at this point, there's less of a need to rush since
where you are rushing is not the next big job or insight or adventure.
Instead, you're rushing to your last post, your more in-depth perspective and, despite your best efforts to deny it, you're moving through a
roster of your priorities which—whether consciously or unconsciously—
you've grown increasingly aware of:

To see your favorite artist perform one last time.

To decide whether that trip to Manchu Picchu is as crucial as a month at the cabin with your wife, your mountains and your books.

To realize you'd rather be at home fixing dinner with a couple you've wanted to get to know instead of attending that conference where you're increasingly viewed as the Old Guard to be challenged and not that Young Turk, posturing and threatening the established hierarchy empaneled on the stage, because alas, you are the one on the panel forced to listen to the reflections of your fellow panelists. You wish you could be on the floor, feeding questions to your younger self, calling others to account in the same way you have personally been confronting your own life and time over recent months...

With the right perspective, this process of rolling time, the passages from youth to elder to child, may be viewed as continuous and never-ending. As the Native American spiritualist and Cowlitz Chief, Roy Wilson, says:

"The circle is one of the most powerful symbols in Native American spirituality. It speaks to us of the eternal nature of life. You can find neither the point of beginning nor the point of ending to the circle. This teaches us that life is unending. We can have a hope in eternal life. These lessons of life come to us from the Medicine Wheel, the Native American's Bible. The Medicine Wheel is known to many of our people as the Wheel of Life. We see life as being beyond the concept of "time consciousness." It is outside of time, cycling forever and forever."[1]

Or, when managing wealth for generations to come, many families with significant assets say they think of long term as operating within a fifty to one-hundred-year time horizon. In truth, this can be something of an inter-generational pretense since in reality the performance of a portfolio is assessed at annual rebalancing meetings of the investment committee. These meetings may be used to affirm moving outside of any particular stated range or set of strategies if conditions (financial crisis, war, executive idiocy at a Presidential level—however defined from whichever side of the aisle) are felt to justify it. While we may voice a commitment to operating within a long-range perspective, reality, bias, and impatience often intrude upon efforts to work within such a commitment.

Family planning on this level is indeed tricky, for, as John Lederach observes:

> "Herein lies the paradox: The journey of life moves toward physical death, which is a future event. When people die and pass into the sphere of the living-dead, they join the ancestors in the past. As such, the journey is toward a past that lies before us…The past and future are not seen as dualistic, polar opposites. They are connected, like ends of a circle that meet and become seamless."[2]

In light of these realities, perhaps as a middle ground between the ongoing cycle of time and time as a subjective, life limited idea defined as that period between my birth and my death, we could take a more genuinely inter-generational approach. Elise Boulding suggests we view ourselves as living in the two-hundred-year present.[3] This concept would be calculated by "subtracting the date of birth of the oldest person we have known in our lives from the projected passing-on date of the youngest person in our family."[4]

Instead, our society has opted to break the circle, to bend it flat and straight, a dead, and for many deadening, line pointing off into the future and back to the past. For those of a Western heritage, it's interesting to note it was the introduction of the idea of good versus evil gods engaged in a battle over the cosmos (which came from the Zoroastrians of Persia) that moved our current sense of time from a cyclical framework, based upon our observation of the cycles of the seasons, toward a linear understanding of time wherein there would be an eschaton or end-time, toward which humanity was marching and which would determine the outcome of the world.[5] And so we each are then tied to a personal end of days from which we cannot escape save for the potential salvation of a higher god of spite, anger, and supposedly redeeming love.

Another perspective is that the Old Testament introduced a linear notion of time—it has a beginning and end and parts in between that progress and develop. Before this framing, a cyclical-Sisyphean understanding of time, of circles wrapped in infinity was the dominant framework. History does not go in any direction, but instead, it moves in cyclical repetition like the seasons and turns of life and death.[6] And of course, this was key in that, "The idea of progress, which would later become the moving force for the creation of science and the hope of our civilization in general, only came about due to a linear understanding of history. If history has a beginning as well as an end, and they are not the same point, then exploration suddenly makes sense in areas where the fruits are borne only in the next generation. Progress gains new meaning."[7] (Sedlacek)

Regardless of the specifics of how it occurred, without that shift in our Western understanding of the nature of time, we would have had no development of our present knowledge of the notion of 'time value of money' around which we now structure our lives and loves. Such an idea states that, in chunks of time, a dollar today is worth more than a dollar tomorrow and upon this artificial conceptual structure we might then build mortgages and life debts in payments of interest, perhaps later, principal. These pieces of our lives, these payments and measures of our value, flow rationally and are then used to move our worth from those who seek to create it in their lives, for the benefit of self, family, and community to a whole cast of others oceans away from our time, to those who now store our value of having lived.

The value of time moves over quarters and years, passing us by, stripped out of our lives, aggregated in the accounts of the lender, whether financial firms, impact investors in far away nations or into charts of accounts of families of wealth flanked with advisors from trillion dollar firms carefully managing the process, structuring strategy and taking their fee, all in good contracted increments. These large, new managers of wealth seeking impact will in turn seek their reward in amounts of two and twenty blackbirds set on a wire stretching out against our Western sky, from here to there, from past to present, from that first entrepreneurial prophet to final, terminal and publicly traded corporate profits.

In the end, our ideas, passions and insights are all destined to be categorized, divided and distributed with an assessed value and future worth imputed by those who have no idea and nary a clue concerning the visionary source or original purpose of the wealth and capital they now seek to manage and direct, seeing only the result and not past origins of that which they now covet today.

Blame the Zoroastrians for the inequities of modern financial capitalism, if indeed anyone is to be blamed for the long-term consequence of time being split, divided and sold to those who would then parse it out for sale to others down the line; for sale from Self to other—lower case, of a deadened spirit 'o' in this context.

To review:

From the perspective of finance, the measure of money's performance is pegged to its relative value over various points in time during predefined investment periods; as stated, this is then referred to as The Time Value of Money. One has Present Value, Future Value and Discounted Value each of which measures the financial value of money today relative to its potential future earnings and the risk that those earnings will or will not materialize in your life or that of others you will never see.

With this connection of time to money, with this valuation of our ideas and energies, with this measure of our real worth, life itself begins to change.

According to James Buchan,

"Once time can be bought and sold through interest, there comes a new urgency to temporal existence: by the turn of the sixteenth century…the church clocks of Germany are striking the quarter-hour. Time, once a calendar of agricultural events, cycles of birth, humility and death and the unfolding of God's will, begins to tick away in units of money: in hourly rates and per diems, weekly wages, monthly salaries, half-yearly dividends, annual raises or bonuses, superannuation pensions, perpetual stock and, eventually, in that redemptive eternity economists call 'the long run.'"[8]

And one may, therefore, understand how time is, in point of fact, money.

But from the perspective of physics, present time is a relative thing and does not exist in objective terms at all, much less monetized. The theoretical physicist, Carlo Rovelli, asks:

"What is the 'present'? We say that only the things of the present exist: the past no longer exists, and the future doesn't exist yet. But in physics, there is nothing that corresponds to the notion of the 'now.' Compare 'now' with 'here.' 'Here' designates the place where a speaker is: for two different people 'here' points to two different places. Consequently 'here' is a word the meaning of which depends on where it is spoken…'Now' also points to the instant in which the word is uttered…But no one would dream of saying that things 'here' exist, whereas things that are not 'here' do not exist. So then why do we say that things that are 'now' exist and that everything else doesn't?"[9]

In ancient Rome, only the wealthy could compress time and distance, since they were the only ones with the resources to store grain over many months, and thus time markets for the best pricing, or pay the significant costs of moving grain over land and sea to where the best prices were or the greatest demands of those in famine or engaging in war.[10] In our time, perhaps the wealthy—as the ultimate owners of a wealth only lent to and managed by others—may still benefit from an ability to compress time into smaller and smaller increments for, time-space compression[11] is "the increasing speed and ease of business travel and transactions which take place as if geography and distance no longer matter. When a currency transaction can be conducted between New York and Singapore in a matter of seconds, for all intents and purposes both space and time have been overcome as barriers to commerce."[12] (Goldman/Papson)

We should take solace in the reality that time itself, as experienced in the moments of time as opposed to maintaining a focus on the long, piling up of time, does not exist outside of the individual moment within which you experience it. Dainin Katagiri, founding abbot of the Minnesota Zen Meditation Center, observes:

> "We believe that we can make time meaningful because we usu-
> ally suppose that time is running on a road from here to there,
> toward a certain destination, from 12:00 AM to 12:00 PM. We
> believe there is a stream of time that flows continually from the
> past through the present to the future, so we say that there are
> one beginning and one end of this world. Then we think that
> time goes from a beginning to an end with a particular purpose,
> and we expect that we can make progress and feel satisfied as
> a result. But if you are seeking to know the time in its naked
> nature, you cannot believe this because time is not a succession
> of constantly connected moments going toward a certain des-
> tination; in the transient stream of time, moments appear and
> disappear. Impermanence constantly cuts off your life, so every
> moment is separate."[13]

Within this understanding of the nature of time, there is no past or future; merely the now of the current moment.

I find this comforting, but then…who knows and who needs it?

We are each on our own again, marching toward that end time; as ever, as you started and as you will conclude for despite our efforts at escape we experience time by ourselves, in the context of our own lives

and those with whom we intersect for brief moments, each approaching, now bright before us and next fading behind as we crane our necks and attempt to freeze that moment—the early age of a child, the first kiss, the last glimpse of a loved one curled in pain in anticipation of approaching death draining life out of her bones and being—each image held in the mind as they are now gone, having fled the present.

Generations build like curlers off the shore, massing first, swelling up and then breaking over the generation that came before, leaving them spread out over the hard packed sand, weak and receding under a frothy surface, washing backward into the time to come, back down into the next wave already building and refreshingly unconscious of its unbroken connection to the waves that came before—to the energy *you* unleashed—for the next generation, the next wrinkle in time, is mostly unaware of the actual life and time of you and yours, much less do they care about those who come from behind, those lives around the world that already shadow them, looking for breaks in the curlers through which to make their growing presence felt. At that moment, *they* are the New Wave[14] and all that matters.

You are nothing.

The Historian Arnold Toynbee observed that each generation thinks itself to be the pinnacle of human evolution and development, and of course they are. The latest technology, thinking and insights regarding the challenges of living alone together are theirs to own, control and interpret for those too young or too old to understand the current reality a present generation is creating within their slice of our time. Yet, this very truth (that you are smarter, wittier and better looking than your parents and their generation, yet quicker, more knowledgeable and offering greater insight than your younger brothers and sisters) is, of

course, the generational Achilles heel
Time will use to slice your tendon
with its knife of experience and bring
you crashing to the ground.

Time will take its sharpened tool
and cut you.

Time will bring you to your
knees as you see colleagues and family fall to your left and right. You are
only here for a flash and are not the
transcendent truth that in your finest
hours you dare think yourself. Your
insights and wisdom are no more than that sad self-improvement poster
plastered on the wall above your head, where you sit in your generational cubicle, all lined up and competing as to form with your peers, each
of you focused, head down, working and now existent, flowing through
your individual experiences of life, out of fear or faith, paying little real
attention to the fate to come.

We deny the ravages of time by purchasing creams and treatments,
to be sure, but also engage in collective efforts to inject what we know
to be a point in time and space that may have no permanence with various decorations, shiny baubles of commerce and capital transactions
that distract our eye and occupy our mind, convincing us of the hoped
for protection offered by those structures we build around us—investment strategies, metrics, conceptual frameworks and beliefs we create
on the inside (our interior landscape) of an impermanent world (their
exterior landscape).

Consider Katagiri's observation that:

"Since human beings have been born in this world, we have
decorated our lives with lots of ornaments to make time more
meaningful. We develop remarkable civilizations of culture,
politics, beauty, and pleasure. We create ineffectual disciplines
such as history, economics, science, philosophy or psychology,
and then we believe that they make life meaningful. Maybe we

believe that spiritual life can help us find meaning. So we create ideas such as God, Buddha, unreal energy, the last judgment and paradise after death, theology, mythology or morality and ethics and then we try to spend on them to make us feel that life is worth living. Century after century we have done this, trying to find real spiritual security through making time meaningful. But still, there is no solution because they are all just ornaments. We still ask: How can you make human life meaningful? What is spiritual security?"[15]

You are merely here in your time, in your place, with a dawning understanding that each generation will have its day's brilliance that will slide under the dusk of its ignorance, arrogance, and ambition. You cannot free yourself from the binds of the past, of your history and the cultural perspectives that convince you of your righteousness. This righteousness blinds you to the fate that comes ever closer as you join with the past and give birth to a future that will itself look upon you with pity and condescension since they are now the ones who inherit the torch of brilliance you carry today. And so time is a function of relationship and relativity between you and others, between you and the timeless Other.

We are brought back once more to our notion and relationship with the Other, and this then is the beautiful wisdom of time that is at once so thrilling and yet so humbling.

This wisdom of Time frees you from hurry and helps you have greater compassion for many—not all, but many—of those who have explored these shores before you. Your parents are one example. Moving back in time, we may have compassion for the individuals and communities and century upon century of humanity upon whom you now surf and tend to judge harshly as you in turn look forward, riding your own wave as it curls toward crashing, and sense how beneath and around you the weight of that history and experience builds behind you, gathering as a storm. The waters come, flow and spray as they drag you down into the mix of swirling sand and foam and ever decreasing minutes.

Your understanding of your life, time and presence is real for you— but it is merely a particle or pulse in a more significant flow of energy, experience and perspective which when taken together make up the broad arc of history and human experience that simultaneously connects you with past and future and so, as has been said, one should merely seek to find one's place within that flow and be here now, peacefully present and thoroughly grounded in what, for you and in this time, is.[16]

This is why the shared concept and individual experience of Time may only be thought of as beautiful if one reflects on the implications of physics and its concepts such as quantum entanglement (which states that "particles that are 'entangled' however distant from one another, undergo the same changes simultaneously."[17]). As has been said, "We are having to call into question our mainstream notions of what are very linear ideas, such as cause and effect, evidence or fact, for these are each ephemeral and temporary, falling in the future just as they had emerged from the past. Many of these new, proven theories of the structure of time and matter call into question our present common and mainstream understandings of what "is."[18] (Robinson)

As one of my favorite authors, Marilynne Robinson, wrote, these ideas imply "a cosmos that unfolds or emerges on principles that bear a scant analogy to the universe of common sense. (This) is abetted by string theory, which adds seven unexpressed dimensions to our familiar four. And, of course, those four seem suddenly tenuous when the fundamental character of time and space is being called into question. Mathematics, ontology, and metaphysics have become one thing. Einstein's universe seems mechanistic in comparison, Newton's, the work of a tinkerer."[19]

From the perspective of physics, we may be forced to forge a new understanding of not only time but our relation to it as being something both personal and subjective while at the same time (literally, at the same time!) being beyond comprehension. David Papineau says:

"In the early 20ᵗʰ century, J.M.E. McTaggart argued that every event has the property of being past, present and future at some time or other. Since these properties are incompatible, and since nothing can have incompatible properties, past, present and future do not exist. The four-dimensional picture given by modern physics also denies the reality of past, present, and future. In this picture, events can be said to be earlier than or later than each other, but no event ever has the privilege of being in 'the present' or 'the past.' This is because being in the present is the same as happening now. In the four-dimentionalist picture, happening here, and objective reality no more contains a 'hereness' than it contains a 'now-ness': whether an event is 'here' or 'now' are matters of a person's perspective on reality, and not a part of reality itself."[20]

As hard as we attempt to maintain some semblance of balance in our lives, we stumble through various realities of what is and how we understand the nature of time itself. While I had a certain perspective on the event, in my SOCAP2016 talk, I expressed the notion that the past is future and present is past, so we should be grounded in our understandings of current reality, which is the concept of Be Here Now promoted by Baba Ram Dass several decades ago—as if the years matter.

The trick is that the Age of Enlightenment advanced a linear and segmented understanding of time and progress where the future is disconnected from the past or may be considered as mostly separate from it, when in fact history is embedded in our experience of the present. In a commitment to advancing positive change in the world, we are injecting ourselves into the flow of time and history—the conditions that have created whatever reality upon which we seek to have impact—and yet our structures are grounded in Western, "enlightened" concepts of time, change and value creation, so we come to believe that a traditional, PE fund structure of 10 years plus two one year extensions with a fee of "two and twenty" is an appropriate vehicle through which to not only explore but advance social change and create situational impact.

How can that be so?

What we are doing is merely operating in a reductionist framework that attempts to separate and artificially simplify the very elements of life we are trying to improve upon. The whole conversation—from investment strategy to fund structure and investment instrument management to our understanding of exits and returns (indeed, what do those terms each *mean* in the full context of change and impact, much less within our evolving experience of time?) comes to be distorted and separated from any real level of meaningful change and sustained impact.

In the absence of this larger perspective, I conclude that for many the song and dance of impact serve mainly to accommodate and normalize the capitalist system that has created many of the very situations of injustice and un-sustainability upon which we seek to have an impact in our time, and right the negative impacts advanced by generations past and the historic legacies carried into our present.

In the end, with all this to be considered, maybe Ghandi had the most important understanding of time:

"There is more to life than increasing its speed."[21]

CHAPTER NINE

OUR FAITH IN FINANCE

I N HEBREWS 11:1 WE FIND THE BIBLICAL DEFINITION OF FAITH AS "...THE ASSURANCE OF THINGS HOPED FOR, THE CONVICTION OF THINGS NOT SEEN."

Simply put, the biblical definition of faith is 'trusting in something you cannot explicitly prove.' This definition of faith contains two aspects: intellectual assent and trust.

> "Intellectual assent is believing something to be true. Trust is relying on the fact that the something is true. A chair is often used to help illustrate this. Intellectual assent is *recognizing* that a chair is a chair and *agreeing* that it is designed to support a person who sits on it. Trust is actually *sitting in the chair*. Understanding these two aspects of faith is crucial. Many people believe certain facts about Jesus Christ. Many people will *intellectually* agree with the points the Bible declares about Jesus. But knowing those facts to be true is not what the Bible means by "faith." The biblical definition of faith requires intellectual assent to the facts *and* trust in the facts."[1] (Emphasis in original)

Financial capitalism is founded upon an intellectual assent that the "numbers don't lie" as well as trust in what the numbers profess to tell us. Beyond such agreement and trust, our faith in finance calls us to the promotion of the true religion of financial capitalism, to seeking the conversion of others to embrace not only the practices of the church but the foundational tenets, values, and confessions of our faith in finance.

This church of free capital markets even has its clergy of missionaries who over past decades and perhaps centuries has headed out around the world to bring the faith and its values to new lands. There are, of course, countless examples of this, but one of relevance is how in the debates of the early 90s regarding the potential privatization of the German Postal Service, rather than engaging in informed market analysis and business plan development, a team of management consultants were brought in to "spark the imagination of their German counterparts through the promotion of concepts that were transcendent in the sense that they would apply independently of time and space. Universal economic values like deregulation and cost cutting were far more important in the process than economic analyses and studies; those values determined both the questions that were raised and the answers given,"[2] Rieger recounts.

In this way, believers must seek to convert others to the belief, and our Faith in Finance must always try to bring new practitioners into the fold, growing the congregation as the market opportunity it is. The Czech term for lender, *veritel*, literally means believer.[3] History reveals how in times of financial crisis the actors within markets are indeed believers in the true church of capitalism, a church with its own set of rules, rituals, and priesthood.

As the conservative British historian, Niall Ferguson, said:

"What the conquistadors failed to understand is that money is a matter of belief, even faith: belief in the person paying us; belief in the person issuing the money he uses or the institution that honors his cheques or transfers. Money is not metal. It is trust inscribed. And it does not seem to matter much where it is inscribed: on silver, on clay, on paper, on a liquid crystal display. Anything can serve as money, from the cowrie shells of the Maldives to the huge stone discs used on the Pacific Islands of

Yap. And now, it seems, in the electronic age nothing can serve as money too."[4]

Harari further observed,

"The sum total of money in the world is about $60 trillion, yet the sum total of coins and banknotes is less than $6 trillion. More than 90 percent of all money—more than $50 trillion appearing in our accounts—exists only on computer servers... Money isn't a material reality—it is a psychological construct... money is the most universal and most efficient system of mutual trust ever devised."[5]

We take wealth's existence on faith and trust and our belief that a series of zeros and ones is, in fact, wealth. This is why the financial crisis of 2008 brought our economic system to a standstill—we lost our faith in finance as a result of a betrayal of our trust in the shaky financial scaffolding we had built around our Church. Rieger continues:

"While for some the notion that finance is a form of faith tradition (with its own wisdom literature, cathedrals and priesthood) may seem like a jump, for many others it is self-evident. The leading U.S. economist John Kenneth Galbraith stated neoliberal laissez-faire economics is built upon theological grounds, while the University of Maryland economist Robert Nelson has published two books exploring the topic. Michael Novak of the American Enterprise Institute has even gone so far as to promote the notion of a 'Christian Theology of Economics.'"[6]

As an economically driven society wrapped in the embrace of unquestioning faith in financial capitalism, we refuse to acknowledge the degree to which those economic beliefs are then translated into financial ritual and the extent to which our understanding of reality is defined by this faith in finance. We describe ourselves as operating within a secular society of science and rationality, but that is just not the case. Instead what we have done is create a world founded upon what the historian Arnold Toynbee termed "man-worship" [sic],[7] a world in which we trust the rationality and quantitative analysis of humanity as superior to all other perspectives and practices *of* our humanity; perspectives and practices not grounded within a trust in the primacy of numbers. But we tell ourselves this faith in numeracy is not faith at all, but the rational way of the universe—and not simply a social construct of humanity.

One implication of this faith in finance is how our understanding of modern financial capitalism has moved from thought and an original knowledge of 'dogma' to rigidity and a Christian institutional knowledge of dogma as revealed truth. We are expected to take as truth the perspectives and understandings preached to us on CNBC, Fox Business News, Bloomberg, and all that comes to us from any number of other electronic pulpits—to say nothing of the witnessing we receive from traditional financial advisors and a host of others in the congregation

Our expression of the Church of Financial Capitalism is now globally dominant and, as much as we may decry it in private, is our public facing worldview. Within the mainstream while the tenets of neoliberalism have come under review, those of financial capitalism remain One, Absolute and Unquestionable. As is true of all dogma, we may not challenge its underlying assumptions nor refute its analysis and perspective.

By way of but one modest example, in a recent finance committee discussion, a senior financial advisor from a major firm was heard to say, "I'm not comfortable with and don't personally accept the [social] implications of what the data tells us, but our perspective as a firm is based on analysis of the economic facts and this is what the data conclude...".

Imagine my response, if you will, for I was fully and completely gobsmacked. Here we are, paying this guy a ton of money and he punts based on the *data*? He dials it back based on metrics any junior associate could have assembled—in fact, most likely *did* assemble?

What we need are not advisors who simply read the numbers, but those capable of real interpretation, who see the story within the quantitative analysis behind which their peers and competitors hide. The idea one should set aside what one knows to be right to advance a professional—or worse, *firm*—perspective that contradicts what one "knows" is to set dogma over broader insight. It is to live based not upon a variety of inputs, but upon a single line of analysis and, as it would appear, faltering capitalist faith.

By contrast, others are called to the true faith, to use quantitative, rational and grounded analysis to challenge, inform and infuse our professional insights with a sounder, more fully informed perspective which integrates evidence and quantitative analysis *with*—dare I say—thoughtful, intelligent, insightful wisdom. To do otherwise is to live with financial data as dictate, not input. It is to operate with data as railroad track, not guardrail. It is to live to take quaking, tentative steps, one following the other, up the stairs of a fiscal gallows as we pass from the quick to dead. By contrast, we are called to walk a path seeking true value creation and dynamic innovation.

Back to business divinity school, my friend...

RATIONAL FAITH

My apologies for that divergence but we mostly gloss over the assumptions that underscore the liturgy we're asked to accept with its methods and processes of so-called objective economic and other analysis when it is these assumptions that are key. As the economist Tomas Sedlacek observed:

> "The anthropological difference between scientific and prescientific man is that prescientific man explicitly knew the assumptions referred to (articles of faith and myths) and actively accept them (or rejected them). In contrast, modern man bears his (scientific) faith more or less unconsciously. Religion is accompanied by an explicit profession of faith but not science (although it is clear you must use belief in science as well)."[8]

Operating within a framework that positions data as the determinant and comprehensive measure of reality (in this case, financial data and economic reality) is to surrender one's life to financial algorithms and economic calculation as opposed to living on the basis of instructive, quantitative analysis *informed* by wisdom, culture and human history. Our lived, collective human experience together with our rational self, much less the data generated from the frameworks created by that self, cannot be separated one from the other. One must operate in service *of* the Other; challenging, questioning and exploring the underpinnings of our financial myths but advancing our overall understanding of the deeper meaning and purpose that underscores our lives and how we further understand the role, place, and purpose of capital within it. We must embrace data as an infusion to enrich additional perspectives on life, not data as life itself.

Maslow said, "The theory of science which permits and encourages the exclusion of so much that is true and real and existent cannot be considered a comprehensive science. It is obviously not an organization of everything that is real. It doesn't integrate all the data."[9]

And, according to the Scottish historian, James Buchan,

> "Though in their own existences, most people recognize that money and happiness are not coterminous; yet they will accept whatever money quantities are fashionable with the economists—national product, balance of payments, consumer price indices or whatever—as measures of national welfare... That economists can't measure any of their quantities even to their own satisfaction, can explain neither prices nor the rate of interest and cannot even agree what money is, reminds us that we deal here with belief not science."[10]

This worship of rational analysis and free, lightly regulated financial markets as a collective expression of that analysis has several implications:

First, is that it blinds us to the real wonder and miracle of numeracy and data. It prevents us from truly appreciating the near mythical magic of math. The physicist Eugene Wigner, commenting upon the virtually inexplicable power of math to capture and explain the wonders of the universe, wrote:

"The enormous usefulness of mathematics in the natural sciences is something bordering on the mysterious and there is no rational explanation for it. It is not at all natural that 'laws of nature' exist, much less that man is able to discover them. The miracle of the appropriateness of the language of mathematics for the formulation of the laws of physics is a wonderful gift which we neither understand nor deserve."[11]

In the mid-90s, when leading a team that first explored a formalized approach to a methodology of social return on investment, it really struck me (as one who in the '70s required tutoring in high school algebra and in the '80s preferred receiving grants of $100,000 since they allowed me to divide them easily into four entry-level staff positions, let's admit, I was late to the show...) that there was a narrative quality to numbers, what I termed *narrative numeracy*, which allowed one to see flows of time and activity, which permitted one to actually *see* the story of how organizations operated, how decisions were made and to what end. This was the gift of quantitative story telling which, when combined with qualitative analysis and reflection, allowed one to see—to actually *see*—with greater comprehension than either words or numbers might allow on their own. And this is indeed a beautiful alchemy in which to participate.

Second, by placing data, mathematics and quantitative analysis in dominant positions over what we then believe or understand to be true we see only half the analysis possible and we are then blind to the rest of the theorem we should apply to our situation. As the previously referenced senior financial advisor has done, we allow "The Numbers" to define our understanding of what is real. Yet we are called to operate in this manner as individual adherents of the financial capitalist faith and as a society operating under the strictures of this faith tradition of capitalist economics and finance, now over 400 years old and mostly dominant despite the variety of ways our faith has fallen short of serving our individual needs or those of the broader community and world of which we are a part.

Yes, while those reading these words are most likely the economic beneficiaries of this system and benefitting from it on terms significantly greater than the 99% and while millions of others around the world have improved their economic circumstance incrementally through adherence to the doctrines of the church of capitalism, *billions* now and in the future will continue to confront the implications of global wealth aggregation by the few and environmental ecocide of a planet wholly managed on the basis of economic interest alone, as opposed to the interests of Earth as living being. While our faith in finance has served many of us well, it will not save us from the economic and environmental dystopia unfolding before our eyes. Despite this, the church of financial capitalism and rituals of our faith in finance advance mindlessly forward under the guise of old-school, linear progress, its adherents clear eyed and committed as we ever so slowly come to be forced to acknowledge the exact fate such a faith has brought upon us as we now slowly walk the plank, soon to drop—arms, mouths, and minds bound—into the dark, ever warming, and putrid waters below.

In another conversation, among countless of a similar type held over the years, yet one more of the faithful, in response to a statement critical of recent positive stock market response to yet even more significant opportunities and license to pollute or violate human rights, as being immoral, emphatically stated:

"Markets are *amoral*. They do not reflect anything more than rational behavior in response to a set of inputs given them. There is no 'moral' imperative asking market actors do anything more than pursue their own self-interest and the financial interests of those they represent. You cannot describe markets as being moral nor should they be. They simply exist; they simply are."

This perspective reflects the reality referenced by Rieger that:

> "There is a firm belief in the moral benevolence of the free-market system and private property, combined with a common acceptance among liberal, neoliberal and neoclassical theorists that this is the only system that works. This system takes on quasi-divine and transcendent qualities when it begins to block any and all alternatives and challenges."[12]

By acting simply to advance their own self interests the individual investors and collective that is the market manifest what is its own set of normative imperatives and assumptions. They are operating with reference to their own code of morality, just not one cloaked in social mores or assumptions one should take anything other than financial advancement into account. Harari says:

> "The capitalist-consumerist ethic is revolutionary in another respect. Most previous ethical systems presented people with a pretty tough deal. They were promised paradise, but only if they cultivated compassion and tolerance, overcame craving and anger, and restrained their selfish interests...In contrast, most people today successfully live up to the capitalist-consumerist ideal. The new ethic promises paradise on condition that the rich remain greedy and spend their time making more money, and that the masses give free rein to their cravings and passions—and buy more and more. This is the first religion in history whose followers actually do what they are asked to do."[13]

In the early years of the rise in our algorithmic life with Google and Facebook, many thought such big data platforms to be truly objective and independent of human bias, bringing forward only what the numbers themselves generated as fact not fantasy or prejudice. We now know the algorithms of our modern life carry embedded deeply within them—how, exactly, they do this, we're not yet sure, but somehow they do—our own racial, sexual and other prejudices, buried within their rolling rows of coded, numeric DNA.[14] Why then is it so hard for us to accept the reality that capital markets—which are simply the financial infrastructure of our social order—also carry within them our social and class assumptions, bias and mores? How is it we can convince ourselves of their amorality in the context of what is at heart a socially determined, numeric operating system?

If capital is a social construct, it should not be so hard to believe aggregations of capital upon capital carry embedded within their various trenches and derivative instruments our social morals, woven deeply within their framing of economic and financial reality. For example, it was an analysis of the "objective" allocation of lending capital by mainstream banks which demonstrated the then socially validated practice of redlining (wherein inner-city and predominantly minority communities were systematically deprived of investment and debt capital due to the class and racial biases of Church of Capitalism's money lenders) that led to the enactment of the Community Reinvestment Act of 1977.

Our faith in finance simply asks us to promote our self-interests over those of others or the community at large in the belief that it will all work out in our collective best interest. We have created a whole media infrastructure to reinforce and promote our ideology and dogma. As a consequence, for years—even to this day—I have heard missionaries of financial capitalism say the nonprofit sector needed to become more business-like, that we must all adopt a belief in business approaches as being superior to all others and embrace its rituals of practice. The assumption was that by being more supposedly disciplined and analytic, more rational, those of us working to create change in the world would better manage not only ourselves but our organizations and in the end the change agenda to which we aspire. We are all asked to believe the numbers don't lie and with a more business-like approach to our work we would be more effective and efficient in its execution—despite the continuous cycles of boom, bust and obliteration documented throughout our modern economic history.

I do not know what it must have felt like in 1929, but as the days of 2008 unfolded, what came to pass was not a rational process of individuals modifying financial analysis and taking careful, appropriate steps to navigate short-term, choppy economic seas. Instead, our collective experience was one of panic, betrayal of trust and the emotional reactions that come with such fundamental deception. This is reflected in terms of how the financial priesthood responded to the unfortunate turn of events in the economic world we had created:

"Lawyers for the Treasury Department went even further [than Robert Rubin's recommendation that regulation of derivatives be taken out of the hands of the Commodity Futures Trading

Commission] arguing that merely *discussing* new regulations would pose a threat to the derivatives market. This argument exposed the faith-based mechanism undergirding the whole situation without acknowledgment: we cannot even afford to critique the market without turning it against us. The slightest insinuation of lack of faith in the free market would be a mistake—a mistake that would almost be as bad as the lack of faith that manifests itself in calling for economic regulations."[15] (Emphasis added)

The financial crisis shook our world to the core, the numbers upon which we relied were shown to be false, to have been based upon lies and to have been used by our priests in their promotion of a fabricated reality. The ratings of the investment houses and instruments were wrong, and as a result, our world was wallowing in error and strung upside down. In the wake of such betrayal, banks stopped lending capital, institutions previously thought to be sound, fell and we called into question our understanding of what is real and fair.

Yet, rather than taking that moment to go beneath the modern myth of financial capitalism and explore what was real, what in actuality had become of our Church, we skated over the surface, suddenly calling upon government policy and public funds to paper over the shortcomings of our faith; turning to the tools of Satan, as it were, to relieve us of our suffering.

Rieger writes:

"The strength of this faith is demonstrated by the fact that it is maintained even in situations of obvious failure and downturn. The market takes on a central role here that assumes transcendent qualities, as it is the ultimate guide not only for economics but also for politics."[16]

And Eisenstein follows with:

"Looking down from Olympian heights, the financiers called themselves 'masters of the universe,' channeling the power of

the god they served to bring fortune or ruin upon the masses...
Like the clergy of a dying religion, they exhort their followers
to great sacrifices while blaming their misfortunes on either sin
(greedy bankers, irresponsible consumers) or on the mysterious
whims of God (the financial markets)."[17]

What should we do if we are addicted to materially mechanistic
financial capitalism as our religion?

It drives how we spend the energy of our lives and places blinders
on our eyes to see and accept only that which may be proven, demonstrated, measured, and valued economically. It has its high priests of
Wall Street with their pronouncements of trends and benedictions recit-
ed following the closing bell together with their statements of what we
should value and how it should be allocated in daily, quarterly or annual
increments with lock ups determined by this selfsame priesthood and
salvation assessed based upon financial performance with no consideration of elements and externalities beyond the purview of the doctrine of traditional market-based economics. That which lies outside
our understanding of the faith is dismissed as soft, immeasurable and
not rational.

Our faith in finance is an addiction to a mindset, way of life and
identity that blinds us to the ultimate damage we are bringing on our
bodies, communities, world, and selves.

OUR FAITH IN VALUE

As previously discussed, we know there is a thing we now call dark matter. We "see" this as a cloud of material that is revealed in its effect upon
the gravitational pull on surrounding actors—stars and other celestial
objects—and by the way it deflects light. But while there have been
numerous proposals regarding how we should think about what dark
matter is we don't really know for sure and for now may only circum-
navigate around our awareness it exists.[18]

Our understanding of the true nature of value is somewhat the same:

We may propose it consists of various components (economic,
social, environmental). And we may observe and assess parts of each

of these. At its core, we just cannot adequately describe its fundamental nature and elements. Quite literally, words truly cannot describe. We know that real value—deep, blended value—exists beyond what we can adequately measure, assess or comprehend. We know our present approaches to understanding what "it" is fall short of a specific definition or enabling us to understand what it "is." As with dark matter, we know value is something other than can be described with econometrics or biological measures or philosophical constructs alone…actual value is something more, something more profound, a thing or phenomenon, just there, yet not within our grasp. This is a value we may only take on faith—despite what the high priests may describe within current doctrine and celebrate in their Eucharist and related rituals of Wall Street.

For those who call themselves impact investors and social entrepreneurs, we must recognize ourselves as members of a new Reformation. We are members of a happy heretical tribe advancing fundamental aspects of our central faith and creating new metrics to explore its implications and pronouncing a renewed liturgy to celebrate our Eucharist.

This truth is in some ways best seen from the perspective of those holding on to the faith of the Old Church, since their rejection of ESG materiality and impact analysis comes from their seeing us for who we are: an emergent sect pronouncing the marriage of a narrative numeracy with capital performance, a Church of the New Capital, seeking multiple returns and deep, sustained value creation that is part financial and in greater parts just, equitable and regenerative.

Jesus Saves.

God Invests.

Now is the time we should open the doors of our ancestors' temple, to receive the winds blowing from a new world we sense beyond its walls, a world waiting for us, a world that might yet come into view should we discover we have the eyes to see and ears to hear.

PART THREE

BEING PRESENT IN THE CREATION OF POSSIBLE PASTS AND POTENTIAL FUTURES

CHAPTER TEN

ON SCALE AND
THE IMPACT COMMONS

E ARE TOLD, THE GOAL OF ALL OF THIS—IMPACT INVESTING, USE OF CROWD FUNDING, EFFORTS AT BUILDING MARKETS AND SO ON—IS GEARED TOWARD ONE THING: SCALE.

From a business perspective, it is at scale financial markets are thought to operate most efficiently with the most significant promise of profit, and it is at scale that modern business may lay the greatest, most widely accepted and celebrated claim of success:

"Our sales have grown, our profit soars, it is time for us to go public!"

For those of a socially concerned bent, poverty is already at scale so our approaches to alleviating poverty must also be substantial, massive and at comensurate scale. Despite Christ's admonition that the Poor we will always have with us (not necessarily by virtue of any divine short-coming as much as that humanity can't seem to overcome our funda-mental, broken human nature and deficits), we continue to try righting our wrongs and solving the problems of capital with, uh, capitalism as traditionally managed through the infrastructure we've spent decades investing in, operating, and profiting from. But when all is said and done, we hope to optimize markets and impacts through ever more significant applications of investment and capital.

And who wouldn't want that?

Whether you're seeking to dominate a world market or global social problem, scale matters!

Or does it?

Scale as a function of grand size may work at odds to attaining quality impact and the creation of sustained value. Gibson Guitars operates at scale, but Santa Cruz Guitars creates deeper, higher quality musical value while producing as many guitars in a year as Gibson does in a day (and, of course, due to economic overreach and taking on too much debt, Gibson may well be in bankruptcy by the time this book is published…).

In the mid-nineties, I made the argument one could scale for either breadth or depth—working to touch millions of lives lightly or thousands of lives with a greater degree of sustained transformation. Twenty-five-some years later, I would argue this is still the case. I suppose one may enter a discussion about the moral righteousness of depth versus breadth, but I will hold that for another day (although, do know there is an entry in this document under Other Impact that also touches on issues of scale). For now, let's merely say that for me, unless I'm pursuing the broad impact of vaccinating children or promoting a reading literacy program, I'm personally more interested in Deep or Mutual

Impact at scale and social change as opposed to Postal Service-Veterans Administration-Trump Towers-WalMart scale.

Just sayin'...

In conversation with a friend who is founding partner of a venture fund located on Sand Hill Road, we began discussing the notion of scale—both regarding investment funds and the amount of capital entrepreneurs sought (or are encouraged) to raise. She observed that an issue which arises for funds is that as they take on higher amounts of capital they then need to begin to make decisions based not upon what was best for a given enterprise, set of investors or fund but upon the need to deploy and *service* the capital they had raised.

If you take in hundreds of millions of dollars of investment capital and tell your investors you're going to generate many multiples of financial return for them, you then have to manage your relationships with your companies on that same basis, and in that way influence the size and type of firm you seek to invest in as well as the factors you consider in managing the fund, defining its performance or understanding its purpose.

Of equal consideration is the reality that often with grander scale comes greater distance between and among the various parts of the investment constellation. Good, sound private equity and venture investing have always been built upon close, connected and supportive investor relationships. In this case, I'm not talking only about good investment practice, but something more subtle, more profound and challenging of our current system of traditional financial capitalism.

Remember:

Impact investing is not regular investing gussied up with an impact patina; it is focused upon transformation and change as opposed to the simple economics of growth and market dominance. Being mindful within a Buddhist practice requires being present and being present requires being with, engaged and connected to the Other. Compassion in Latin means "to suffer with"—not to engage in 'drive by' investing or modified acts of charitable giving and philanthropy. In the context of impact investing, the relationship we should strive to create together with our investees is not one of a traditional investor/investee relationship, much less one of distance and disengagement; it is one of true presence, connection and "suffering with" one's entrepreneurs (for God knows, they do sometimes suffer!) in the course of being fully engaged in the process of blended value creation, of creativity and of bringing transformative ideas to reality, in the form of impact within community and in support of Planet.

It is not that large funds or wealth management firms are necessarily "bad," for as we know money may be thought of as neutral and valueless until we place it in motion and thereby put it in context, in connection, between various actors and agents which then use it toward specific ends and via certain means and practices which take on the form of greater or lesser effectiveness in pursuit of blended value creation—of intentionally and strategically generating various types of return: financial, social and environmental. With its release as a form of directed energy, capital may well come to manifest the particular kind of impact its stewards intend. The challenge for these firms is one of culture, incentive and vision, which are hard to alter once established and understood by advisors, managers and clients. This refers to how the firm and its various stakeholders understand issues of the scale and depth of potential impact as well as the degree and nature of financial and other returns generated.

Just as there are Eight Levels of Philanthropic stewardship within Judaic tradition (see *Six Lists to Live By* in this document's appendix) and various levels of operationalizing loving-kindness within Buddhist tradition, the impact tradition is understood through degrees and kinds of change one may intentionally layer into any given investment opportunity via the term sheet (for private investments), relations with management (for public investments) or in the course of how one makes decisions—how one manages for impact—internally for a privately held company. Real impact is intentional and never merely business as usual or incidental—regardless of the degree of scale in question.

The greater size of an investment fund or company or community organization does not in and of itself mean positive, sustained impact cannot be attained. However, it does mean the intentionality of that impact, of connecting and of advancing a changed order (economic, social, religious, hierarchical or what have you) will be more complex and require all the more focus and discipline on the part of those man-aging the fund and invested ventures. Whether or not the implications of scale and its pursuit are fully realized by some of those now entering the practice of impact investing, only time—and the relative transpar-ency of those impact actors—will tell.

Having made it this far into this text, it should not surprise you, dear Reader, that whatever we may choose to tell ourselves in the cur-rent time, the above process of exploring notions of scale has played itself out over the course of history...

Before the early 1800s, as Rudolf Steiner observed:

> "...there were true economic impulses present in the whole
> system of loan and investment. Then, through the instrumen-
> tality of the banking system, these economic impulses began to
> change into purely financial ones; and in this process the whole
> thing became not only impersonal, but also unnatural. Every-
> thing was drawn into the stream of money, as it moved itself
> along. Our money business, without any natural or personal
> subject—that is the end toward which, as the nineteenth centu-
> ry drew to a close, everything which had originally been upheld
> by a personal and natural subject was gravitating."[1]

This process then came to be carried forward in our continued prac-tices of imperialism and colonization which drove states to operate with sole reference to maintaining and generating capital and wealth sep-arate and apart from considerations of social and environmental fac-tors. This played out and was interwoven with the evolution of religious institutions that focused upon salvation as an act of individual faith and interest rather than social and community experience.

Against this backdrop, I see the challenges and potential dangers of scaling impact investing in the following observation from Grant con-cerning the eventual evolution and denigration of the new age movement:

> "The great commercial success of the new age movement was also
> its downfall as a philosophy to be taken seriously, as complex

and profound ideas were often appropriated by the lowest common denominator and flattened to fit into a modern mentality,
neutered by poor aesthetic taste, simplistic, self-centered spirituality, and overly credulous commerce in tacky paraphernalia.
All of these elements that many of us find so worthy of ridicule
have served to diminish some of the most significant ideas of
the last few centuries to caricatures in collective understanding,
often buried behind atrocious pastel book covers, embedded in
absurdly grandiose and imprecise language, and inextricably
linked with preposterous and unprovable assertions."[2]

While as far as I know, we have yet to see the first Impact Report
published in light blue pastel, we must guard against a future time of
flattened expectations and lowest common denominator impact performance, though it is no doubt already in the immediate offing.

As we move to scale impact, we will feel pressures to introduce new
investment products and practices that are 'conforming' with the other
investment strategies and instruments in the market so they may easily
be managed at a distance or distributed via the existing infrastructure
of mainstream finance with little effort or need for accommodation of
our impact agenda. As a result, some may be tempted to respond to the
need to soften the terms of what impact comes to mean, how deep we
care to go in its pursuit and the degree to which we will need to accommodate the existing economic order to advance our investment agenda
as opposed to our working to challenge the base assumptions and practices of that agenda, the economic order within which it operates and its
economic much less broader philosophical concepts. This is not a question of perspective or opinion, but rather history and experience. Impact
investing will integrate within mainstream capital markets. And impact
investing will need to maintain its critical posture as a tool in our efforts
to address the challenges of our time or it—and we—will become tools
of traditional financial capitalism itself.

Impact investing is not traditional investing and does not entail the
easy 'bolting on' of a few modest, additional impact investment practices to accommodate traditional investing assumptions or the modest

aspirations of a 'new' impact agenda. Impact investing is about changing the economic systems that have created today's problems and led to
a world in which fewer and fewer actors control the vast majority of the
Planet's wealth, financial forces increasingly distanced from, yet dominant over, our world's local communities. And despite our best efforts,
asset owners will no doubt continue to be tempted to understand value
and return as a function of growing their asset base at the expense of
others and the Earth itself.

I believe James Buchan to be wrong when he says,

> *"For that is the end of economics:*
> *the world reduced to a scorching slum,*
> *its women to whores, its men to murderers."*[3]

But it will remain to those advancing our future impact investing
agenda to in fact prove him so.

THE IMPACT COMMONS

As we step back and reflect upon the scale of crowds and markets, one
has to then reflect upon the whole notion of who owns it all—what is
the source and structure of the resources and flows from which our
wealth arises? As we do that, we must, in turn, ask questions regarding
the Commons and the process by which it was all initially divided,
parsed out and allocated to individual from collective ownership. A
great deal has been written about the history of the Commons and it
is not my intent to revisit that history here.[4] That said, we should not
merely assume the idea of individualized wealth and ownership has
been with us from the start. As noted by the environmental journalist,
Mark Dowie:

> "Earlier settlers, who had occupied the Americas for so long they
> eventually became known as the Native Americans, had regard-
> ed the land as a commons for at least 10,000 years. To them,
> stewardship of the commons was an assumed tenet of the social
> contract, not something that needed to be debated, preached

or taught in school. The 110
million or so hoofed animals
that grazed the commons—the
bison, deer, the elk, caribou,
antelope, wild sheep, goats
and boar—were the peoples'
livestock, to be culled when
needed for food and clothing."[5]

Even within Western Christian traditions, there were those who
argued individual ownership was not consistent with God's plan. As
Saint Ambrose wrote:

> "It is not anything of yours that you are bestowing on the poor;
> rather, you are giving back something of theirs. For you alone
> are usurping what was given in common for the use of all. The
> earth belongs to everyone, not to the rich...Hence Scripture
> says to you: Incline your soul to the poor, give back what is
> owed, and answer him with peaceable words of gentleness."[6]

(Parenthetically, I do not recall which one of our newly minted
Saints of the Silicon Valley once also said—before learning how to use
his PR folks to more judicious ends— "I don't believe in having to give
anything back, because I do not believe I have taken anything away!"
My response—maybe yours, too!—is that my taxes that paid to teach
his employees to read and write, my roads and bridges upon which he
drove to work, my police and fire departments who service even his community, would beg to differ—setting aside any greater consideration of
community or social context. One cannot help but conclude our modern,
tech saints who we worship so completely are not in one way or another—
despite our incessant celebration of them—found to be wanting when
compared with Saints of old; say, a Saint Martin Luther King, Jr. or
a Saint Dorothy Day or a Saint Malcolm X or a Saint Theresa, to say
nothing of the modern saints I know who still walk amongst us. With
such comparisons, one cannot help at times but pine for an earlier day...).

Later in his writings, the more ancient Saint Ambrose goes on to say:

"For nature generously supplies everything for everyone in common. God ordained everything to be produced to provide food
for everyone in common; his plan was that the earth should be,
as it were, the common possession of us all. Nature produced
common rights, then, it is usurping greed that has established
private rights."[7]

The historian Peter Brown, in speaking of Saint Ambrose, helps us
understand that,

"Behind his views on the common rights of nature lay an ancient
person's sense of the numinous fecundity of the earth, a view
shared by Christians and pagans….For humans to have divided
up among themselves so luxuriant a source of common wealth,
so teeming with life, was an act of hubris as absurd as attempting to measure out properties on the face of the heaving ocean.
Human avarice had done the one and was quite capable of trying to do the other."[8]

By the time Columbus came upon what was to be called the Americas, he stated, in describing the practices of the First Nations People
concerning their understanding of property, that, "I could not learn if
they possess private property, but I seemed to discern that all owned a
share of what one of them owned and particularly with regard to vict-
uals" (February-March 1493).[9] And earlier he had stated that "They are
without covetousness of another man's goods."[10]

However, in the second voyage, Christopher Columbus' son
observed what happened when the culture of the native tribes came
in contact with their own: "Certain Indies which the Admiral had
brought from Isabella went into those cabins [which belonged to the
Indians] and made use of whatever they pleased; the owners gave no
sign of displeasure, as if everything they owned were common property. The people, believing that we had the same custom, went at first

among the Christians and took whatever they pleased; but they swiftly discovered their mistake."[11]

A half century later, however, it was a Christian sect, the Hutterite Brothers, formed in Moravia in 1556, that was based on the early chapters of the Acts of the Apostles, who would promote the idea that what was provided by God was the property of all and the notion that "community of goods was that practice of true Christians. 'We think it wrong to buy something and sell it and take the profit, so making the thing more expensive to the poor and taking the bread from their mouths, and thus the poor man cannot but become the mere servant of the rich.'…All that a man used reverted on his death to the community."[12] And, of course, there is any number of other intentional communities—and a long history thereof—one should be aware of as well, many of which are with us to this day.

Later on, it would be Thomas Berry who, taking a broader view of our living community, would observe:

> "The basic orientation of the common law tradition is toward personal rights and toward the natural world as existing for human use. There is no provision for recognition of nonhuman beings as subjects having legal rights. To the ecologist, the entire question of possession and use of the earth, either by individuals or by establishments, needs to be profoundly reconsidered. The naive assumption that the natural world exists solely to be possessed and used by humans for their unlimited advantage cannot be accepted. The earth belongs to itself and to all the component members of the community. The entire earth is a gorgeous celebration of existence in all its forms. Each living thing participated in that celebration as the proper fulfillment of its powers of expression. The reduction of the earth to an object simply for human possession and use is unthinkable in most traditional cultures."[13]

And as reflected in a comment from one of our times' leading business gurus, Peter Drucker:

"For partisans of capitalism, it is often convenient to pretend
that property is some naturally occurring fact, but it is really a
social construction the must be delineated and enforced by the
power of the state. And the very idea that all of the physical
and social worlds can be divided up into discrete parts, each
tagged with the name of an owner, is a part of capitalism's ideological infrastructure that had to be painstakingly constructed
over many years."[14]

By the mid-1800s there was a widely shared belief, grounded in the
writings of John Locke and rulings of Judge James Kent, that land not
under development was not actually owned by anyone. For the property
to be judged as rightfully owned, it had to be developed, managed and
cultivated—put to the good use of society and nation. Accordingly, Vat-
tel could then go on to promote the idea that "farmers enjoyed a natural
right to displace nomadic hunters."[15]

The history of how Western settlers and government agents removed
First Nations and Native American tribes from their lands is one of
genocide and empire, well beyond the scope of this book, but for one
account I would direct you to Peter Cozzens' heartbreaking volume, *The
Earth Is Weeping: The Epic Story of the Indian Wars for the American West.*[16]
And the multi-century history of the European Enclosure Movement—
the process by which power elites converted the commons to individual
ownership—is a closely related and tragic history, tellingly explored by
Alastair McIntosh in his classic, *Soil and Soul: People Versus Corporate
Power.* Finally, the recently published, *Ramp Hollow: The Ordeal of Appa-
lachia* by Steven Stoll offers an excellent review of the Commons and an
American version of the Enclosure Movement. However, as example,
we will touch on this specific notion of use and ownership as it relates
to capital in the form of water rights and ownership of natural capital
in the United States.

In the United States, Congress passed prior appropriation laws
in the mid-19th century to settle water disputes during the California
Gold Rush. For example, what came to be called the Colorado Doctrine was based on a Supreme Court ruling of 1872. Prior appropriation

states that the first person or economic entity that makes "beneficial use" of water assumes then the
rights to that water for the settlers
but not Indigenous People of the
period. "First in time, first in right"
came to be the law of the land for
white settlers, ranchers and farmers.
These rights are then the property
of the stakeholder to use, buy, and
sell. This is a great example of the
notion that the only use that might

be beneficial is that put to human, economic development—industrial,
agricultural or household—and that the right of nature to use that water
or to simply let it be is not considered.[17]

Out of this, then, it is easy to see how the basis of water rights in
the American West became not only founded upon notions of "first use"
which determined seniority of rights, but also the idea that if one forgoes
the use of a resource one also surrenders the rights to that resource. As
a logical outcome of this line of thought, under today's Bureau of Land
Management, those bidding for oil drilling rights are not allowed—by
law—to simply secure the rights and let the oil lie undisturbed in the
ground. As, under the current Administration, the BLM moves to lease
greater amounts of public property for fracking, coal mining and other
development, environmental activists bidding on the leases with the
intent of allowing the earth to remain as is find themselves pulled up
before the court and subject to serious fines, and even imprisonment.

The logic that land must be put to 'productive' use has its roots in
how we initially understood the place of land relative to our own identity and life. Snyder says,

"The idea that 'wild' might also be 'sacred' returned to the
Occident only with the Romantic movement. This nine-
teenth-century rediscovery of wild nature is a complex European phenomenon—a reaction against formalistic rationalism

and enlightened despotism that invoked feeling, instinct, new nationalisms, and a sentimentalized folk culture. It is only from very old place-centered cultures that we hear of sacred groves, sacred land, in a context of genuine belief and practice. Part of that context is the tradition of the commons: 'good' land becomes private property; the wild and the sacred are shared."[18]

We must ask, who truly does own nature and must ownership be viewed solely as it relates to use?

Consider what it means to discover something and then how we act to claim that discovery as our own, whether in the form of real asset, Amazonian plants or intellectual property. If the Earth and its mysteries are already there—the Americas existed before Columbus and were known by the People of the First Nations, gravity existed prior to Newton, fractals were a reality before Mandelbrot, Pythagoras's discovery of how numbers and mathematics were natural elements of the universe— each person who discovers these and so much more is merely uncovering what we did not know or were not aware of, not creating something new that did not exist. What they discover and reflect is more accurately described as our own ignorance.

Natural resources rest in the Earth, and indigenous peoples acted as stewards of the land on a sustainable basis for millennia before the European notion arose that if not put to good use, a resource could not be claimed to be owned. And please do not talk to me about the "tragedy of the Commons" for that is a distortion of truth, dead and gone. There was no tragedy until the rise of individualist culture, the enclosure movement of the Scottish Highlands and the Indian Wars waged by the United States against Native peoples. We created as a social construct the idea it was the process of converting a resource from passive to active, "productive" use that constituted its conversion from commons to private good, managed for the benefit of an individual or perhaps family but no longer accessible to or to be maintained for the common, shared interest of a local community or greater society.

As we think of the purpose of capital, we must reflect on the question of whose capital it is to begin with and what economic and political order made it possible for one to amass wealth at the level upon which it is aggregated well beyond the living requirements of a single family. Before we can discuss responsible wealth stewardship or the end toward which we make investment decisions, before we consider questions of use, we must first consider questions of source, control, and economic dominance within a financial system unconcerned with advancing a sustainable world.

One model to be considered relative to the Impact Commons comes from the ownership structures of cooperative organizations where, as described by Alison Lingane of Project Equity, there are three types of participation one may create:

- Direct ownership of underlying assets and value of assets (stock value, asset value, etc.)
- Profit or Loss participation you might receive from that asset (dividends and profit sharing), and
- Control and Voting rights.

One might invest in each of these levels of ownership, and yet the control, participation and expected financial return vary, allowing for worker ownership, community participation, outside investment and various other ways to structure partnership.

Thorstein Veblen's view of property, presented in his 1899 book, *The Theory of the Leisure Class*, "...(referred to as 'a debunking of classical economics so caustic that some readers mistook it for a satire'), was that property originates in theft and that its acquisition beyond necessity has nothing to do with survival and nearly everything to do with status."[19] Veblen believed humanity was made up of actors and that we were social and connected: "In the organic complex of habits of thought which make up the substance of an individual's conscious life, the economic interest does not lie isolated and distinct."[20] Therefore, in our connection with each other, with the Other, the wealth we create from the Earth is jointly sourced, the benefits of which should be viewed as common to all; its greater purpose commonly shared for, as we say, planet and people.

We must rethink our understanding of the concept of ownership and explore various new (and in some cases, traditional) approaches to structuring capital and understanding who may lay claim to the variety of returns generated therefrom, revisiting our understanding of the Impact Commons, how we think about the nature of returns and what is owned by the investor, the investee and the Commonweal.[21] As authors Sloman and Fernbach wisely observe:

"Every farmer knows that the hard part is getting the field prepared. Inserting seeds and watching them grow is easy. In the case of science and industry, the community prepares the field, yet society tends to give all the credit to the individual who happens to plant a successful seed. Planting a seed does not necessarily require overwhelming intelligence; creating an environment that allows seeds to prosper does. We need to give more credit to the community in science, politics, business, and daily life."[22]

The Norwegian beliefs that underscore the rule of law regarding land use and access are based on the notion of *Alle Manns Retten*, translated as "The Right of Access Law" or "The Right to Roam."[23] According to these laws, while private ownership exists and land may be managed for private gain, access and use remain open to all.

From a view out of our cabin window, where I sit and write this text, one sees a Norwegian alpine landscape, but from this single perspective one may view a massive nature reserve, range land for domestic animals and private property—all of which may be crossed and accessed by any citizen and each of which exists while allowing the Earth itself to remain in good health. In this way, there may be a better approach for how we think about ownership itself, its impact on our community and the purpose of those assets generating from it.

In the end, we must acknowledge that

"The fruits of the earth belong to everyone; the earth, to no one."[24]

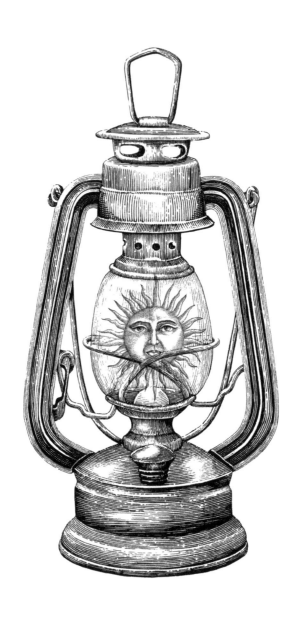

CHAPTER ELEVEN

THE GIFT OF FIRE:

The Purpose of Capital as Freedom

P LEASE NOTE: AS IS TAUGHT IN BUSINESS SCHOOLS THE WORLD OVER,

"The purpose of capital is to seek its highest and best use."

What professors mean by the phrase "highest and best use" is that different types of capital seek different levels of financial return in exchange for various levels of assumed risk and liquidity lock ups. Capital's highest and best use is to seek that combination of highest financial return and lowest assumption of risk possible to optimize financial returns. The thinking is that fixed income—debt, bonds and various forms of lending secured by an underlying asset and first position in the event of bankruptcy—are understood to generate levels of lower financial gain in exchange for lower levels of assumed risk exposure. Equities (public or private) carry greater risk and therefore will seek—and deserve—higher financial return in exchange for that increased risk exposure. In creating a portfolio of investments, one deploys a certain amount of capital into various types of investment instruments across an array of asset classes to achieve the overall returns a portfolio needs to reach the investor's goals, some investors being more or less risk averse than others in their pursuit of total financial returns for any given portfolio.

All of it—the notion of capital, the metrics by which we divide and track the performance of that capital, and the measures by which we assess its volatility, risk, and financial returns—is merely a conceptual framework upon which one set of actors has come to agree and with which we all must finally come to terms. In defining parameters of financial performance, we state capital seeks its highest and best use and in that way are asked to embrace a financial faith that believes capital itself to be neutral; it is viewed as assuming no moral, social or other character. Capital is considered as existing within some Swiss neutrality until being released in pursuit of its own highest and best use as defined by the asset owner or asset owner in collaboration with an advisor, but it does so outside of any consideration or assessment of social, ethical or probative value.

Folks in mainstream finance take this point very seriously. As previously discussed, I recall one conversation with a good colleague of mine who became downright incensed when I stated the run up in the public markets over the months since Trump's inauguration to be 'immoral' since it represented investors' greed in anticipating a President who would roll back taxes, environmental protections, and pretty much everything else save defense spending. My friend became as emotional as I'd ever seen him, exclaiming, "Markets are *amoral*…They merely exist; they just are."

Within this frame, capital is viewed as a vehicle, or again, more accurately, a transparent social construct we've created as a proxy for a reality we have built in our world; a fact based upon materialism expressed in economic terms to the exclusion of social or environmental considerations. As described elsewhere in this document, it is a reality understood to be rational, quantitative and objective, while review of social and ecological aspects of our world have traditionally been interpreted as subjective, qualitative and fleeting—and therefore existing outside a logical framework of economics and finance—in some ways, outside of reason itself. (Give up financial return for greater equity and justice? Why, that's just *crazy*!! Who would leave money on the table for someone else to benefit?? Who would do *that*??)

We have the hidden potential to invest in good or bad...but at any one time, we and what we come in contact with is empty and neutral regarding whether or not the object under observation becomes "good" or "bad." One could say, therefore, at risk of sounding like an NRA commercial, capital is viewed as neutral—it is a tool, a vehicle through which we may pursue something or bring something about. Its relative quality, its essence, comes not from what it is but rather what it becomes as a result of our putting it into motion, our releasing its energy upon the world. Accordingly, our ad would be along the lines of: Capital Investing doesn't kill people—people kill people!—or something like that?!

As has been said, it is not money that is evil, but rather the love of money. It is how we manage, deploy and utilize capital in the world that it manifests as good or bad or degrees in between. However, I would argue capital markets, in reflecting the character of those within them, do also assume that character (and therefore, if humanity is greedy, than capital markets are greedy—if immoral, they are then to my mind, immoral). The irony in all this is that of the well known phrase, "Markets function in response to one of two things: fear and greed." Well, if that is true are not these both examples of human, social emotions? But for now let's accept the premise that markets simply reflect the values and practices of those within them and move on to the next part of our discussion, that of the social foundations of capital.

It is within a conceptual framework, inside this intellectual boundary set of what we take for a collective reality, that we define what is true for us, in this time—that capital and by extension capital markets reflect the purpose we're driving toward and how we will understand whether we have achieved that purpose. And we as a society recognize the use of capital as author and environmentalist, Jerry Mander, presents it:

> "Our society is characterized by an inability to leave anything in
> nature alone. Every piece of land, every creature, every mineral
> in the oceans, every growing plant, every mountain, every inch
> of desert is examined for its potential contribution to com-
> mercial development and exploitation, and to the expansion

of technological society. Even the essential building blocks of nature—the atom, the proton, the electron—are subject to commercial scrutiny. Where science can intervene, science does so; corporations then package the process and sell it."[1]

Many asset owners accept without question financial performance, that which we seek to do with our wealth, as its fundamental purpose, as simply a question of preserving and generating greater amounts of its self. The purpose of capital is to grow exponentially over time and increase its value in the form of financial wealth. To "win" is to generate more wealth whereas to "lose" is to reduce the amount of capital under our immediate control. We fear nothing more than society's cold description of our selves or our progeny as having trod the well-worn path from "shirtsleeves to shirtsleeves in but three generations," as the saying goes. The only measure of not only our capital but also our performance is the amount with which we began versus that with which we conclude our journey at life's end or the greater overall economic value we generate in the course of a life. The purpose of money is to be applied to its preservation and growth; any other outcome is a shame and a disgraced result of our entrepreneurial inabilities or fiduciary failures. Within this mindset, the purpose of capital is to make more capital.

By extension, many impact investors, with their commitment to doing well and good, enter the arena of capital considerations with the understanding their investments must first and foremost generate market rate, risk adjusted financial returns, together with the creation of social and environmental value. Some embrace this goal to convince traditional, mainstream investors focused solely upon financial performance that the pursuit of social value does not have to be at the expense of financial return, because as just stated, to end with less capital than one started with is assumed to be failure. Others embrace this notion of doing well as a possible way of preventing the potential loss of their capital, viewing consideration of impact factors as a form of risk mitigation. These asset owners do not want to be the ones who lost the family fortune on their watch or may not trust their capacity to create other forms of value in the world and so hold fast to this notion of financial return as the sole measure of their worldly worth or goal as fiduciary.

That said, one must still ask what the highest and best use of capital indeed is—its *ultimate* purpose and not that measured by financial performance alone. If one does believe capital to be merely a value-neutral demonstration of financial performance within an exclusively economic framework, than our inquiry should conclude and be done. With the pride of the Chicago School, Milton Friedman (and perhaps, Friedrich Hayek) beaming down upon them, the current and historic practices of asset owners, mainstream financial advisors, fund managers and investment institutions may be celebrated and affirmed, whilst any notion of social value as commensurate with monetary value rightly turned aside and, having been briefly considered, now placed in a wholly subordinate position to the goal of maximizing financial returns to asset owners of all stripe and nature.

However, if one accepts the idea that capital is itself a neutral substance, void of moral or social considerations, and if we take as valid the idea that capital only assumes the measure of social attention we are willing to assign it, than the phrase "the asset owner is the market" is, in fact, correct and each investor is free to define the character, financial terms and any other parameters of capital as she sees fit. The mainstream, institutional, Wall Street and Chicago School definitions are merely that—the descriptions of institutional and social lemmings driven to the edge by warped crowd wisdom, seeking to organize themselves to squelch consideration of social or environmental factors and squeeze such notions right out of any financial deal. But if capital is neutral, we must embrace an understanding of the purpose of wealth as being whatever we see fit to assign it, with us each free to refine our definitions, boundaries, and parameters as we like.

Each age is also then free to define the purpose of capital, its highest and best use, as it prefers. And we must acknowledge it is in each age, culture, and nation, that such has been the case. The aberration rests not with the past, but the present for in the past the purpose of capital was in points of history and within certain communities broadly understood to be that of service to society, to family and, lastly, to self.

Other sections of this document explore this further, but for now, please reflect on a few observations:

> During a presentation made in 2003 at the World Economic Forum in Davos, Switzerland, when the concept of Blended Value and impact investing was outlined, a man stood from the audience to say, "This is fine and good—as a businessperson I support it—however, it is nothing new…What you're describing is simply the structure and practices of the traditionally privately held German family firm."

Going back a bit further, within the Christian tradition, the theologian Walter Brueggemann says:

> The Book of Acts speaks "about having 'all things in common.' It did not and does not mean living in a commune, but rather that the property of all is situated in a social-moral context of community. That ancient world of course did not practice possessive individualism; it did, however, legitimate social stratification and distinct social classes and legitimated inequality of social access, social power, and social goods. The common good of the early church spoke deeply against such stratification that was embodied in the imperial pyramid, even as it speaks now against unregulated possessive individualism and accumulation."[2]

Or within Muslim finance, as the legal scholar Umar Moghul notes,

> "The Shari'ah is clear that the purpose of business is the preservation of life (non-human as well as human) as well as the preservation of wealth—both community and individual. Concepts (and the practices which come out of them) such as *Muhasabah* (self reporting and constructive response) and *Muraqabah* (focused on practices of transparency, trust, and confidence) are both examples of how Islamic religious practices may inform business management practices. And several schools of religious

teaching include consideration of Earth's resources as falling within the notion of preserving and stewarding wealth for both individuals and community."[3]

Or heading further East (that is, East of me…not necessarily East of you!),

"…The Buddha had a lot to say in praise of wealth and money. The issues for him concerned how you get it and what you do with it: whether you are using its energy to make yourself happier or to make the world better…The Buddha told his banker disciple Anathapindika that wealth—well used—should first and foremost give pleasure to our families and us. Then there's the pleasure we can give to our friends and others who live around us. And there's more—having wealth means that we can recover when things go wrong for us. Wealth means that we can keep up a good reputation in the community (by making ritual offerings in the Buddha's day, which were no doubt costly) and it means that we can enable the good causes we find most worthwhile….The crucial point is that we make full use of our wealth: to engage happily with others and with the world," says Houlder.[4]

Many intuitively know all this and seek something else. Our stated intent of "doing well *and* doing good" is the place where many now enter the conversation of impact investing. When it was simply a practice of doing well and *then* doing good, it was an issue of charity and philanthropic giving where the questions were "How much do I need to have before I have enough to give away? What exactly do I need to give up in order to do something of true value in the world?"

With doing well and doing good, we believe we may provide for our own needs and desires without having to give up anything in return. While there are discussions regarding what this means and whether it is true, the general idea is that we may have our cake and eat it too, as opposed to having to make any real financial or other sacrifice or alter

our circumstance in exchange for a
sense of morality and, dare we say,
justice. We can save the world and
save for our Selves all at the same
time…Such a deal!

One is reminded of the para-
ble of the Christ being asked by a
wealthy, young inheritor what it will
take for him to enter the Kingdom
of Heaven, wherein Jesus is harsh
and tells him he must give up all he owns because it is as possible for a
rich man to enter the Kingdom of Heaven as for a camel to pass through
the eye of a needle.[5] Jesus was harsh because the questioner showed no
interest or concern for the poor but only for his own damned soul.

Those carrying the impact investing banner need take care we don't
assume the same posture when asking whether we might do well and
do good through our investments. Those of us who claim a commitment
to advancing impact investing—to creating various levels of financial
return together with the generation of diverse social and environmental impacts—need be quite cautious regarding our base motivations for
engaging in this work. We need to understand whether our motives
are genuinely grounded in an interest in generating Mutual Impact on
behalf of the Other or is our concern really what Richard Rohr calls
"disguised narcissism"[6] wherein we cloak our real intent within the gar-
ments of concerned impact upon the world when we are only willing to
pursue impact as long as there is no requirement we alter our expectations, behavior, or life in our pursuit of Bonhoeffer's Cheap Grace or my
own notion of Cheap Impact.

Some simply seek to sleep well at night regardless of where our capital rests or the actual use to which it is put, its traditional purpose of
seeing to itself, of seeking its own highest and best use as defined merely
by financiers and arbiters of what our society takes to be sound economics. As long as the noise of the destruction it creates is softened by this
cloak of impact piety we don't have to worry about hearing the cries of
the poor and oppressed. We may celebrate our good selves as we dance

to the tunes of millionaire rock stars and with the traditional investors who have now joined our ranks in this quest to profit while pleading our economic innocence. We seek to justify our own ego and sense of self without challenging our true Self to grow or move deeper in our understanding of impact much less to embrace the opportunity before us to develop a more meaningful engagement with the wisdom of the world which promises to open us up, to show us what is more real than either our capital or our present understanding of truth.

At the institutional level, organizations we create must come to be managed as vehicles of impact, advancing greater justice in the world and not merely acting as receptacles of capital until we have no option but to engage in change as a result of some personal or institutional crisis of meaning. One of the more sobering examples of the devolution of organization as change agent is the Christian Church itself. In the early centuries of the church—before Christianity was adopted by the Roman Empire—communities often did share wealth among members, operate with female leadership and seek to fully manifest Christ's teachings in the world. Over the course of centuries, Rohr says:

> "...the mainline church organized itself around structural charity and almsgiving, but the church lost a deeper sense of solidarity, justice, simplicity, and a basic understanding of the poor. No longer were we called to become poor like Christ but to help the poor through charity. It became acceptable to get rich personally, even for the clergy, with the idea of passing on that wealth to the poor. But as good as charity is, it largely became an avoidance of basic concern for justice."[7]

Financial institutions seeking to be active in impact investing will certainly have the opportunity to pursue that path. As they do, they will need to look deeply within themselves as organizations, examining their cultures and motivations, engaging their clients in new dialogue, to assess their capacity to take their place among others working to reshape the very character of capital as we know it—or may come to undertand it.

THE CHARACTER OF CAPITAL, REVISITED

What is required of us is a new definition of the purpose of capital that we can, if you will, bring to the bank, though a *community* banking institution in this case. The closing section of this document will explore a possible understanding of that purpose in greater detail, but before we may advance a new vision of the implications of an alternative understanding of how we might manifest the intent of capital, we must first explore how we think about the nature, the broader character of capital; the idea that capital—whether in illiquid assets such as land or liquid investments such as cash—is always in motion, even when we think it is not.

We need do this for two reasons:

First, the money we put in our accounts is not money in the bank, for as soon as it hits our accounts, it bounces off and onto the Street; moving dynamically, going into and out of deals. Of late, people have talked about impact investing as a form of "portfolio activation," but in fact, our capital has always been in action. Like the bank in *It's a Wonderful Life!* my money isn't in my account—it's in Bob's business and Mary's mortgage and on and on.[8] Capital is in various and diverse ways, always in motion, in action, in the world—for better or for worse—and, for many of us, mostly worse.

Second, objects—in this case, capital—sit in restful motion. Objects at rest are not still but active within their given point in time. In this context, capital wants to be engaged in the world and seeks to be in motion even when it is at rest. The concept of Buddhist action speaks to the reality that when sitting at rest, in reflection, molecules move and atoms circle and minds, while calm, focused, and clear, are connected to one another at deeper levels of being and nothingness. Objects are at rest but simultaneously flow in directed movement as they interact with each other, as they gather in various new forms and growing forces. They are then unleashed to flow and move and become their former potential that now is transformed from still sitting to active task while yet at rest, from potential possibility to being or settling yet again over there, away from where it once was, now connecting in new ways, with new momentum, with new Others.

Under our management, capital seeks to grow in the form of collective acquisition, contribution or construction of something new, a newly constituted mass of capital potential now realized, of objects directed to move, of buildings consisting of various parts previously at rest but now in new locales. Capital may also act to release humanity to move in new ways, creating yet more experiences of life on multiple levels, some seemingly at rest and others visibly moving toward the creation of new realities and forms of being. All this is the result of deliberate, intentional movements of wealth in pursuit of impact and blended value creation, in contrast with our traditional financial pursuit of the static goals of gold or capital's simple replication and cancerous growth. This mindset is an understanding of the purpose of capital as community and impact as opposed to capital as economic growth and traditional, financially driven commerce alone. If, indeed, money reflects merely the nature of those who own, manage and deploy it, let us default to this vision of *living capital* as opposed to one of its own replication, expansion, storage and final decay on economic terms alone.

Consider this:

Researchers have demonstrated that sub-atomic particles do not exist in the absence of their relationship to other particles and outside observation.

Note to Reader: The following is to be read all at once, at a good clip...

Capital rests in accounts and columns, is housed in forms of bytes and bits and chameleon bites of zero and one, and one and zero, over over over and over again, stacked in digital columns of ones and zeros in charts and ledgers of accounts and code—until, suddenly, they are not, after investors, fund managers and asset owners set them in motion, set them off through the ether to be placed in another column, another account, another entity, often to take form in counties and countries far away from the asset owner who supposedly lays claim to what has been put into motion; lays claim to what

they thought was theirs to be owned, and gathered tightly to
one's chest but which is actually like sand flowing through
fingers, possessed in part, yet held by others in moments before
the next market shift, the next statement of returns, the next
tide that moves against one market in favor of another, lift-
ing up what was formerly supposedly valueless and sweeping
it off along the shore, out to the ocean's larger market, toward
new owners, toward new purveyors of opportunity and risk
and impact in the hopes of reward to be counted by whomever
finds that capital now manifest in this one chart of accounts as
opposed to another, new owners, who now themselves find they
must surrender to new circumstance perhaps better, perhaps
worse, but always different, always with dynamism and action
whether in immediate motion or at dynamic rest for now until
unleashed again, in pursuit of capturing yet another perceived
opportunity or chance or interest, whether 2%, 10% or 20%,
financial returns that waiver depending upon the final calculus
applied and its numeric elements…depending upon whatever
is considered to be on the table or off, internal or external, to
any given investment; it is a moving line, after all, based upon
whatever rules of the game you choose to govern you.

A brief aside:

*Did you know that in the late Middle Ages, mathematical
considerations and mistakes were so common that in French, 'faire par
algorisme', 'to do it with algorithm,' came to mean 'to miscalculate?'*[9]

One reflects upon our present chart of national accounts and decision to include only that which is measurable in economic terms within
our current metrics and framework of value, regardless of relative value
or importance; is this not miscalculation? A profound algebraic error of
global proportions? The more it changes, the more it remains the same.
But I digress…

I would have to conclude *capital is <u>not</u> neutral or pure or void of indications of its origins.* It carries the shadows of its source as we bring the source code of our genes forward in our DNA, down through generations. Why else would it need to be laundered, after all? And depending upon our capital's provenance, it may give off an odor, a stench, which despite our best efforts may not be laundered away as it flows from bank to bank or continent to continent. The lingering odor of capital is still discerned by bonded bloodhounds bounding after it through dark woods within which such jaundiced money seeks to hide from the dogged steps of financial forensic analysts, tracking and trailing their way through scrolling digits and bytes and columns of capital spread from declining company to decrepit countries which seek to horde the ever massing piles of wealth, now positioned in futile efforts to protect the One Percent from the ceaseless entreaties of the global Other from which we cannot escape, in this life time or any other.

How capital performs has less to do with objective numerics than with who is watching and who does the counting to determine what is on the balance sheet versus left under the table or passed into the grey netherworld economy, opaque like a Trump business deal or, alternatively, counted only as faux externalities on some green balance sheet, like the Earth—there but not present according to the financial auditor of record.

Which is it or which might it be? Which *should* it be? That is ours to decide.

> And then it occurs again, where suddenly capital in motion
> calls other objects to move—organic produce is gathered, dirt
> turned; pots thrown, glazed and fired, now set aside to be still
> and calm again, waiting in motion on the shelf, waiting to fall
> and shatter on our manufactured ground that is the floor of our
> house of cards. Iron caterpillars move across a former Amazoni-
> an Eden, flowing, crushing, themselves in motion up stems and
> leaves as they consume and chew one form of energy. This then
> changes into another form of capital energy in the way of new
> resources, setting free a new horde of Caterpillars, once more

to move across a distant landscape, converting more resource from passive to active use, more trunks and limbs of branches of trees set aside, moved from upright and reaching to stripped and stacked, resting elsewhere anew on trucks moving toward processing or in slash piles to be burned (potentially thoughtfully tempered with carbon offsets) but instead, in the absence of the deal, becoming multi-particulate pollution settling on branches nearby, in lungs far away or cast out and up and above, existing as microscopic weight but a growing burden upon the Earth nevertheless, to be carried in the clouds where they gather to darken the sky, and then move as significant storm, unleashing the natural energy of capital now swirling upon itself in its vapors, looking for its next place of touch down, releasing flooding rain and now capital again in the form of destructive force and changing climate.

Capital at rest in accounts in motion across the world. After all: it's not personal, it's business. The majority, the woolen crowd as guided by its shepherding experts, appears to believe money and capital markets are not moral or evil or good. We are asked to believe they simply *are*, absent any influence of source, future use or potential for value integrated with values. We're asked to believe capital markets

exist outside of the social interactions and deliberations that brought them into being and give them daily life.

If that you can believe...

CAPITAL AS FREEDOM

Freedom is a state of liberation, self-determination, and human agency. It is a centering of self within the Other as our awareness of deep relationship—how we are defined by and come to define the Other—puts us in meaningful context of Life. We are defined not simply as we choose to see, style and make ourselves within this world but as we relate to others and the Other. Our final purpose, then, is to be in the world in whatever manner best supports our journey toward freedom as we, in turn, support that mission in others.

> *The Purpose of Capital is to*
> *support, augment and energize our freedom to engage in*
> *a shared process of continual becoming.*

As previously discussed, we have taught that the purpose of capital is to seek its highest and best use, by which we have traditionally meant the highest financial return for the least amount of risk within a given asset class. If, however, one understands capital to be not an economic concept, but economics as but one component within a more significant, more complicated process of value creation, than, as Milton Friedman asked us to reflect, a critical consideration beyond the financial performance of capital is our understanding of the degree to which wealth attains its potential as a vehicle for increasing freedom and the way in which our various political and other systems advance that freedom.

The questions we focus upon then become:

What is the purpose of capital beyond its function as fuel for corporations and capital markets or a component of economic return?

What is capital's place in the creation of real, authentic freedom and our pursuit of deep blended value in our world?

Who is it that is to be freed and in what ways?

If we understand capital as a tool, a resource, a form of energy, than one may easily see the purpose of capital is in turn to function as a means of promoting freedom; specifically, the use of wealth is to advance the liberty of those entities through which it courses and the freedom of those individuals with whom it comes in contact:

- At an individual level, it is the freedom of an entrepreneur to create a firm to capture a perceived community and market opportunity.
- At the organizational level, it is the freedom of a group of individuals to gather and resource themselves to advance a common goal or objective, to capture a shared vision of value.
- At a more profound level, the purpose of capital is to enable humanity to move toward the realization of its potential on this planet; to be free of poverty, to function in the present experience of living, to support and sustain not only human existence, but to place that existence within the context of shared systems of optimized human *and* non-human life.

The purpose of capital is to be free to allow us to achieve our full potential as individuals and as a community of beings intertwined with the forces of life on this planet. If we are to realize this purpose, we must know that power of life of which we are a part and of which capital is a resource for us to use to rediscover our true nature of being in the world.

Ancient Greeks believed in a time before time called the Golden Age[10] when humanity lived in harmony with the gods; a time when we were truly free, a time to which we must seek a return. Our purpose then, and that of the resources and tools we control, such as capital, is to help us find our way back to that period of ancient enlightenment, actualization, and freedom, as individuals and as a global community of humanity and Planet. Aristotle spoke of how all things in the world had a purpose, a *teleos*, and for centuries this idea was how we structured our understanding of purpose. *Teleos* is a relevant concept even regarding chaos, relativity and field theories given the nature of the entity is defined only in regard to its relation relative to other objects and, at a subatomic level, its being under observation.

By extension, capital performs best when viewed relative to its context, its portfolio and market community; its nature is determined as a function of its relation to other entities. The value of capital is best appreciated as when we understand it as economic *and* social *and* environmental with each of these components, in turn, interacting and intertwined. Value manifests in diverse and various ways but is always more than economic value alone. Capital is about more than money; it is about freedom.

The idea of capital naturally seeking its highest use is still valid, save for the reality that our traditional understanding of "use" is only partially correct. It is not merely highest and best use of economic value creation potential but rather its *total* value creation potential. It must be put to use but applied in the *fullness* of its potential—not merely toward economic value creation. In the end, capital seeks to be deployed in pursuit of its highest potential optimization; and in that way to be free, to energize freedom. Capital tries to connect in as many forms and ways possible in pursuit of attaining its true, holistic and integrated natural state, which traditional, mainstream understandings of capital, markets, and organizations (as vehicles through which financial capital is deployed) do not adequately consider, allow for or advance.

Value and Use are relative terms—defined in relation to other opportunities and the larger portfolio of which any specific investment is a part. The highest and best use of a portfolio is a function of our comprehending the aggregate impact that may be generated through the effective allocation of our capital into each investment we make. In this way, Total Portfolio Management is a first step toward attainment of capital's best use toward the end of capturing opportunities, catalyzing change and generating positive impact—each of which is a degree of greater freedom to realize what one is or may become—as an individual, as an investment opportunity, as a community.

THE POLITICS OF IMPACT

The Chicago School economist, Milton Friedman, wrote a seminal piece on the topic, *Capital and Freedom*, in which he describes the connection between democracy and capitalism. His focus on the interplay between the two as well as his understanding of the potential of capital to be a vehicle for freedom is insightful, yet the blinders of an old school, bifurcated economist with near-sighted vision limit Friedman's perspective. His understanding of capital as freedom is correct but hindered by being couched only in individualist, economic terms (which we know is simply a construct, so we may critique it as such and add to it not only economic considerations but social and environmental ones as well).

More than economic principles and consideration drives capital. It is fuel and energy, a flow that when constricted is limited and inhibited from attaining its full freedom and value creation potential. It may be restricted to a single portfolio and set of practices and grow on economic terms but will never fulfill its real potential when understood on financial terms alone. It may be "successful" but not attain significance relative to overall human experience or the intentional generation of value beyond an economic understanding of what value is. A strictly economic knowledge of the purpose of capital is, by definition, one that will underperform its real potential.

One must take care, however, since when placed within a political frame, capital as freedom can take on a nationalistic bent, as expressed by investment firms such as Freedom Capital that seek to take the notion of impact investing and re-direct it toward an "America First" agenda, placing capital into investment strategies focused upon "national security," economic "independence" for the United States and so on. Regardless of one's individual, political posture, vision or agenda, as Naess says,

> "Any analysis of economic activity presupposes that there are certain norms which have to be satisfied in the analysis. The most prominent economists until this century, including Francois Quesnay, Adam Smith, John Stuart Mill and Karl Marx,

have been engaged as much in moral philosophy as in detailed economic affairs. In this century there has been a dangerous narrowing of the scope of textbooks on economics, so that very little of the normative philosophical basis of the field is left. Economics is dried up. We are left with a kind of flat country of factual quantitative considerations, with no deep canyons or impressive mountain peaks to admire."[11]

Spinoza believed the legitimacy of the State comes from the self-interest of individual actors within society and that all beings are driven by self-interest and that this competing self-interest is best mediated via an ordered State, based upon a social contract, similar to that described by Hobbes. Spinoza even went so far as to say that "the purpose of the state is freedom."[12]

Similarly, we extend this notion of the role of the state to that of capital by saying the purpose of capital is freedom—to act as the fuel, if not vehicle, to support the creation of the world one seeks to create—and view that freedom as focused upon the individual but the individual in the context of community and planet. The values we embrace may manifest in a variety of forms as moderated by a democratic process—which, in its purest form, is our expression of and experience in community. Spinoza views his social contract as continually up for renegotiation, in the same way, the previsously referenced impact term sheets outline specific conditions upon which each investment of capital is to be managed, deployed and its performance assessed.

Within this framework capital becomes that fuel of freedom upon which individuals, organizations, and society each may draw. And, as previously referenced, Friedman also stated that concentrated power is not rendered harmless by the good intentions of those who create it. No doubt he was most likely referring to the consolidation of power within government, but one must wonder what he might make of the concentration of economic power we're witnessing today. For impact investors, we are called to reflect on those words and challenge the systems of finance working to consolidate wealth, extract value from community and planet, and inhibit individuals from realizing their potential and freedoms as healthy, fulfilled members of our communities and diverse ecosystems.

We must also acknowledge that if we are going to engage in impact investing and operate within a framework of individual lodged within community and planet, we must ask:

How do we get there?

Namely, what *are* the political implications of impact investing in this day of partisan politics and, within the United States, our nation's drift toward a strong government rolling back protections for the environment while simultaneously running roughshod over individual human, social, and our planet's natural rights?

Some claim it inappropriate to combine politics with investing, but this is farce. To take no position is to endorse the present status quo; not to vote is to vote in favor of the current order, just as not to discuss the politics of capital is to affirm its present form and use in our world. Capital investment is a political act endorsing, supporting, and fueling our present system of financial capitalism as it exists and as it has evolved over past decades. If one knows enough to invest capital, one knows enough to grasp the implications of investing in either stasis or transformation, investing in business models of the past centuries or the centuries to come. You should not only know what you own, but own what you know to be the power of your presence as an investor, as an agent of your actions and as a force in the world.

As mentioned above, some have already stepped forward to embrace impact investing as an act of conservative capital deployment and so-called America First investment practices. Others have claimed that as wealth advisors, their obligation to clients is to deploy capital on whatever terms those clients desire—and that therefore investing in strategies that are "right wing" or conservative are just as valid as investing with "social" screens and priorities of progressive, "liberal" values.

This may be correct if one is investing via screened funds, aligning the individual values of a single investor with the value creation potential (as the client defines it) of any given investment opportunity. In that case, the only tensions to be resolved may be those of wealth advisors themselves who might have to grapple with the ethics of facilitating investments into strategies antithetical to their own personal beliefs. In traditional investor terms within a bifurcated, "do well and then do good" framework, this would be fine since historically we've pretended one may separate what one does during the week from who one is, personally, on the weekend. I suppose if you can sleep on that basis, it is your life and career—not mine—and you will have to find your own way through that swamp.

If, however, we are going to call this *impact* investing and we are doing so in order to have a positive *impact* on the world, then by definition what one is trying to impact is the status quo, the world as it currently exists and the direction in which we are now headed, a direction from which we must turn. What we seek is a changed society, a valued planet and greater justice among our various relationships of power, hierarchy, and politics. This means we believe the current state of the world is *not* what we want it to be and we are acting to resist forces promoting and seeking to protect traditional financial capitalism and the social and environmental injustices upon which it is built and our traditional investing practices advance.

This means impact investors seek to promote a change agenda and not one of conserving, defending or maintaining the status quo, much less freeing financial institutions to have yet greater advantage over consumers or liberating companies from regulation of the amount and form of pollution they can generate to the detriment of our communities and ecosystems.

This means we seek to structure our capital to advance greater individual choice within our communities—not support policies restricting the choice of individuals to live their lives and manage their health decisions as they see fit.

Impact investing means expanding our understanding of justice to include not simply those who are citizens of our nation, but those with whom we share our citizenship of the Earth.

Impact investing means defending not the unlimited free speech of corporations as "people" but rather the promotion of truth, scientific and experiential evidence and the real facts upon which we must base the words we seek to speak freely and use to promote our agenda of justice.

Impact investing means protecting those not able to stand to protect themselves, whether they are a refugee family, a line worker in a manufacturing facility or voiceless animals being processed through factories, wandering in the woods or moving through the world's rivers and oceans.

This does *not* mean impact investors are Democrats as opposed to Republicans.

Impact Investing is active and political in pursuit of an agenda of social justice and sustaining environmental relationships and neither of the two dominant parties presently active in the United States owns that agenda. As individual impact investors bring our values to the fore—as we work to integrate values with value creation—we may indeed find ourselves fundamentally at odds with much of the current Washington agenda and certainly not part of the "Me First!" culture now running rampant within our society. That does not mean we go by default to the other side of the aisle, but rather must work to use our capital to hold both sides of the aisle to account.

The politics of impact are those of change, empowerment and shared self-determination for those presently standing outside our walls as well as those within our borders seeking greater participation, opportunity and equity—in both senses of the word. The politics of impact are those of challenge and transformation, of working to attain our true potential to advance a just and sustainable planet to the greatest benefit of human and non-human beings. Impact Investing is as political as it gets—just not on the terms of our present partisanship which asks us to believe future answers will lie within the old framing of what we used to take as "political" or the simplistic and selfish framing of what it seems to mean to now be "conservative" in this Trumpian era.

Impact Investing returns us to the very roots and foundations of engaged, truly populist democracy as renewed by a new generation of thought, practice and vision that transcends party doctrine and dogma. Impact Investing is about change in and of the current economic and political order, but is also about bringing a sense of presence and witness to our process of political engagement. The politics of impact investing is that of Buddhist Action and the Quaker and Christian philosophies of bearing witness to oppression as we seek to bring great-er compassion and justice to the world.

In the end, the politics of impact investing is that of putting your assets on the line to finance a new order, a new world and a new reality. Much of today's politics is loud and abusive, which we must recognize, call out and appropriately respond to in the manner of, "I can't hear what you're saying cuz your actions are speaking so loudly." We must seek to get behind and around our rhetoric to affirm and advance our agenda of sustained, deep engagement and socio-environmental justice.

We are called to envision and advance an approach to politics that in some ways will take us back to our historic fundamentals and in oth-ers will require we transcend the dualism of our current political order in the same way we are transcending the dualism of financial capitalism as we've known it these past centuries.

IMPACT INVESTING AS CHANGE

Capital must be managed, deployed and assessed based upon its total, whole value creation potential—its ability and potential to generate returns on financial, environmental and social terms. We are called to manage capital as a resource to optimize the full potential of living beings and our planet, not to be gripped tight in one's fist, with increas-ing amounts draining through dry, cracked fingers and pale skin but released to generate new levels of total performance and impact. Capital is to be invested to realize its full, value potential. It is to be managed to optimize freedom and creative experience of our living in the world as we are called to live. It is capital understood as liberator, not oppressor.

Capital may also be a tool that can turn on itself and destroy our tra-ditional understanding of what wealth is for and how it is to be deployed. The German historian and philosopher, Karl Jaspers, reflected upon the idea that history is a process of annihilation in that to advance each age had to be built upon the destruction of previous thinking and practice.[13]

We now live in a culture that claims to celebrate disruption of tra-dition and established economic order, whether in the form of trans-portation or technology or energy. One hears consistent if not constant references to Schumpeter's vision of capitalism as a form of creative destruction and we claim that is what makes for innovation, progress and the future health of our society. If we truly believe this to be the case, than we have only yet to begin to fully appreciate the coming disruption of our economic systems. Management of capital via Impact Investing will serve as a sledgehammer to annihilate traditional, financial capitalism.

Impact Investing is not some augmented approach to capital management and investing. It is a means by which we may first acknowledge, then begin to heal and then seek to create new, positive value out of the damage we have created in past centuries through our having taken a bifurcated approach to finance. Capital is an instrument by which we may deconstruct the gods of traditional economics and finance, returning their parts to the soil to nourish the new growth of whole system economics. Impact investing builds upon but deconstructs and then transcends traditional investment thinking and practice.

As actors responsible for how capital moves in our world, we need to understand the importance of ourselves moving through the stages necessary to advance our vision of capital as a vehicle for human freedom and natural self-determination. We need to learn how best to engage in constructive social change, defined as:

> "The pursuit of moving relationships from those defined by fear, mutual recrimination, and violence toward those characterized by love, mutual respect, and proactive engagement. Constructive social change seeks to change the flow of human interaction in social conflict from cycles of destructive relational violence toward cycles of relational dignity and respectful engagement. The flows of fear destroy. Those of love edify. That is the challenge: how to move from that which destroys toward that which builds,"[14] according to John Paul Lederach.

As we turn from the oppression of our currently ahistoric and exclusively economic understanding of our world and the place of capital within it, to one that affirms capital as a vehicle of freedom and abundance, we need to replace the violence of historical financial capitalism with life affirming, peacemaking investment strategies. We can bring such an approach to wealth management through the following stages of capacity building, as outlined by Lederach:

- Have the capacity to envision oneself in relationship to another;
- A willingness to embrace complexity;
- An ability to operate within a non-dualistic/non-polarizing understanding of the world;
- A capacity to be open to a process of creativity;
- A willingness to take meaningful and real risks[15]

Moving through our financial version of these stages is the goal of the successful impact investor, but the steps are also critical to each of us living a life that is engaged, dynamic, empowered, and impassioned.

When all is said and done, capital has the potential to catalyze movements in the world in the same way a pebble dropped into water has the force of its impact upon the surface yet is measured and assessed on the basis of the concentric circles emanating out from the place of its initial entry into the water. Capital may be viewed as an initial investment of energy at the point of its first deployment, and it is this energy that moves out into the world, making things happen, causing things to occur. It takes the strength of its initial deployment and radiates it out from there, like swells moving across water. Its performance may be simultaneous as emanating from its origin, its original investment, but may also be understood as rooted in its past while having the potential for evolving further into a future yet to be created. The effort of impact investors to unleash capital as freedom places that capital within a given point in time—where it is—yet simultaneously connects it with its past and possible alternative futures. It is capital as impact potential; at one and the same time, impact possibilities and impact realized.

JUSTICE AS IMPACT
With the recognition of the potential purpose of capital as freedom, we may then turn to reflect on our history and the place of injustice within

that history as a precursor to our attaining sustained freedom within our communities and society. As with other concepts we've explored, the interplay between justice and real security is no new insight:

"Keep the country secure and look after the people righteously,
for justice is the bedrock of the kingdom."
—Persian inscription hewed into a cliff face in
three languages at Behistun (in modern day
Iran) by Darius the Great, 522BCE.[16]

Steps toward justice and equity are always within our reach. Over the centuries we've seen time and again wherein the action of those controlling capital has been to seek more and more significant ways to consolidate, maintain and grow their wealth, at the cost of the poor and the expense of community. While Adam Smith, a moral philosopher come economist, raised numerous considerations and concerns regarding the social implications of his economic ideas, those concerns were not and are not heeded by those who profess to be his followers.[17] The result of our global and historical process of wealth aggregation is in the papers daily and recognized by many, regardless of political stripe or bent. We have various ways to document it, but in the end, it is evident when we live in a world where "(a)ssets of the world's three richest people are greater than the combined GNP of 600 million people in the world's poorest countries."[18] I will forgo citing a litany of additional numbers and data[19] that despite the light-hearted and self-amused claims of some (Pinker) document our many and diverse global and local community challenges.

With the possible exception of the Golden Age of pre-history, human history has been an ongoing process of ebbs and flows from periods and places with greater justice and equity to periods and places wherein financial extraction by the wealthy from the poor reigned and was allowed to operate on an unfettered basis. This is not just a function of the tides of time but has been built into the economic orders created by humanity—wait, scratch that—created by the wealthy and powerful as they have managed a global march toward

wealth consolidation and, by extension, a progressive limiting of freedom for the majority of the world's population down through the ages.
These events are not the natural course of human history, but are the
logical outcome of power, control and wealth consolidation; it is structural and it is systemic.

These are systems which evolved as power worked its way through
societies and down through time. As Rieger observed,

> "What is overlooked most frequently is that these gaps [in wealth
> and income] are not primarily about income levels as such; look-
> ing at numbers often leads to this misperception. These gaps are
> ultimately about differentials of power and influence because big
> money equals big power in the current economic system. Such
> power and influence determine who gets to shape the world,
> who gets recognized, and whose ideas count."[20]

This modern reality has its roots in the progressive surrendering of
common interest to private ownership, first of land and later of financial capital itself. Alastair McIntosh tells this story, documenting how
in Scotland the Clearances of the 1500s, together with the Enclosure
Movement that was then made possible, consisted of clearing the Commons of both small, local farmers and indigenous animals, making the
way for herds of sheep and the textile mills to come. It is in this way
Pierre-Joseph Proudhon is correct, that all wealth is theft.

And it is also in this way that wealth—that capital—came to be
separated from the earth and common ownership as those in power—
whether kings of throne or commerce—came to clear lands of natural peoples, not only in Scotland but in the Americas and around the
world as the power of capital began to make itself felt in our new age of
financial capitalism regardless of the particular political order of nations
around the world. The table upon which capital rests may be set for
different actors in different times, but the table remains ready for those
with the capital to buy a place setting.

Accordingly, there are diverse implications of global climate change
for communities of wealth and poverty around the world. One reflects

our history as much as our past in that, "Natural catastrophe amplifies existing inequality,"[21] as seen in flooding of low-land agricultural areas, spreading of disease to those unable to access vaccines and lack of food during periods of famine.

As Jedidiah Purdy observes,

> "The global atmosphere is a great launderer of historical contributions to and benefits from, inequality. Everything washes out in the weather…It is too anodyne to say that climate change creates hazards for which wealthy countries are better prepared. It is more accurate to say that it creates a global landscape of inequality, one in which the already wealthy people who have contributed most to the problem see their advantages multiplied."[22]

Much as we might care to decry this reality, in truth, the vast majority of us, of those most likely to be reading these words—regardless of the absolute size of our net worth—are complicit in this historic consolidation of wealth. While war, economic depression, and pestilence may act in the short-term to redistribute wealth (or to at least reshape the ranks of wealth holders), on balance our progress over centuries has been one of ongoing accumulation and concentration as opposed to equitable distribution and mutual benefit. Many have described this process, but for one recent and excellent exploration, the reader is directed to Walter Scheidel's *The Great Leveler: Violence and the History of Inequality from the Stone Age to the Twenty-First Century.*[23]

St. Ambrose, writing in 380CE, said,

> *"What a splendid thing justice is…(to be) born*
> *for others rather than for oneself."*

And, as has been stated, within a Buddhist tradition one is not able to attain true enlightenment unless all have attained such.

The question for those engaged in the management and deployment of capital must begin with this reflection on the purpose of capital and from there we may be positioned to explore its implications for a life, for a community and for a planet.

We are each called to this pursuit of freedom.

We are each called to burn for and embrace this gift to self and Other.

CHAPTER TWELVE

LIVING IMPACT:

Purpose as New Progress, Presence as Our Value Manifest

T HE CONCEPT OF PROGRESS FIRST CAME TO CENTER STAGE AS PART OF A "NEW PARADIGM OF HISTORICAL CONSCIOUSNESS" THAT EVOLVED IN THE PERIOD BETWEEN 1750 AND 1850, A TIME WHICH GERMAN HISTORIAN REIN-HART KOSSELLECK TERMED SATTELZEIT ("SADDLE TIME").

At that point, historians began to make observations of what they came to call the Axial Age (800-200BCE), but on its own, it was a transition period thought to mark a clear delineation between the past and the future of modernity.[1]

More recently, the cultural historian and eco-theologian Thomas Berry wrote:

"A central value word used by our society is "progress." This word has great significance for increasing our scientific understanding of the universe, our personal and social development, our better health and longer life...But then we see that

progress has been carried out by deflating the natural world.
Human beings are degrading the earth as this degradation
of the earth is the very condition of "progress." Industrialists
and capitalists are co-opting the language we use...It is a kind
of sacrificial offering...The language in which our values are
expressed has been co-opted by the industrial establishments
and is used with the most extravagant modes of commercial
advertising to create the illusory world in which the human
community is not living."[2]

The Norwegian philosopher Arne Naess takes this idea one step
further when he says,

"Technical progress is sham progress because the term technical progress is a cultural, not a technical term. Our culture is
the only one in the history of mankind in which the culture
has adjusted itself to the technology rather than vice versa...we
have the motto, "You can't stop progress," you can't interfere
with technology, and so we allow technology to dictate cultural forms.[3] ...It is interesting but disturbing to note that certain
techno-industrial sides to existence are now accepted as unal-
terable and objective. We don't say 'progress requires that slums
be eliminated, there's no sense to try to stop it!' Slums may be
eliminated by the time we arrive at commercial space flight, but
why do the words 'development' and 'progress' have so little
appeal here? Or: we do not say that 'progress requires that each
and every one of us has access to nature and agreeable milieu
for our children. There's no sense fighting against progress." Or:
'Progress requires a change from constitutional democracy to
a democracy of true living together (*samliv*).' Just when do we
choose to make use of this term 'progress'? Why not speak in
terms of progress of life quality?"[4]

From the perspective of social value, Toynbee writes:

"Since the dawn of civilization there has been a disparity between Man's technological progression and his social performance. The advance of technology, particularly the most recent advances during the two centuries 1773-1973, has vastly increased Man's wealth and power, and the 'morality gap' between Man's physical power for doing evil and his spiritual capacity for coping with this power has yawned as wide open as the mythical jaws of Hell. During the past 5,000 years the widening 'morality gap' has caused mankind to inflict on itself grievous disasters."[5]

Or, as Martin Luther King, Jr., observed more succinctly:

"Our scientific power has outrun our spiritual power. We have guided missiles and misguided men."[6]

As we reflect on humanity's development, growth is often equated with the notion of progress, but they are not the same. As Sivaraska stated,

"We have lost the power of discernment and cannot differentiate between need and greed."[7]

In contrast to these perspectives, as is true of many aspects of empire building, many modern writers believe there are no real limits to growth and expansion, focusing not on qualitative, but quantitative growth. For example, Harari, in an otherwise robust analysis offered in his book, *Sapiens*, states:

"The modern economy grows thanks to our trust in the future and the willingness of capitalists to reinvest their profits in production. That does not suffice. Economic growth also requires energy and raw materials, and these are finite. When and if they run out, the entire system will collapse. But the evidence provided by the past is that they are finite only in theory.

Counter-intuitively, while humankind's use of energy and raw materials has mushroomed in the last few centuries, the amount available for our exploitation has actually *increased*. Whenever a shortage of either has threatened to slow economic growth, investments have flowed into scientific and technological research. These have invariably produced not only more efficient ways of exploiting existing resources, but also completely new types of energy and materials."[8] (Emphasis in the original).

This unbridled faith in technology as progress to solve problems together with our belief the Earth exists to be exploited for human desires and ambition combine to create a dangerous blind spot in our modern world view and perspective with regard to the planet, our relation to it and the future, destructive reality we are creating.

Technology does not in and of itself solve all our problems and especially not when it comes to the question of resource depletion; not when one considers what is known as "Jevons Paradox." As Peter Frase tells us,

"Stanley Jevons, a British economist writing in 1865, made the argument that increasing efficiency does not lead to less consumption since consumers would simply use more of the cheaper energy made available by the increased efficiency of production—and over the many decades since he posited this paradox, Jevons has been proved to be correct. While many argue that "technology" will solve our problems of energy resource and development, in fact, there is a high likelihood the inverse may be true when viewed on a global basis and even within discrete markets."[9]

Davies points us toward another issue related to this "limits to growth" conversation:

"Business as usual can be passed off as "sustainable development," while green politics is reduced to an anemic clinging to the past, reliant on a pastoral fantasy about the perpetual harmony of

unspoiled nature. At worst, it does not even need to be co-opted,
since the tool of sustainability is already an explicit defense
of the status quo: a managerial, efficiency-seeking principle
with the avowed aim of securing the flow of natural resources
required for the continued accumulation of capital."[10]

It would appear we will proceed with our commitment to growing
consumption and (by extension) capital as our measures of success and
progress, compounded by the fact that our metric for that growth—
the metric by which we celebrate our understanding of economic
development—is itself flawed. Again, as Naess, Jonathan Rowe, and
many others have observed frameworks such as Gross National Product and other measures of financial exchange do not help us approach
an understanding of value creation, but rather transactions—the social
value of a divorce or marriage may be viewed as equal and yet clearly
not. Such metrics assess economic exchange or perhaps growth but not
meaning, impact or true, integrative value creation.[11]

And, of course, growth is *not* value creation, despite our tendency
as a society to conflate the two. And so we will seek continued growth
cloaked as progress, unrestrained and ill-considered until we can grow
no more; and the growth we promote will be such that we will, in the
end, choke to death, both metaphorically and literally. As Edward Abbey
said, "Growth for the sake of growth is the ideology of the cancer cell."

A better future may not lie in growth at all, but rather in the
opposite direction, in progress defined as smaller size and deeper relationship with each Other and Planet; in progress as measured in a
variety of forms of presence. As EF Schumacher wrote, "The keynote
to Buddhist economics is simplicity and nonviolence. From the economist's point of view, the marvel of the Buddhist way of life is the utter

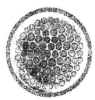

rationality of its pattern—amazingly small means leading to extraordinarily satisfactory results."[12]

As we consider the question of limits and growth, we need also consider issues of whether we take to that discussion a mindset of abundance or scarcity. Within a scarcity mindset, we are asked to live in fear and, indeed, the current financial capitalist system promotes this notion of scarcity over abundance. This 'either-or' decision, in this case between scarcity and abundance, but also reflected in the notion of doing well or doing good, making a grant or an investment, working for a nonprofit or a for-profit, and so on are each logical outcomes of the ancient tension between material and spiritual purpose, which we carry into today's modern life and economy. As Hans Binswanger said:

> "This growing entropy in the physical sphere is matched by a growing disorder in all spheres of life that come under the economy's pull. As humankind breaks ever-new ground in the economic sphere, our disorientation in other spheres becomes all the greater. The economy deprives a man of forces that, like the sun in nature, have always reestablished the original order. Goethe particularly stresses three areas where man is becoming disastrously disoriented, and economic gains are therefore countered by vital losses. The first great loss suffered by humanity in the march of economic progress is the loss of beauty."[13]

IN PURSUIT OF DEEP ECONOMY

To overcome our loss of beauty and security, we must reframe our understanding of what sustained growth means as well as our measures of progress. We will only do this via a reconceptualization of our knowledge of economics itself and evolution above and beyond the current practices of traditional financial capitalism and—by extension—our knowledge of current impact investing practice. We must "jump track," as it were, to rise a good notch and move from simply continuing on this course of doing well and doing good to turning upward, to set a new direction, to rise to our next level of being and consciousness in our understanding of the purpose of capital.

This new understanding will be grounded within two principles.

First, is the concept that we have obligations to others—beyond our selves, to families, community, and nation to be sure, but also to Planet and all sentient beings living upon it. There is no option for us to be the last one standing, to become Sapien triumphal yet alone upon a charred Earth.

Second, is the idea we must value not merely human life, but the diversity and richness of humanity in the context of a Living Planet. We celebrate our freedom and the variety of ways humanity chooses to live—the freedom human beings have to explore and express themselves, yet we must only celebrate this freedom in connection with other living as well as natural entities; we cannot be free if others are not. The purpose of our capital cannot be our purchasing of freedom for Self and not Other, for Self cannot be made free in absence of the Other's liberation.

In this context, the purpose of capital is revealed in our exploration of community, humanity, culture and ecosystem, each and all woven within an understanding there is no single answer. This is not a matter of cultural or ethical relativism; instead, we must—with others—explore how various responses fit within our time, place and comprehension of the value we are called to create in this world. If we are to be forever linked with forms and variations of capitalism, than we must seek to be cosmopolitan capitalists, managing assets as part of a globally simultaneous celebration of cultural freedom and biological abundance and diversity. This is something we cannot achieve on our own and cannot capture in pursuit solely of individual self interest and the traditional measure of financial returns alone.

This will require our creation of a new approach to economics, that of Deep Economy, a term most recently used by Bill McKibbon, who presents the idea in the context of human communities, which is a critical consideration, of course, but not the type of Deep Economy to which I refer for deep economy grounded upon an understanding of economics of human community is an anthropomorphic perspective, placing humanity at the center of the world.

In contrast, I would argue we must view humankind as simply one part—perhaps a small part—of the whole. We are the species that is the source of the current problems we face. We must generate the solutions to these problems if our children and societies are to survive in the future. Yet if we are to be successful, we must surrender our egoistic infatuation with our selves and our technologies as being the measure of all that is good and positive in our world. We must turn to technology and capital in service not only of Self but of Other.

To be successful in all this, we must place the Earth and other species on at least equal footing with our own good selves if we are to operate within an evolved understanding of our world and life. Only then will we have the possibility of bringing the proper conceptual and scientific frameworks to bear upon our current and future problems. What we need is an approach to our understanding of the purpose of capital and a system of Deep Economy rooted more centrally within the principles of the deep ecology philosophy that inspires the concept to begin with.

Deep ecology was introduced and defined by Arne Naess in his 1973 article, *The Shallow and the Deep, Long-Range Ecology Movements* (Inquiry, Vol 16, pages 95-100). Naess states:

> Deep ecology is based on the "...rejection of the man-in-environment image in favor of the *relational, total-field image.* Organisms as knots in the field of intrinsic relations...and embraces the notion of *Biospherical egalitarianism—in principle.* The 'in principle' clause is inserted because any realistic praxis necessitates some killing, exploitation and suppression. The ecological field worker acquires a deep-seated, even veneration, for ways and forms of life. He reaches an understanding from within, a kind of understanding that others reserve for fellow men [sic] and for a narrow section of ways and forms of life. To the ecological field worker, the equal right to live and blossom is an intuitively clear and obvious value axiom. Its restriction to humans is an anthropocentrism with detrimental effects upon the life quality of humans themselves. This quality depends in part upon the deep pleasure and satisfaction we receive from close partnership with other forms of life. The attempt to ignore

our dependence and to establish a master-slave role has contributed to the alienation of man from himself."[14]

We see possibilities for the development of Deep Economy in the sound work of The Capital Institute, The New Economy Coalition, BALLE, The Buckminster Fuller Institute and literally countless others active in communities, ecosystems and markets around the world. And while this work is sound, we must recognize it takes place against a backdrop of centuries of debate and discussion regarding the place of humanity in our world and humanity's relation to Earth and other species. Such an exploration is beyond our capacities in this reflection, but the historian Keith Makoto Woodhouse, in his recent publication, *The Ecocentrists: A History of Radical Environmentalism*, offers an excellent overview of this topic as debated within today's community of environmentalists and ecocentrists of recent decades. For our purposes, it should be noted that while Arne Naess, no doubt with others, first framed the concept of deep ecology, he did not view humanity's place as being separate from that of the Earth, but rather as a part of and actor within its ecosystems.[15] And we would also adopt such a perspective.

In the end it is about advancing a connected framework of understanding Earth, our Sentient Community, Economics, and Self through the practice of a rediscovered personal and social alchemy. This alchemy includes considerations of economics and its tool of finance, but is not itself defined by them. This transformation blends diverse components of being and materiality to optimize our experience of life within the pursuit of self realization, social freedom and verdant ecologies inclusive of yet not dominated by humanity. In this new economic order which we may already see manifest around us in diverse ways and forms across the world, capital functions as but one fuel for the vibrant alchemy of life.

Within this understanding of its true essence, capital is simply a form of blood continually moving through an emergent, regenerative Deep Economy, converting from one form to another, flowing through various and diverse organizations (cooperative, for-profit, nonprofit), stewarded by various and diverse temporary asset owners (institutional

and private, communal and individual) who view themselves as
stewards of capital in a continual
process of deployment, use, renew-
al and endless regeneration. Capital flows from one manifestation to
another as part of a constant conversion from its initial element to
second, third and fourth elements,
constantly in motion, shape shifting from grant to debt to equity
and back, yet always consisting of
the same fundamental constitution
as fuel for freedom, self-realization
and life.

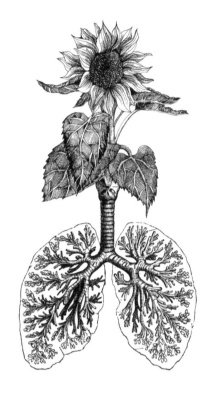

Like Spinoza's notion of substance or that of the pre-Socratic
Greek philosophers of the Axial
Age, capital continually evolves
through social structures, eco-sys-
tems, and earthen soils. Within this framework, capital becomes personal progress manifest, in transition from our historic understanding
of capital and economics into that of an ever-renewing future of humanity's diverse and various capitals in application and action. Our call is
to advance and realize our full vision and vibrant, potential freedoms
as we sit present in this evolving process of contemplation, innovation,
exploration, engagement, and, finally again, reflection.

THE PURPOSE OF CAPITAL AS
CONTINUING JOURNEY, RESTORATIVE
JUSTICE AND MUTUAL IMPACT

I began this most recent leg of my own journey with some level of frustration with the realization many of those promoting impact investing
and any number of other proposals for connecting capital to community
and planet seemed largely unaware of the path behind and those who've

trod it. I would argue many of us have not understood how best to think of these issues within the larger context of total human experience, history and wisdom—and we are each the poorer for that ignorance.

As my inquiry has evolved, I've realized we must redefine our understanding of the next step for impact investing and the evolution of our own understanding of the purpose of capital. Instead of basing our sense of progress upon notions of the big investment ideas, ongoing refinement of strategies for building upon bifurcated notions of doing well and doing good, the organizing of yet additional impact initiatives and raising yet more massive impact investment funds, I would submit what we as individuals and as a community that professes to care about the purpose of capital must first do is stop and reflect upon one very basic question:

How are we each called to act to remove injustice and its related barriers to each member of our human and non-human community and ecosystems attaining sustained freedom in our world?

I would suggest the correct response to this question may be that there is not a single solution or framework within which we might operate or that we might promote at our conferences and through our various collaborations. Rather, the answer is that there are multiple answers and that, first, we must each commit ourselves to a deeper, more humble practice of living, while affirming that "The best criticism of the bad is the practice of the better."[16]

This is why we are called to create model impact portfolios, to be transparent in our investment practices, to be accountable to our own selves as well as to the Other and our extended personal community, and so on. As a community we must accept that we are each called to play many and diverse roles over the course of a life, over the course of our lives, and in this way debates and discussions regarding the "best" approach to impact or the relative place and role of social enterprise versus mission driven, for profit, versus state-sponsored enterprise is that, well, it depends—upon context, actors, resources, capacity and a host of related factors we may not even see until we're in the midst of the new becoming.

This is not a question of lacking an enhanced vision, paradigm or new set of operating principles—for we will require each—rather a question of openness and inquiry, humility and innovation within varying contexts and with diverse stakeholders requiring better ways to understand their unity than more contentious debates regarding which is the "right" and "proper" way to pursue our progress or define our purpose. We must be transparent and engaged, one with the other, and seek to challenge ourselves to continually drill deeper and rise higher in terms of how we hold ourselves and each other accountable for advancing a true and not distorted, opaque or weakened impact agenda. Again, Broad Impact is fine, but not enough to address the challenges before us. We must be open to new perspectives and alternative strategies, but hold our selves to account for advancing real, Deep, and Mutual impact through our collective efforts.

I take as one example the work of Rudolf Steiner, who offered a way of thinking as opposed to a prescriptive outline of what to do. At the same time, his ideas were rooted in the notion that one must act; one must take the concepts and ideas of a new way of economic thinking and put them into practice. As Economic Historian Christopher Budd observed,

> "...Steiner's ideas belong more to kinetic than to potential economics; they are in movement and call to be led over into action. They are wasted on those who neither wish to act, nor to change their way of acting. That is as true now as it was in 1922 [when Steiner gave his lectures on economics], and so the question remains: How are such ideas to be put into practice? And by whom?...Economics can get nowhere as a merely contemplative activity."[17]

In light of this and as the culmination of related concepts explored in this book, I would argue we're each best served by engaging in a form of personal *paradoxical curiosity* which John Paul Lederach describes as approaching

> "...social realities with an abiding respect for complexity, a refusal to fall prey to the pressures of forced dualistic

categories of truth, and an inquisitiveness about what may hold together seemingly contradictory social energies in a greater whole. This is not primarily a thrust toward finding common ground based on a narrowly shared denominator. Paradoxical curiosity seeks something beyond what is visible, something that holds apparently contradictory and even violently opposed social energies together."[18]

Our task is not to grapple with how to do good and well, it is not to founder in the shoals of our existing economics of bifurcated value creation, but to rise above that economic Yin and Yang of investing versus philanthropy or grant versus investment to embrace the more abundant energy and opportunity of the Impact Tao, of a commitment to the creation, affirmation, and advancement of the whole that is the central nature of the blended value we seek to optimize within a community and over the course of a life.

It is an integrative, ongoing, and flowing understanding of the purpose of capital that fuels our efforts at optimizing art in the context of community, of placing supports and structures beneath our actions to realize the full potential of not only humanity but humanity as a partner and collaborator within the process of the natural unfolding of which we are a part.

What could be more appropriate for both the process and practices of managing and integrating financial, social and environmental components of value creation through the deployment of capital?

While we may be parts of communities of interest and work, advancing various aspects of our respective activities, in the end, it is all a dynamic process of personal commitment, exploration, and vision as explored in the context of community and with the Other. Our personal and professional integrity is found in the intentional, mindful manifestation of how we show up in the world, how our actions reflect our values and how efforts at separating our material from our spiritual is a negation of our very selves.

Instead of, as the ancient philosopher Lucretius says, "running away from ourselves,"[19] we must seek to stand and be engaged in a more profound, more intentional manner—to find ourselves in the course of how we apply all of our worldly assets in pursuit of both the temporal and transcendent reality we seek to be in this world. At its core, it is a simple, though complex, process. On the material level, it is less a process of getting rid of 'things' (though that may certainly be a part of it) than it is one of identifying a potential source of personal energy and empowerment that may be of benefit simultaneously to self and Other.[20]

Let us reduce the drag on our lives by paring down and minimizing the physical and psychological burdens of this world—inclusive of a traditional understanding of how to invest and to what ends. This can have the effect of freeing us, generating new levels and forms of energy which in turn positions us to do more with less, to live better with fewer material things and to think more clearly, with an uncluttered mind—to be free. This is less a call to voluntary simplicity than one of clarity of purpose and first principles by which we might better value our worth beyond measures of financial wealth and against those of personal aspiration and vibrant meaning.

We may seek to do the same on an intellectual level. As the biologist/philosopher Edward O. Wilson said:

> "[Reductionism] is the search strategy employed to find points of entry into otherwise impenetrably complex systems. Complexity is what interests scientists in the end, not simplicity. Reductionism is the way to understand it. The love of complexity without reductionism makes art; the love of complexity with reductionism makes science."[21]

We are called to be creative scientists and artists of an infused rationality that seeks to liberate us as individuals and communities striving to realize our potential highest and best presence in this life. In this pursuit, we could do a lot worse than aspire to live our lives as a modern form of Charles Darwin's. He left his studies in the science of medicine to pursue a career as an Anglican priest since it was Natural Theology, the study of how God acts in the world, which at that time allowed students to explore both biology and theology as a single course of work.[22]

Such a path reminds me of those leaving traditional finance in order to explore, practice and become actualized within new approaches to impact investing as the management of capital and career. I'm reminded of the hundreds (if not thousands I've not met) of financiers who have left finance and business people who have left traditional business in order to pursue profit with purpose and a more deeply rooted self within a society of personal and social changemakers. I'm reminded of social workers going to business schools in order to drive enterprise opportunity as vehicles for advancing justice and capital as energy for empowerment.

In the end, however we understand it, we each in our own way might benefit from the intentional integration of theology and spiritualism with science and finance and social liberation with community empowerment as the guard rails for moving us toward a new place of blended value realized, operating in and of the world as we know it or might experience its future course.

Within this context, our end goal is to create a diverse community, self actualized, engaged and connected as deeply as possible in multiple manners, in various ways and countless forms. In this way,

> "Naess is focused on the concept of 'Self-realization!' as a central idea—but he does not intend this within the singular frame of an individual's own personal development of self, but rather a "wider" Self, "one with a capital S that expands from each of us to include all." This also relates to how he understands the idea of communication and 'relational thinking' which is the idea that 'nothing exists apart.' In this way, words only have meaning in the interplay between how they are simultaneously understood by the individual in the context of the community and eco-system of which they are a part."[23]

This is why understanding, connecting with, and living within the flow of the many traditions, forms of wisdom literature and diverse schools of philosophy is critical to understanding ourselves, our world and the role of investing in a world in search of healing.

We do all this since our goal is not merely to create impact upon and within the lives of others, but in a genuine sense to save our selves. Justice is a two-way street, a relationship of connection and engagement rather than a charitable act we perform upon the Other.

> "If the Sanskrit word translated into English is *atman*, it is instructive to note that this term has the basic meaning of "self," rather than "mind" or "spirit" as one usually sees in the translations. The superiority of the translation using the word self stems from the consideration that if your self (in the wide sense) embraces another being, you need no moral exhortation to show care. Surely you care for yourself without feeling any moral pressure to do it—provided you have not succumbed to a neurosis of some kind, developed self-destructive tendencies or hate yourself."[24] (Sessions)

In so doing we come to be liberated from boundaries; we come to be free.

RESTORATIVE JUSTICE AS MUTUAL IMPACT IN ACTION

While we tend to think of justice as an act of making things right, of advancing greater equity in the world, from the perspective of the asset owner and investor, we must also keep in mind the concept of restorative justice—justice that speaks to our condition and prospects for being made whole through the process of advancing greater equity in the world and challenging the very systems which may benefit us, in our role of relative wealth and privilege.[25] Within the concept of restorative justice, we view our mistakes as the opportunity for us to grow, transform, and become more of the whole people we are called to be.

It is through this process we are allowed to become more fully aware of the wisdom that awaits us, that will emerge out of our engaging more deeply, of moving first from the letter then to the prophetic voice and only later to the deep wisdom and sustaining spirit of the Law, of being more fully present in our impact investing process. In this way, the relationships our capital offers us are avenues to collaborative free-dom—not separated, isolated and individuated from the Other. It is, as we discussed in our reflection on Other Impact, the opportunity to become engaged with and restored by the experience of Mutual Impact.

Dialogue is key to this change, for as Sulak Sivarakas offers: "...(g)enuine dialogue requires active listening. We need to abandon our idea of a particular outcome and remain quiet within. When both sides feel heard, creative problem solving can bring unanticipated results. Reconciliation is key. Acknowledging the past alleviates suffering, heals injustice, and fosters transformation. Called restorative justice, victim, and perpetrator listen to each other deeply—difficult as that may be—and, as a result, both change."[26]

Many advisors today are stuck in a legalistic approach to impact investing. They are focused on fulfilling the term sheet notion of impact which spells out our expectations, the definition of performance and ini-tial statements of what specific result they will generate. This entry-level approach is important, but only takes us so far in that it focuses only upon the "how" of impact investing. It has us look at the mechanics of the practice and from there attempt to define what our purpose is as opposed to looking up, out and beyond to discern intent and purpose and only from that point practice.

As we move toward that place, a Prophetic approach to Impact Investing is one that acknowledges the challenge that even if we fulfill the terms of our investment contract, injustice is still resident within the current financial capitalist system within which we operate, a system that allows us to extract economic value from low-income communities in the name of and working within the bifurcated construct of doing well and good. The practice of restorative justice allows us to be reinstat-ed to a deeper level of human connection and community, while open-ing our selves to receive a deeper, more profound experience of what it means for us to be the objects of impact of our investments as much as those who are our investees or stakeholders with particular interest in the outcomes of how we structure our impact investments.

Restorative justice places us in a position of exploring our healing and growth simultaneously with the healing, growth, and opportunity we hope to bring our collaborators and stakeholders. We do this by leveraging capital for more than the generation of only financial returns to us. In this way, our wealth is regenerative not only of environmental or social value but of the personal value we may accrue to the benefit of our journey or that of our family, community and the greater whole of which we are each a part and through which we may only then come to sit in the presence of transcendent wisdom.

Along these lines, it has been said,

"You fix your life, and your business, and your world by fixing yourself."[27]

Restorative justice as experienced in the possibilities of impact investing is one vehicle through which that goal may be attained. As is often the case, we may learn something from Native traditions in this regard:

"Native spirituality is circular. The Medicine Wheel is a circle. The alter is in the center, and the human race sits in the outer circle. We all have different views of the altar: God. We all see it from different angles…The fundamentalist is the static one who never moves around the wheel and believes that his or her view is the only valid view. The eclectic moves freely about the wheel and soon realizes that all of the views are valid ones. All of the visions in the chart are valid. We can learn from each one of them. As we sit in the circle with all of our fellow human creatures, we discover that we have differing views of God and life. God is reflected through each of us through our own individual experiences.…The more we can move freely about the wheel, the more balance we find in our spiritual walk and the more spiritual depth we experience in our lives.[28]

What's interesting is that we may set out to "do good" but can't adequately do so in the world if our intentions and motivations and self are damaged. It is our intentions and our selves we bring forward which have the highest potential to create positive change in the world. As we are ourselves wounded, our capital might create some level of good and positivity, but it may never create Mutual Impact if we are not fully engaged in that process of being and becoming.

I'm reminded of John D. Rockefeller, whose philanthropy left a legacy of positive impact in the world, and yet not a year after he first received a state charter to create his foundation, on April 20, 1914 he ordered Pinkerton forces to confront striking coal miners in Ludlow, Colorado, which, whether intentional or not, resulted in a massacre wherein two dozen people, including the wives and children of miners, were killed and many others wounded.[29] Today, his progeny, in the management of their own capital and building upon the significant philanthropy of previous generations, have initiated a process of divestment from fossil fuel investments and are exploring how to engage other wealth holders in impact investing and sustainable finance.

The family has evolved and changed as the world is evolving and changing.

The circle turns and turns again...

THE PURPOSE OF CAPITAL:
IMPACT INVESTING AS VALUE MANIFEST

How do we best act to remove injustice and other barriers to attaining freedom for ourselves and the Other?

The first thing we need do is recognize every action we take creates impact in the world. All investing creates impact; all philanthropy creates impact; all capital creates impact. What we must focus upon is the type of influence and connection we have and make in our world and the degree to which we work to ensure it is a fully positive action. It is a question of the nature and level of our intentionality, awareness, and ability to be present within an investment process as opposed to being detached managers of one.

For investors, methods focused upon defining, understanding, assessing, and measuring the value add of our investments is a fundamental challenge and one that carries the risk of limiting our comprehension of the full manner in which we have an impact upon our world. Along these lines, Fred Wolf says, "'Knowing is disrupting. Every time we go to measure something, we interfere. A quantum wave function builds and builds in possibilities until the moment of measurement when its future collapses into only one aspect. Which aspect of that wave function comes forth is primarily determined by *what* we decide to measure."[30] The more we focus on solely quantitative metrics assessing "impact" the more compartmentalized and removed we become *from* that impact and the more impact becomes something we do to others as opposed to something we ourselves engage in and with. By contrast, the more engaged we are and understanding of the representational, narrative value of our investments the more significant connection we might have *with* the value created and the more open we may become to the life giving flows unleashed through our capital deployment.

What we do is create impact—where and how we engage in making that impact reflects our value manifest in the world and is our choice. We know while we must reflect upon the meaning and purpose of capital—which is a big idea!—as we explore and decide upon how to advance our understanding of the use of capital; we are not necessarily required to do it all at once or to only act "at scale."

> "Purpose sounds big—*ending world hunger* big or *eliminating nuclear weapons* big. But it doesn't have to be. You can also find purpose in being a good parent to your children, creating a more cheerful environment at your office, or making a giraffe's life more pleasant."[31] (Emphasis in original)

Many of those within the impact investing and social enterprise arena speak of the critical importance of scale—by which they usually mean growth, size, and impact in huge numbers. But, as previously discussed, one may also scale for depth, for Mutual Impact, for connectivity in one's family, community, and personal world—together and in partnership and collaboration with the Other, however that Other presents itself in our lives.

Impact investors with smaller assets to invest shouldn't focus on thinking about their investment strategy or impact as having to be weighed against the scales of great wealth. To do so is to fall into the trap of so-called personal growth, self-promotion, and progress as a direct line from small to large or tiny to great, of moving ever toward some vaguely stated goal of temporary success. One's impact purpose may be as focused as helping a local food bank become more sustainable financially or buying the seeds for a local community garden. Impact may be broad and distributed, but our pursuit of impact is optimized when we seek to be deeply embedded in the relationships and networks of both our own and the Other's life and communities.

The more fundamental challenge for those mobilizing capital for impact and attempting to gain clarity concerning the use of capital as freedom is in understanding the outsized role today's capital markets play in fueling the economic system of financial investment and monetary returns that are the life blood of companies and communities at the heart of unsustainable business practices and rapacious treatment of the Earth and its various human and non-human communities. The employee and resident earning a living off the supply chain represent nothing relative to the power and energy unleashed by aggregated, rent-seeking capital in regions, forests and communities around the world. Snyder comments that:

> "...Our conservationist-environmentalist-moral outrage is often (in its frustration) aimed at the logger or the rancher, when the real power is in the hands of people who make unimaginably larger sums of money, people impeccably groomed, excellently educated at the best universities—male and female alike—eating fine foods and reading classy literature, while orchestrating the investment and legislation that ruin the world."[32]

Or as Martin Buber said,

> "The origin of all conflict between me and my fellow men is that I do not say what I mean, and that I do not do what I say."[33]

The threat to the future of impact investing is that we will settle for Branded Impact as opposed to Mutual Impact. And by investing in the absence of consideration of capital's deepest purpose, we thereby constrict its possibilities and potential. We limit its force as energy and potential as freedom, confining it within our admittedly circumspect understanding of life, reality and possibility as defined by self and not Other.

We can only function effectively if we function with an understanding of our *inability* to fully ascertain our potential; our *inability* to ever construct frameworks capable of capturing the fullness of life and experience. We must approach the practice of impact investing and the management of our diverse assets from a place of humility, openness and quiet reflection.

As The Dark Mountain Project seeks to use art as a tool to explore how we are called to be present with Nature and community during what we may take as these end days, impact investors must be mindful, deliberate and reflective in their process of understanding the purpose of capital and their efforts to deploy capital in the pursuit of multiple returns—various levels of financial returns together with the generation of environmental and social impacts. It is from such a place of presence where we may then be able to truly see and experience the freedom capital might bring to individual, community, and Planet.

This is why the impact metrics conversation may only be effectively entered into with an awareness of the reality that we will never be able to assess the full, integrated value of our investments for we can never know what forms of sustained impact we may generate. We will never know what wave of energy we convert to a particle that is received as a pulse, many communities away, many lives down the road. We must sit quietly with the reality of our shortcomings while we open our eyes and minds to take in the full potential of what may be generated by way of our diverse and many efforts, and through the application of our countless resources and energies.

Within ecology, a trophic cascade occurs when one animal's presence in the food chain sets off a waterfall cascade of benefits to a host of other animals that are a part of an eco-system.[34] The wolves' reintroduction to Yellowstone was not initially great for the elk they killed, but over time the herd became healthier and the carcasses the wolves left behind benefitted grizzly, fox, coyote and a host of other animals and microbes. The wolves forcing the elk herds to move out of the low-lands and into forests and other terrain enabled bushes and leafy trees to regenerate, which in turn made it possible for bird and other populations to become re-established to the benefit of the overall ecosystem.

Within social ecology, our engagement with the Other in a supportive, beneficial, and respectful manner—what Buddhists call the practice of loving-kindness or what Christians call being the Living Christ in the World or what First Nations people celebrate in the event of the Potlatch and so on through various other traditions—are all forms of our creating a trophic cascade of Mutual Impact first for our Selves, our friends, family, community, eco-systems and ultimately societies and world. Seeking to create such a cascade of kindness is of simultaneous benefit to Self and Other.

We are each part of a larger eco-system. We should each seek to initiate such trophic cascades, small and large, over the course of our lives.

Our personal purpose must be that of our capital:

To create deep blended value through the extension of living freedom to all beings and elements of the Earth.

THE READING LIFE:
Limitations of Self

ONE OF THE CHALLENGES OF WORKING ACROSS SILOS OF KNOWLEDGE AND PRACTICE IS THAT ONE KNOWS PERHAPS JUST ENOUGH TO BE DANGEROUS OR STUMBLE INTO INTERNECINE CROSS-DISCIPLINARY WARS, YET NOT ENOUGH TO BE TRULY HINDERED BY EXPERTISE OR TEMPTED TO PASS DEFINITIVE JUDGMENT ON THEMES AND ISSUES WHICH TO THE LAYPERSON APPEAR TO BE BRIDGES BETWEEN THOSE SAME SILOS OR DISCRETE AREAS OF PRACTICE.

I am not an economist or historian. I am not a philosopher or scientist. I am a reader in reflection, floating over and across worlds inhabited on a full-time basis by others and not fully grounded in any particular, single perspective on what "is" or doctrinal belief in how the world operates.

But this—the limitation of one's ability to fully understand a single framework—is the situation shared by each of us, even the professed experts, since in addition to the challenge of fully comprehending any one discipline, there is always more knowledge to absorb, more wisdom to divine, more information to take in, to process, to integrate into what one believes one already knows. Over seventy-five years ago, the Austrian psychoanalyst Otto Rank is said to have temporarily stopped writing, stating, "There is already too much truth in the world—an over-production which apparently cannot be consumed!"[1] I doubt whether the challenge has subsided in this age of the incessant noise of over sharing, crowd sourced knowledge and a time when each and every person feels they have something worth offering regarding their lives and loves, much less their deeper truths, which seem far less frequently plumbed.

At the beginning of my intentional quest of reading and modest reflection, I was naive enough to think I had something new or unique to share. Instead, I've found time and again that just as I thought I understood in some distinct way, someone else—a person or a community of thought—had arrived well before me. The experience of quite literally finding several books in a row that were *my* books to be written but had already been authored was at first humiliating for someone often introduced as a thought leader and yet later, calming. The truth is nothing I experience has not been experienced before. The rush of discovery and insight that surges through me as I come on a new piece of work or have what I think is a new insight is not mine, but ours, coursing down through centuries and across many multiples of generations of mostly faceless and often nameless others.

All one need do is pause to absorb it, reflect upon it and receive it as the gift that is mine, ours and, with consideration of the Other, theirs. All I need do is turn off the computer, shut down the iPad and await its revelation. I would submit, with great appreciation of its irony, that those of us who speak constantly have less to say than we presume.

In contrast, those who retreat into both our historic journey and their own sense of a deeper, exposed Self have more we might hear, if we simply stop talking, producing and consuming in favor of calm reflection and possible reception of the revelations that await in the stillness.

Or, as Jimi Hendrix is supposed to have said, knowledge speaks, but wisdom listens.

A good reading life begins with a good life of quiet and reflection in order for one to hear and appreciate the questions—the *real* questions—one is grappling with. In that quiet, you may hear your true Self and understand more concerning what you are and are not, what you know and know not, which then feeds directly into how one sets the course for a life of more intentional reading, exploration and personal reflection. Saint Augustine famously said,

> "Do not go outside; return into yourself.
> In the inner human being dwells the truth."

For me, what began as a research endeavor to connect dots in new ways and promote supposedly new perspectives has settled into a reading life, a way of connecting what was with what we seek to create anew within this our time before we pass. One studies a body of thought and area of inquiry, thinking you get it and understand its fundamentals only to discover later—whether months or years—that your insight was mistaken or fell short of its potential and there was more to discover and appreciate within the countless currents that make up the deep human river.

As Peter Orner says,

> "Stories fail if you read them only once.
> You've got to meet a story again and again, in different moods,
> in different eras of your life."[2]

This is true not only of narrative and fiction but of the big stories of human history. What I read as a youth had a different meaning to me than when later in life I returned to read the same story (whether of philosophy or history or politics or science).

Or as Susan Sontag observed,

> "No book is worth reading once if it is not worth reading
> many times."[3]

This is why The Reading Life is so critical to one's development and evolution of understanding of self, society and humanity. All this—economics, philosophy, science, spirituality and more—already exists. It is simply layer upon layer of a fabric pulled back but found to be now layered again, exposed in time worn ways and shiny as it flows from past to future, all as one. The Reading Life makes one acutely aware of the limitations of the Self as much as the fundamental connection to the Whole as the means by which we may overcome our individual borders. All one need do is be open to the process and willing to surrender to what awaits. Our egos and identities are the only obstacles to be overcome. Everything else is free to be received.

During my recent year of thinking dangerously, I spoke at a gathering of multi-millionaires, saying a few words about how I was reflecting upon the need for us to focus on the "Why" of impact investing and how I'd gone off the conference circuit for the previous year in order to commit myself to a life of focused reading and reflection, while continuing my client advisory work. Following my comments, a gentleman came up to me and said: "I can't tell you how much I admire what you're doing…I would love to be in a position to take the time to read the way you are, but I just can't—I simply have too much else I need to be doing.…"

I smiled and thanked him for his support, but what I wanted to say was how is it possible I could find a way to engage in a journey of reading and reflection while still carrying a full complement of client families I was advising when he, a man of significant financial wealth, could not step back in any way to try to do something of the same in order to go deeper in his own journey? What was the purpose of his capital if not to give him the freedom to pursue his journey more fully?

I wanted to remind him of the passage from the Pirke Avot, a book of Judaic Wisdom Literature, which states, "Don't say, 'When I have leisure, I will study—perhaps you will never have that leisure…'".[4]

A second interesting encounter I had was with a colleague (a well-known impact investment advisor, at least within my circle), who upon seeing a short stack of New York Review of Books on a table in my home commented, "Wow—great to see you reading those! I have to say,

I've tried, but the articles are all on things I don't know anything about; they were too hard to get through, so I stopped reading them..."

I couldn't help but cringe at his words, but also agree the NYRB often took me places that were challenging—but it was all I could do not to reply with a bit of shock and wonder in that the very reason I *do* read NYRB religiously is because it expands my world and brain, while opening up periods of our history, culture and shared experience I've not been exposed to and introduces me to new perspectives I'd otherwise not encountered. Some of my best reading is there, as well as many of my most exciting literary discoveries that have helped guide my present journey of personal development.

The difference between taking a sabbatical and engaging in a reading life is that in the sabbatical one's time is spent away from work and usually focused upon a given end or product—to study a particular period in time, to produce a book or article—whereas in the reading life, one looks to integrate reflection, the groomed and tailored thoughts of others and the wisdom of the ages, into and within your life.

My reading is a form of praxis wherein the new perspectives I'm exploring come to be integrated within the new experiences and work in which I'm engaged which then come to be informed by my reading, the direction and form of which is then shaped in turn by the improvement and refinement of my work, and on and on. The reading life has become a part of my effort to integrate my activities with my reflections into a more holistic approach to being in the world in both my personal and my professional capacities. In the end, this may all be a question of adhering to the following:

Pause often along the ridgelines of the ranges we explore and meadows we inhabit, listening for those who have tread this path before.

ADDENDUM

Acknowledgments

I offer deep thanks to the many ancient and modern prophets, activists, philosophers and writers whose work over past centuries has directed my journey and informed my path over more recent years. I pay tribute to those many colleagues and collaborators whose comments, work and pushback have shaped my life reflections on our shared experience. And I give thanks to those many elders who have guided me in my growth.

While there are many deserving of my recognition—the complete number of which would fill its own book of acknowledgment—this list would certainly include such positive teachers as Minoru Yasui (a civil rights activist who, after being convicted of breaking curfew during World War II and incarcerated in an internment camp for Japanese Americans, went on to take part in a class action lawsuit against the United States Government regarding the incarceration of his community and later was founding director of the Commission on Community Relations in Denver, Colorado, where I worked as a teen and received critical mentorship from Min) and George R. Roberts (co-founder of the private equity firm Kohlberg Kravis Roberts & Company and whose personal and philanthropic investments opened new avenues for me in my early thirties, placing me on this present life course). My life would not be the same where it not for these and other mentors who have directed me on my way.

A list might also include those who otherwise influenced me over past decades, such as Bull Connor (Commissioner of Public Safety in Birmingham, Alabama, whose decision to set fire hoses and police dogs on citizens defending their civil rights stirred the conscience of America—as well as my own) and, of course, our current President, who by living as our Shadow has given me and others opportunity to focus on becoming more fully woke, going deeper in reflection, cultivation and action to realize our true purpose.

In a more positive posture, I offer my thanks to those who served as advisors and reviewers of this document. These include:

Danny Almagor, Marc Epstein, John Elkington, Jim Emerson, Tim Freundlich, Andrew Kassoy, Ivo Knoepfel, Charly Kleisner, Berry Liberman, Lindsay Louie, David McConville, Bill Meehan, Bernard Mercer, Jack Meyercord, Lorrie Meyercord, Sara Minard, Halvor Namtvedt, Alex Nicholls, Diana de Propper, Jason Scott, Don Shaffer, Evan Steiner, Volker Then, Rabbi Batshir Torchio, Brian Trelstad, Fay Twersky, Matthew Weatherley-White, Adam Wolfenson.

While their advice and suggestions have been important to the development of this effort, I remain responsible for the final content.

My thanks also to The William and Flora Hewlett Foundation and Ms. Annie Chen for their critical strategic partnership, personal feedback and other support that helped provide the opportunity for me to engage in this work over the past three years.

My thanks to Herb Schaffner. I also thank Domini Dragoone, who executed the layout and design of the book as well as its cover. And deep thanks to my long time friend and artistic collaborator on this project, Dana Smith, whose enthusiasm and openness to exploring the intersect of my writing with her art made a world of difference in the quality of this offering. My appreciation also goes to my Research Associate, Adam Isbiroglu, for his invaluable assistance in organizing the books, materials and work environment to assist in expanding my knowledge on these various topics explored.

My thanks and love to my wife, Mia Haugen, whose grounded perspective, gentle questions, editorial suggestions and boundless support are what have made this document possible. And thanks to our Norwegian family who put up with my writing periods at our hytte in Ustaoset, Norway. Love to my father, the Rev. Dr. James G. Emerson; in addition to his own books, this one is also part of his intellectual legacy. And, of course, my love to Bella for her pure engagement of the journey.

Author's Note

CULTURAL CONTEXT

This book is an inquiry into the purpose of capital as explored against the development and current practices of modern, financial capitalism. While its themes and topics are ones common to many cultures, the basic framework is what could be considered Western cultural as rooted in the Enlightenment and various schools of thought arising from that period. This book is also written from the perspective of an older, male, white American, with all that might entail.

This is not to say other cultures I touch upon and may draw from are not worth highlighting and exploring in greater detail than I was able to do in this initial inquiry as much as to acknowledge many of the current social, environmental and other challenges we face have their roots in assumptions, mindsets and perspectives of a Western cultural framework. In the future, it is my hope to collaborate with others in exploring more deeply how various cultures have responded to issues of meaning and the purpose of capital.

SOURCES AND USES

This manuscript is the end result of nearly three years of reading, reflection and research, during which I read scores of books and traced a variety of concepts down through the centuries. I created a reference library of 4,000 books and would often pull a volume, read a section and find a spark I would carry into my own thinking.

To manage this process, I created an initial research manuscript which exceeded 420-pages of tight text and included a large number of excerpts from a host of sources. That document then formed the basis for this present manuscript, which has now itself gone through many multiple drafts, culling and condensing of many other writers' work that informed my thinking.

I have made a genuine and sincere effort to ensure I accurately tracked sources, quotes and ideas and yet recognize much of what I say has been explored by others over years and years. In fact, it should be obvious questions of meaning and purpose are at the center of the human experience over millennium. The following sections document specific quotes used in the text and highlight a collection of books and writers whose work was important in my own writing and exploration. My deep thanks to each of you.

In addition to this footnotes section, the reader is directed to this document's Bibliography and "Best Books" sections for additional information regarding books I drew upon in this process, as well as those I felt were especially worthwhile in my reading and reflection.

On Words and Images

When presented with the possibility of working with Jed to illustrate his latest writing I thought we were two unlikely collaborators. How do a fine artist and a philosopher/economist find creative synergy? But, as Jed says, dissonance leads to breakthroughs. Happily, Jed's willingness to engage with "the Other" extends to myself and that is the spirit in which he approached me to create an image-based dimension for this book.

As an artist I often work collaboratively, which always requires adaptation. In this case, Jed asked me to provide images to reflect his manuscript that is in part biography and in part an historical critique of financial capitalism. This text initially appeared difficult to illustrate. But, one of the fundamental ideas Jed discusses is that the heart must inform investment decisions along with the brain—they are two parts of a whole. I saw that brain/heart dichotomy reflected in the relationship between word and image presented by the project. I wanted the images to engage the text in conversation, not just to illustrate. I did not want my images to be a pretty place to rest from Jed's fiery discourse, but to confront the reader/viewer with the same inescapable economic, social, and personal dilemmas that are presented in his text.

An artistic strategy I often work with is collage. When two or more source images are placed in juxtaposition they form a conversation and together acquire new meaning. It is the viewer that creates that new meaning upon viewing the collage. An unexpected juxtaposition of images invites an active form of seeing which frees the brain to interpret rather than just identify. Thus the viewer is actively involved an ongoing process of (re)interpretation which expands—while at the same time personalizing—the collage's meaning.

For each of the illustrations included in this volume, I selected two images that when combined create a tense visual conversation, which is most eloquently described in Jed's exploration of the many dualistic elements of our society, nature/technology, rich/poor, Self/Other, and how these seemingly oppositional forces may find mutual ground and in the end are simply a blend, an integrated whole of the value we create in the course of our lives.

—Dana Smith,
San Francisco, California,
Dana Smith Gallery

My Best Books

When I come upon blogs with titles such as the "Top 10 books" or "The Top Books You Must Read," I can only laugh and move on. The "best" books are only best for each reader within a certain timeframe and point along one's journey.

I read many classics in my youth—and am glad I did—yet I have concluded my understanding and appreciation of them fell short of what either their authors intended or my mentors hoped for me to take away from their pages. Books—and more importantly, the ideas held within them—connect and reverberate in a soul based upon where that soul is in its own process of evolution. One person's top ten list may be another's worst time spent reading list.

While Truth lies constant beneath the soil, each of us who till the earth do so under diverse skies, with differing mulch, moisture and seed. The experience of resonating with the words laid out in a book is a condition of our own state of mind and potential to understand what is meant versus what we might hear or receive.

I did not engage in my reading process in a logical way, but rather one topic led me to another and to another. I began by simply wanting to understand more of how we got here, our world history and evolution, in terms of religion, social history and economic development. Generally speaking, I began with an exploration of the history of economics, which took me to world history, the history of natural science, philosophy and religion, finally landing me into a whole host of readings having to do with physics—which, interestingly enough, brought me back to religion.

Accordingly, the following are some of the more significant authors and books I read in this process, however first and foremost, I went back and read many of the "original" philosophers; Pre-Socratic philosophers and so on. This was followed by reading many of the Enlightenment philosophers, of whom Spinoza was my favorite; which was then followed by more modern folks: Arne Naess, Richard Rohr, Gary Snyder and Karen Armstrong in particular.

There were very few books in my bibliography that I read which I did not benefit from in one way or another. However, if you are looking for a starting place to a reading life, I believe reading the following books would enrich your journey.

The Illusion of Separation: Exploring the Cause of our Current Crisis
Giles Hutchins (Definitely one of my favorite reads and one of a set of good books from Hutchins, who also maintains an active blog worth following and reflecting upon).

The Practice of the Wild
Gary Snyder (Love this guy...His writing is excellent and he offers a really nice take on integrating deep reflection with Buddhist practice and human knowledge. Totally worth reading a number of his books, but this one gave me a lot to think about).

How Much is Enough? The Love of Money, And the Case for the Good Life
Robert Skidelsky and Edward Skidelsky (One of my favorites—a great historical overview of our understanding of meaning and money, along with a solid summary of their framework for the Good Life. Definitely worth reading!)

Walking On Lava: Selected Works for Uncivilized Times
The Dark Mountain Project (After spending six weeks off line working on this project, I returned home to find my 'hot off the presses' copy of this book and it immediately became one of my best reads...Much of what I read is about finance and impact investing. It is nice to read something that comes at my issues of concern from the left side of the stage and sings).

Fields of Blood: Religion and the History of Violence
Karen Armstrong (Pretty much anything by Armstrong—she is great…
but this one was important in teasing out the contribution of economic
development to class and other conflicts, and contrasting that with religious evolution).

Through the Eye of a Needle: Wealth, the Fall of Rome,
and the Making of Christianity in the West, 350—550 AD
Peter Brown (Probably more in the weeds than many will need, but
fascinating in its detail of this important period of transition)

The Origin of Wealth:
Evolution, Complexity and the Radical Remaking of Economics
Eric Beinhacker (A very strong overview of the development of eco-
nomics and where wealth comes from).

The Silk Roads: A New History of the World
Peter Frankopan (Really fascinating overview of the historic links
between East and West that includes a strong discussion of the global
slave trade which occurred in the first millennium and which should
pretty much put to rest any ideas you have regarding the separation of
our races, creeds and peoples. Spoiler alert: We're all related…).

Sapiens: A Brief History of Humankind
Yuval Noah Harari (He has many fans now and I really like his work as
well—but I do not agree with his conclusions regarding the supremacy
of man or what I felt was his relative dismissal of spiritual experience).

Mankind and Mother Earth: A Narrative History of the World
Arnold Toynbee (A great book on ancient history and tracking our
experience within the biosphere from prehistory to modern times).

The Ascent of Money: A Financial History of the World
Niall Ferguson (This is a great piece of work—but places too much faith
in market economics).

The Myth of the Rational Market:
A History of Risk, Reward, and Delusion on Wall Street
Justin Fox (Perhaps one of my favorite books—this one really opened up a new world of critique for me...and is a great balance to the previous entry!).

Retrieving the Ancients: An Introduction to Greek Philosophy
David Roochnik (A really wonderful introduction to how early philosophy evolved).

The Age of the Sages: The Axial Age in Asia and the Near East
Mark Muesse (Really worth reading—connected a lot of dots for me).

The Axial Age and Its Consequences
Edited by Robert Bellah and Hans Joas (A collection of relatively academic writings by a diverse set of folks; for those who really want to drill into the topic)

The Systems View of Life: A Unifying Vision
Fritjof Capra and Pier Luigi Luisi (Basically a textbook, but worth reading in that it gives one a real grounding in Systems Theory).

The Big Picture: On the Origins of Life, Meaning, and the Universe Itself
Sean Carroll (A really solid offering linking physics with philosophy—but not the last word).

The Evolution of Minds: From Bacteria to Bach and Back
Daniel Dennett (Fairly dense for your armchair philosopher—uh, me!—but just a really interesting read...).

Leadership and the New Science: Discovering Order in a Chaotic World
Margaret Wheatley (This is a classic and really worth tracking down...).

The Myth of Enlightenment: Seeing Through the Illusion of Separation
Karl Renz (The title says it all...really good read!).

Nonduality: A Study in Comparative Philosophy
David Loy (a little dense and detailed, but a great unpacking of the issue of dualism and philosophic approaches to same).

The Collapse of Western Civilization: A View From the Future
Naomi Orestes and Erik Conway (Perhaps the shortest book I read, but one of the most provocative).

The Birth of the Anthropocene
Jeremy Davies (As reflected in how heavily I referenced this work, I thought his framing and presentation of the topic was excellent and definitely worth your reading).

After Nature: A Politics for the Anthropocene
Jedidiah Purdy (In addition to Davies' book above, I read a number of books on the Anthropocene, each of which offered a different perspective and are worth reading. Purdy's work was very solid and a great addition to my collection. Also, see Angus below as well...).

Ecology, Community and Lifestyle
Arne Naess, as Translated by David Rothenberg (The one who coined the term "deep ecology" I have read many of his writings and while he can be hard to get through, he is always rewarding in the end).

Deep Ecology for the 21st Century:
Readings on the Philosophy and Practice of the New Environmentalism
George Sessions (Perhaps one of my favorite books; a great collection from a number of authors that really pulls it all together).

No Rising Tide: Theology, Economics and the Future
Joerg Rieger (One of my favorite books; very challenging in its implications and with a great critique of Milton Friedman).

Economics of Good and Evil:
The Quest of Economic Meaning from Gilgamesh to Wall Street
Tomas Sedlacek (One of the books I thought I was supposed to write, this one pulls together a host of religious and economic thought. Really a great and challenging read).

It's Not About The Money:
Unlock Your Money Type to Achieve Spiritual and Financial Abundance
Brent Kessel (A good reflection on investment practice and how to assess your own "money type"—one of eight—in order to understand more of who you are and what you're trying to attain through your investments).

A Redder Shade of Green: Intersections of Science and Socialism
Ian Angus (Angus offers a set of really solid reflections here. Together with his other book, *Facing the Anthropocene*, he offers one a great deal to consider in terms of how we must advance our work within the context of global financial capitalism).

The Four Nobel Truths of Wealth: A Buddhist View of Economic Life
Layth Matthews (A fairly basic introduction—but a solid review of the fundamentals).

Beyond Religion: Ethics for a Whole World
His Holiness The Dali Lama (This book explores the common values and beliefs which connect each of us to the Other. A really sound exploration of much of what we have experienced over the centuries and points a direction toward where we need to go)

The Wilds of Poetry: Adventures in Mind and Landscape
David Hinton (This is a great presentation of diverse and pioneering poets from Whitman through some of today's best. Hinton offers not only some of the best passages of poetry, but gives the reader the biography and context necessary to appreciate why those he selected are so central to our current understanding of poetry and the world).

The Ecocentrists: A History of Radical Environmentalism
Keith Makoto Woodhouse (This is the last book I've read in this process and I'm doing so as I work on my final edits—but I wish I'd read it amongst my first, though it only just came out. Much of my current thinking regarding capital is integrative of environmental issues and new thinking, which is basically the topic of this excellent history. Well worth the read!).

Dancing Standing Still: Healing the World from a Place of Prayer
Richard Rohr (Rohr does an excellent job integrating reflections on contemplation with being active in the world. His Center and weekly newsletter are well worth exploration as is this book).

The Soul of Money: Reclaiming the Wealth of Our Inner Resources
Lynne Twist (It is only appropriate to end this set of recommendations with a classic in the field. If you have not had the opportunity, you really need to read this one!)

Crumbs on a Path:
A Partial Bibliography

The process by which I engaged in my reading was what I called an "open architecture inquiry." I would read of book of history, philosophy or finance and become embraced by a story of humanity. I would see reference to a book, author or concept I wasn't familiar with or was intrigued by and would search out that book, which would then in turn reveal some other conceptual path of exploration and off I'd go.

In the end, I had created a reference library of nearly 4,000 volumes and have at this point read over two hundred and fifty books over now three years while working full-time with my clients. It has been an incredible experience and is a reading life I hope to continue. That said, while I've tried to keep track of various readings, I've found it harder than I expected to list each book I've explored. What follows is a sound bibliography for the quotes and references in this text, but may not include everything I actually read. Think of the following as crumbs on a path, leading into the dark woods of a warm night. I welcome your own suggestions of additional paths and lights along the way!

1. Abbas Amanat, Iran: A Modern History, Yale University Press: New Haven, CT, 2017.
2. Benedict Anderson, Imagined Communities: Reflections on the Origin and Spread of Nationalism, Verso Press: London, 1983/2016.
3. Ian Angus, A Redder Shade of Green: Intersections of Science and Socialism, Monthly Review Press: New York City, NY, 2017.
4. Ian Angus, Facing the Anthropocene, Monthly Review Press: New York: NY, 2016.
5. Kwame Anthony Appiah, Cosmopolitanism: Ethics in a World of Strangers, Norton and Company: New York City, NY, 2006

6. Karen Armstrong, A Short History of Myth, Canongate Press: Edinburgh/New York, 2005.

7. Karen Armstrong, Fields of Blood: Religion and the History of Violence, Anchor Press: 2015.

8. Hannah Arendt, Eichmann in Jerusalem: A Report on the Banality of Evil, Penguin Classics: New York, NY, 1963.

9. Hannah Arendt, The Life of the Mind, Harcourt Press: San Diego, CA, 1971.

10. Jesse Ball, Notes On My Dunce Cap, Pioneerworks: New York, NY, 2017.

11. William Barber, A History of Economic Thought, Wesleyan University Press: Middletown, CT, 1967.

12. Susan Wise Bauer,The Well-Educated Mind: A Guide to the Classical Education You Never Had, Norton Press: New York City, NY, 2003

13. Mario Beauregard and Denyse O'Leary, The Spiritual Brain: A Neuroscientist's Case for the Existence of the Soul, Harper One: New York, 2007.

14. Eric Beinhacker, The Origin of Wealth: Evolution, Complexity and the Radical Remaking of Economics, Harvard Business School Press: Boston, MA, 2006

15. Robert Bellah and Hans Joas, The Axial Age and Its Consequences, Eds., Belknap Press: Cambridge, MA, 2012.

16. Medea Benjamin, Inside Iran: The Real History of the Politics of the Islamic Republic of Iran, OR Books: New York, NY, 2018.

17. Lee Benson, et. al., Knowledge for Social Change: Bacon, Dewey and the Rvolutionary Transformation of Research Universities in the Twenty-First Century, Temple University Press: Philadelphia, PA, 2017.

18. William Bernstein, The Birth of Plenty: How the Prosperity of the Modern World was Created, McGraw-Hill: New York, NY, 2004.

19. Thomas Berry, The Great Work: Our Way Into The Future, Three Rivers Press: New York City, NY, 1999

20. Joseph Beuys, What is Money? A Discussion, et al., Clearview Press: Forest Row, UK, 2009.

21. Hans Christoph Binswanger, Money and Magic: A Critique of the Modern Economy in Light of Goethe's Faust, University of Chicago Press: Chicago, IL, 1985.

22. John Bloom, The Genius of Money: Essays and Interviews Reimagining the Financial World, SteinerBooks: Great Barrington, MA, 2009.

23. John C. Bogle, Enough: True Measures of Money, Business and Life, John Wiley and Sons: Hoboken, New Jersey, 2009.

24. Dietrich Bonhoeffer, The Cost of Discipleship, Simon and Shuster: New York City, NY, 1959

25. Walter Brueggemann, Money and Possessions, Westminster John Knox Press: Louisville, KY, 2016.

26. Peter Brown, Through the Eye of a Needle: Wealth, the Fall of Rome, and the Making of Christianity in the West, 350—550 AD, Princeton University Press: Princeton, New Jersey, 2012.

27. Robert Mcafee Brown, The Essential Reinhold Niebuhr, Yale University Press: New Haven, CT, 1986.
28. James Buchan, Frozen Desire: The Meaning of Money, Farrar, Straus and Giroux: New York, NY, 1997.
29. Christopher Budd, Prelude in Economics: A New Approach to Economics, Johanus Academy of Sociology and Economics: West Sussex, UK, 1979.
30. Susan Cain, Quiet: The Power of Introverts in a World That Can't Stop Talking, Broadway Books: New York City, NY, 2012.
31. Fritjof Capra and Pier Luigi Luisi, The Systems View of Life: A Unifying Vision, Cambridge University Press: Cambridge, UK, 2014.
32. Matthew Carr, Blood and Faith: The Purging of Muslim Spain, New Press: New York City, NY, 2009.
33. Carroll, Sean, The Big Picture: On the Origins of Life, Meaning, and the Universe Itself, Dutton Press: New York City, NY, 2016
34. Thomas Cathcart and Daniel Klein, Plato and a Platypus Walk Into a Bar..., Penguin Books: New York City, NY, 2007.
35. Owen Chadwick, The Reformation, Penguin Books: London, UK, 1964.
36. Clayton Christensen , How Will You Measure Your Life?, Harper Collins Press: New York City, NY, 2012.
37. Kenneth Clark, Civilization, Harper and Row: New York, 1969.
38. Eric Cline, 1177 BC: The Year Civilization Collapsed, Princeton University Press: Princeton, NJ, 2014.
39. Paulo Coelho, The Alchemist, Harper One: New York City, NY, 1993.
40. Michael Cohen, The Pathless Way: John Muir and the American Wilderness, University of Wisconsin Press: Madison, WI, 1984.
41. Chuck Collins, Born on Third Base: A One Percenter Makes the Case for Tackling Inequality, Bringing Wealth Home, and Committing to the Common Good, Chelsea Green Publishing: White River, VT, 2016.
42. Peter Cozzens, The Earth is Weeping: The Epic Story of the Indian Wars for the American West, Alfred Knopf: New York, NY, 2016.
43. Ray Dalio, Principles, Simon Schuster: New York, NY, 2017.
44. Dark Mountain Project, Walking on Lava: Selected Works for Uncivilized Times, Chelsea Green Publishing: White River Junction, VT, 2017.
45. George Elliot David and Friedrich Strauss, The Life of Jesus: Critically Examined, Restoration Editors: New York, NY.
46. Jeremy Davies, The Birth of the Anthropocene, University of California Press: Oakland, CA, 2016.
47. Ashley Dawson, Extinction: A Radical History, OR Books: New York City, NY, 2016
48. Daniel Dennett, The Evolution of Minds: From Bacteria to Bach and Back, Norton & Co.: New York City, 2017.
49. Dowie, Mark, Losing Ground: American Environmentalism at the Close of the 21st Century, The MIT Press, Cambridge, Massachusetts, 1995.

50. Peter Drucker, Post-Capitalist Society, Harper Business Books: New York City, NY, 1993.
51. Charles Duhigg, The Power of Habit: Why We Do What We Do In Life and Business, Random House: New York City, NY, 2012
52. Will & Ariel Durant, The Lessons of History, Simon and Schuster: New York City, NY, 1968.
53. Freeman Dyson, Dreams of Earth and Sky, New York Review of Books: New York City, NY, 2015.
54. Charles Eisenstein, Sacred Economics: Money, Gift & Society in the Age of Transition, Evolver Editions: Berkeley, CA., 2011.
55. Niall Ferguson, The Ascent of Money: A Financial History of the World, Penguin Books Group: New York City, 2008
56. William Finnegan, Barbarian Days: A Surfing Life, Penguin Books: New York, NY, 2015.
57. Justin Fox, The Myth of the Rational Market: A History of Risk, Reward, and Delusion on Wall Street, Harper Business: New York, 2009
58. Peter Frankopan, The Silk Roads: A New History of the World, Alfred Knopf: New York, NY, 2016,
59. Peter Frase, Four Futures: Life After Capitalism, Verso Press: London/New York, 2016
60. Paula Fredriksen, Jesus of Nazareth: King of the Jews, Vintage Books: New York, NY, 1999.
61. Sigmund Freud, Todd Dufresne, The Future of Illusion, edited by, Broadview Editions: Ontario, Canada, 2012
62. Milton Friedman, Capitalism and Freedom, University of Chicago Press: Chicago, IL, 1962 Friedman, Thomas, Thank You for Being Late: An Optimist's Guide to Thriving in the Age of Accelerations, Farrar, Straus and Giroux: New York, 2016.
63. Susi Geiger, Debbie Harrison, et al, eds., Concerned Markets: Economic Ordering for Multiple Values, Edward Elgar Publishing: Cheltenham, UK, 2014.
64. Robert Goldman and Stephen Papson, Landscapes of Capital: Representing Time, Space and Globalization in Corporate Advertising, Polity Press: Cambridge, UK; 2011.
65. Dane Gordon and David Suits, Epicurus: His Continuing Influence and Contemporary Relevance, Rit Cary Graphic Arts Press: Rochester, NY, 2003
66. Anthony Gottlieb, The Dream of Enlightenment: The Rise of Modern Philosophy, Liverlight Publishing Corporation: New York, 2016.
67. Harvey Graff, Undisciplining Knowledge: Interdisciplinary in the Twentieth Century, Johns Hopkins University Press: Baltimore, 2015.
68. Grant Adam, Originals: How Non-Conformists Move the World, Viking Press: New York City, 2015.
69. Thomas Greco, The End of Money And the Future of Civilization, Chelsea Green Publications: White River Junction, VT, 2009

70. John Michael Greer, After Progress: Reason and Religion at the End of the Industrial Age, New Society Publishers: Gabriola Island, BC, 2015.
71. Stephen Gresham, Advisor for Life: Become the Indespensible Financial Advisor to Affluent Families, John Wiley and Sons: Hoboken, NJ, 2007.
72. Ray Grigg, The New Lao Tzu: A Contemporary Tao Te Ching, Charles Tuttle and Company: Rutland, VT, 1995.
73. Thich Nhat Hanh, Living Buddha, Living Christ, Riverhead Books: New York City, NY, 1995.
74. Yuval Noah Harari, Sapiens: A Brief History of Humankind, Vintage Books: London, 2011.
75. Donna Haraway, Staying with the Trouble: Making Kin in the Chthulucene, Duke University Press: Durham, NC, 2016.
76. David Harvey, Marx, Capital and the Madness of Economic Reason, Oxford University Press: Oxford, UK, 2018.
77. Paul Hawken, Drawdown: The Most Comprehensive Plan Ever Proposed to Reverse Global Warming, Edited by, Penguin Books Random House: New York City, 2017.
78. Richard Holmes, The Age of Wonder, Vintage Books: New York, NY, 2008.
79. Kulananda and Dominic Houlder, Mindfulness and Money: The Buddhist Path of Abundance, Broadway Books: New York City, NY, 2002.
80. Hutchins, Giles, The Illusion of Separation: Exploring the Cause of our Current Crisis, Floris Books, 2014.
81. Vivian Hutchinson, the New Zealand Social Entrepreneur Fellowship, Hong Kong SE Book Hub: Hong Kong, 2011.
82. Jonathan Israel, Radical Enlightenment: Philosophy and the Making of Modernity 1650-1750, Oxford University Press: Oxford, UK, 2001.
83. Pico Iyer, The Art of Stillness: Adventures of Nowhere, Simon Schuster: New York, 2014.
84. Christopher Ives, Zen Awakening and Society, University of Hawaii Press: Honolulu, HI, 1992.
85. David Jaber, Our Historic Moment: Purpose, Planet and Places to Intervene, Self-Published: www.ourhistoricmoment.com, 2017
86. Derrick Jensen, The Myth of Human Supremacy, Seven Stories Press: New York, 2016.
87. Dan Jones, Magna Carta: The Birth of Liberty, Penguin Books: New York, 2015.
88. Fredrik Jonsson, Enlightenment's Frontier: The Scottish Highlands and the Origins of Environmentalism, Yale University Press: New Haven, CT, 2013.
89. Robert Kaplan, The Nothing That Is: A Natural History of Zero, Oxford University Press: Oxford, UK, 1999.
90. James Karman, Robinson Jeffers: Poet and Prophet, Stanford University Press: Palo Alto, CA, 2015.
91. Dainin Katagiri, Each Moment is the Universe: Zen and the Way of Being Time, Shambhala Publications, 2007

92. Aileen Kelly, The Discovery of Chance: The Life and Thought of Alexander Herzen, Harvard University Press: Harvard, MA, 2016.

93. Brent Kessel, It's Not About The Money: Unlock Your Money Type to Achieve Spiritual and Financial Abundance, Harper One: New York City, NY, 2008.

94. Daniel Klein, Travels with Epicurus: A Journey to a Greek Island in Search of a Fulfilled Life, Penguin Books: New York, NY, 2012.

95. Roman Krznaric, The Wonder Box: Curious Histories of How to Live, Profile Books: London, UK, 2012.

96. Satish Kumar, No Destination: Autobiography of a Pilgrim, Green Books: Cambridge, UK, 1992.

97. Hans Kung and Rabbi Walter Homolka, How to Do Good and Avoid Evil: A Global Ethic from the Sources of Judaism, Skylight Paths Publishing: Woodstock, VT, 2009.

98. Dalai Lama, Beyond Religion: Ethics for a Whole World, Mariner Books: Boston, 2011.

99. Misia Landau, Narratives of Human Evolution, Yale University Press: New Haven, CT, 1991.

100. Jeremy Lent, The Patterning Instinct: A Cultural History of Humanity's Search for Meaning, Prometheus Books: Amherst, MA, 2017.

101. Michael Lowy, Ecosocialism: A Radical Alternative to Capitalist Catastrophe, Haymarket Books: Chicago, IL, 2015.

102. John Paul Lederach, The Moral Imagination: The Art and Soul of Building Peace, Oxford University Press: Oxford, England, 2005

103. Les Leopold, Runaway Inequality: An Activist's Guide to Economic Justice, Labor Institute Press: New York, NY, 2015.

104. Emmanuel Levinas, Time & the Other, Duquesne University Press: Pittsburgh, PA, 1987.

105. Alan Lightman and Roberta Brawer, Origins: The Lives and Worlds of Modern Cosmologists, Harvard University Press: Cambridge, MA, 1990.

106. Living Earth: Field Notes from the Dark Ecology Project 2014-2016, Sonic Acts Press, 2016.

107. James Lovelock, A Rough Ride to the Future, Overlook Books: New York, NY, 2014.

108. David Loy, Nonduality: A Study in Comparative Philosophy, Humanity Books: Amherst, NY, 1988.

109. Joanna Macy, Active Hope: How to Face the Mess We're in Without Going Crazy, New World Library: Novato, CA, 2012.

110. John Maeda, The Laws of Simplicity: Design, Technology, Business and Life, MIT Press: Cambridge, MA, 2006

111. Jerry Mander, In the Absence of the Sacred: The Failure of Technology and the Survival of the Indian Nations, Sierra Club Books: San Francisco CA, 1991

112. Manguel, Alberto, A History of Reading, Penguin Books: New York City, NY, 1996.
113. Philip Marcovici, The Destructive Power of Family Wealth: A Guide to Succession Planning, Asset Protection, Taxation and Wealth Management, John Wiley Press: West Sussex, UK, 2016.
114. Scott Martelle, Blood Passion: The Ludlow Massacre and Class War in the American West, Rutgers University Press: New Brunswick, NJ, 2007.
115. A. H. Maslow, Religions, Values, and Peak-Experiences, Penguin Compass: New York City, NY, 1964/1970,
116. Layth Matthews, The Four Nobel Truths of Wealth: A Buddhist View of Economic Life, Enlightened Economy Books: US, 2014.
117. Grant Maxwell, The Dynamics of Transformation: Tracing An Emerging World View, Persistent Press: Nashville, TN, 2017
118. Alastair McIntosh, Soil and Soul: People Versus Corporate Power, Arum Press: London, UK, 2001.
119. Ed McGaa Eagle Man, Native Wisdom: Perceptions of the Natural Way, Four Directions Publishing: Minneapolis, 1995.
120. Jon Meacham, The Soul of America: The Battle for Our Better Angels, Random House Press: New York, NY, 2018.
121. Stephen Meyer, The End of the Wild, Boston Review Press: Somerville, MA, 2006.
122. Louis Menand, The Metaphysical Club: A Story of Ideas in America, Farrar, Straus and Girox: 2001
123. Istvan Meszaros, The Structural Crisis of Capital, Monthly Review Press: New York, NY, 2010.
124. John Miller, A Crude Look at the World: The Science of Complex Systems in Business, Life and Society, Basic Books: New York, NY, 2015
125. Pankaj Mishra, Age of Anger: A History of the Present, Picador: New York, NY, 2017.
126. Umar Moghul, A Socially Responsible Islamic Finance: Character and the Common Good, Palgrave McMillan: Brooklyn, NY, 2017.
127. Jason Moore, Anthropocene or Capitalocene? Nature, History and the Crisis of Capitalism, Editor, PM Press: Oakland, CA, 2016.
128. Brian Morris, Pioneers of Ecological Humanism: Mumford, Dubos and Bookchin, BlackRose Books: Montreal, QC, CA, 2017.
129. Timothy Morton, Dark Ecology: For a Logic of Future Coexistence, Columbia University Press: New York, 2016.
130. Mark Muesse, The Age of the Sages: The Axial Age in Asia and the Near East, Fortress Press: Minneapolis, MN, 2013.
131. Jerry Muller, The Tyranny of Metrics, Princeton University Press: Princeton, NJ, 2018.
132. Arne Naess, Ecology, Community and Lifestyle, as Translated by David Rothenberg, Cambridge University Press: Cambridge, UK. 1989.

133. Daniel Nelson, Nature's Burden's: Conservation and American Politics, the Reagan Era to the Present, Utah State University Press: Logan, UT, 2017.
134. Friedrich Nietzsche, Anti-Education: On the Future of Our Educational Institutions, New York Review of Books: New York City, NY, 2016.
135. Michael Novak, The Spirit of Democratic Capitalism, Madison Books: Lanham, MD, 1982.
136. Michael Novak, Social Justice Isn't What You Think It Is, Encounter Books: New York City, NY, 2015.
137. Naomi Orestes and Erik Conway, The Collapse of Western Civilization: A View From the Future, Columbia University Press: New York City, NY, 2014.
138. Peter Orner, Am I Alone Here? Notes on Living to Read and Reading to Live, Catapult Press: New York, 2016.
139. Frank Ostaseski, The Five Invitations: Discovering What Death Can Teach Us About Living Fully, Flat Iron Books: New York City, NY, 2017.
140. David Papineau, Philosophy, Oxford University Press: Oxford, UK, 2009.
141. Karl Popper, The Open Society and Its Enemies, Princeton University Press: Princeton, NJ, 1994.
142. Eric Posner and Glen Weyl, Radical Markets: Uprooting Capitalism and Democracy for a Just Society, Princeton University Press: Princeton, New Jersey, 2018.
143. Jedidiah Purdy, After Nature: A Politics for the Anthropocene, Harvard University Press: Cambridge, MA, 2015.
144. Steven Radelet, The Great Surge: The Ascent of the Developing World, Simon and Schuster: New York, NY, 2015.
145. Gerardo Reichel-Dolmatoff, Rainforest Shamans: Essays on the Tufano Indians of the Northwest Amazon, Themis Books: Devon, UK, 1997.
146. Karl Renz, The Myth of Enlightenment: Seeing Through the Illusion of Separation, Inner Directions Press, 2005.
147. Ruth Richards, Everyday Creativity and New Views of Human Nature: Psychological, Social and Spiritual Perspectives., editor, American Psychological Association: Washington, D.C., 2009.
148. Matt Ridley, The Evolution of Everything: How New Ideas Emerge, Fourth Estate/HarperCollins Publishers, London, 2015.
149. Joerg Rieger, No Rising Tide: Theology, Economics and the Future, Fortress Press: Minneapolis, MN. 2009.
150. Geshe Michael Roach, The Diamond Cutter: The Buddha on Managing Your Business and Your Life, Double Day Press: New York City, NY, 2000.
151. Andrew Roberts, Napoleon: A Life, Penguin Books: New York City, NY, 2014
152. Marilyn Robinson, The Givenness of Things: Essays, Farrar, Straus and Giroux: New York, 2015, 29.
153. Richard Rohr, Dancing Standing Still: Healing the World from a Place of Prayer, Paulist Press: New York City, NY, 2014

154. David Roochnik, Retrieving the Ancients: An Introduction to Greek Philosophy, Blackwell Publishing: Malden, MA, 2004.

155. Carlo Rovelli, Seven Brief Lessons on Physics, Riverhead Books: New York, 2016.

156. Don Miguel Ruiz with Janet Mills, The Voice of Knowledge, Amber-Allen Publishing: San Rafael, CA, 2004.

157. Peter Sahlins, 1668: The Year of the Animal in France, Zone Books: New York, NY, 2017.

158. Edward Said, Culture and Imperialism, Vintage Press: New York City, NY, 1993.

159. Kirkpatrick Sale, Human Scale, Revisted: A New Look at the Classic Case for a Decentralist Future, Chelsea Green Publishing: White River Forks, VT, 2017.

160. Michael Sandel, What Money Can't Buy: The Moral Limits of Markets, Farrar, Straus and Giroux: New York City, NY, 2012

161. Carol Sanford, The Regenerative Business: Redesign Work, Cultivate Human Potential, Achieve Extraordinary Outcomes, Nicholas Brearley Publishing: London, UK, 2017.

162. Robert Sardello, Silence: The Mystery of Wholeness, Goldstone Press: Benson, North Carolina, 2006/2008.

163. Will Schwalbe, Books For Living, Alfred Knopf: New York, NY, 2017.

164. Walter Scheidel, The Great Leveler: Violence and the History of Inequality from the Stone Age to the Twenty-First Century, Princeton University Press: Princeton, New Jersey, 2017.

165. Roy Scranton, Learning to Die in the Anthropocene: Reflections on the End of Civilization, City Lights Books: San Francisco, CA, 2015.

166. Sessions, George, Deep Ecology for the 21st Century: Readings on the Philosohpy and Practice of the New Environmentalism, Shambhala, Boston, 1995

167. Tomas Sedlacek, Economics of Good and Evil: The Quest of Economic Meaning from Gilgamesh to Wall Street, Oxford University Press, Oxford: England, 2011.

168. Sulak Sivaraksa, The Wisdom of Sustainability: Buddhist Economics for the 21st Century, Koa Books/Chiron Publications: North Carolina, 2016

169. Skidelsky, Robert and Edward, How Much is Enough? The Love of Money, And the Case for the Good Life, Allen Lane Press: Penguin Books London, UK, 2012.

170. Steven Sloman and Philip Fernbach, The Knowledge Illusion: Why We Never Think Alone, Riverhead Books: New York City, NY, 2017.

171. Emily Esfahani Smith, The Power of Meaning: Crafting A Life That Matters, Crown Publishing: New York City, NY, 2017.

172. Jan Christian Smuts, Holism and Evolution, Forgotten Books: London, UK, 2016.

173. Gary Snyder, The Practice of the Wild, Counterpoint Press: Berkeley, CA., 1990.

174. Joel Solomon with Tyee Bridge, The Clean Money Revolution: Reinventing Power, Purpose and Capitalism, New Society Pulishers: Gabriola Island, BC, Canada, 2017.

175. Rudolph Steiner, Economics: The World as One Economy, New Economy Publications/Rudolph Steiner Press: London, UK, 1972

176. Matthew Stewart, The Courtier and the Heretic: Leibniz, Spinoza and the Fate of God in the Modern World, Norton: New York, 2006.

177. Matthew Stewart, Nature's God: The Heretical Origins of the American Republic, Norton Press: New York, 2014.

178. Ira Stone, A Responsible Life: The Spiritual Path of Mussar, Wipf & Stock: Eugene, OR, 2006.

179. David Peter Stroh, Systems Thinking for Social Change: A Practical Guide to Solving Complex Problems, Avoiding Unintended Consequences, and Achieving Lasting Results, Chelsea Green Publishing: White River Green, VT, 2015.

180. Mark Summer, The Evolution of Everything: How Selection Shapes Culture, Commerce and Nature, PoliPoint Press: Sausalito, CA, 2010.

181. Paul Tillich, Theology of Culture, Oxford University Press: Oxford, England, 1959.

182. Timmons, Savy Giving: The Art and Science of Philanthropy, Hardle Grant Books: Melbourne, AU, 2013.

183. D.T. Suzuki, Essays in Zen Buddhism, Rider and Company: London, UK, 1953.

184. Shunryu Suzuki, Zen Mind, Beginner's Mind: Informal Talks on Zen Meditation and Practice, Weatherhill Press: New York, NY, 1970.

185. Brian Thomas Swimme and Mary Evelyn Tucker, Journey of the Universe, Yale University Press: New Haven, CT, 2011.

186. Chris Thomas, Inheritors of the Earth: How Nature Is Thriving in an Age of Extinction, Hachette Book Group: New York, NY, 2017.

187. Tzvetan Todorov, The Conquest of America: The Question of the Other, University of Oklahoma Press: Norman, OK, 1982.

188. Arnold Toynbee, Change and Habit: The Challenge of Our Time, One World Press/Oxford University Press: Oxford, 1966.

189. Arnold Toynbee, Mankind and Mother Earth: A Narrative History of the World, Oxford University Press: Oxford, UK, 1976.

190. Peter Trachtenberg, The Book of Calamities: Five Questions About Suffering and Its Meaning, Little Brown and Company: New York, NY, 2008.

191. Lynne Twist, The Soul of Money, W.W. Norton: New York, NY, 2003.

192. Roberto Mangabeira Unger, The Religion of the Future, Verso Press: London, UK, 2016.

193. Daniel Christian Wahl, Designing Regenerative Cultures, Triarchy Press: Axminster, England, 2016.

194. Julianne Lutz Warren, Aldo Leopold's Odyssey, Island Press: Washington, 2016.

195. Jack Weatherford, Indian Givers: How Native Americans Transformed the World, Broadway Books: New York, NY, 1998.

196. Jack Weatherford, The History of Money: From Sandstone to Cyberspace, Three Rivers Press: New York, NY, 1997.

197. Arthur Weissman, In the Light of Humane Nature, Morgan James Publishing: New York, 2014

198. Margaret Wheatley, Leadership and the New Science: Discovering Order in a Chaotic World, Burrett-Koehler Publishers, San Francisco, 2006.

199. Alfred North Whitehead, Adventures of Ideas, The Free Press: New York, NY, 1933.

200. Alfred North Whitehead, The Concept of Nature, NeoEditions, 2015.

201. Alfred North Whitehead, Science and the Modern World, The Free Press: New York City, NY, 1925.

202. Ken Wilber, A Theory of Everything: An Integral Vision for Business, Politics, Science and Spirituality, Gateway Press: Dublin, Ireland, 2000.

203. Edward O. Wilson, Consilience: The Unity of Knowledge, Vintage Books: New York City, NY, 1998.

204. Roy Wilson, Medicine Wheels: Ancient Teachings For Modern Times, Crossroad Press: New York, 1994.

205. Wohlleben, Peter, The Hidden Life of Trees: What They Feel, How They Communicate, Grestone Books: Vancouver, CA. 2015.

206. Keith Makoto Woodhouse, The Ecocentrists: A History of Radical Environmentalism, Columbia University Press: New York, NY, 2018.

207. N.T. Wright, The Resurrection of the Son of God, Fortress Press: Minneapolis, MN, 2003.

Six Lists to Live By

THE EIGHTFOLD PATH
OFFERED BY THE BUDDHA[1]

1. Right Understanding: Understanding the four Noble Truths
2. Right Thought: Being should bring satisfaction
3. Right Speech: Speaking truthfully and skillfully
4. Right Action: Not killing, stealing or indulging in irresponsible sexual behavior
5. Right Livelihood: Not engaging in a profession that brings harm to others
6. Right Effort: Encouraging wholesome states of mind
7. Right Mindfulness: Awareness of the physical and mental dimensions of our experience
8. Right Concentration: Staying focused

EIGHT DEGREES OF GIVING[2]

"There are eight degrees of almsgiving, each one superior to the other:

The highest degree, than which there is none higher, is one who upholds the hand of an Israelite reduced to poverty by handing him a gift or a loan, or entering into a partnership with him, or finding work for him, in order to strengthen his hand so that he would have no need to beg from other people...

Below this is he who gives alms to the poor in such a way he does not know to whom he has given, nor does the poor man know from whom he has received...

Below this is he who knows to whom he is giving, while the poor man does not know from whom he is receiving...

Below this is the case where the poor man knows from whom he is receiving, but himself remains unknown to the giver.

Below this is he who hands the alms to the poor man before being asked for them.

Below this is he who hands the alms to the poor man
after the latter has asked for them.

Below this is he who gives the poor man less than what is proper,
but with a friendly countenance.

Below this is he who gives alms with a frowning countenance."

—The Rabbi Moses Maimonides,
writing in the middle 1100s.

TEN COMMANDMENTS

1. You shall have no other gods before Me.
2. You shall not make idols.
3. You shall not take the name of the LORD your God in vain.
4. Remember the Sabbath day, to keep it holy.
5. Honor your father and your mother.
6. You shall not murder.
7. You shall not commit adultery.
8. You shall not steal.
9. You shall not bear false witness against your neighbor.
10. You shall not covet.

A PLATFORM OF THE DEEP ECOLOGY MOVEMENT[3]

1. The flourishing of human and non-human life on Earth has intrinsic value. The value of non-human life forms is independent of the usefulness these may have for narrow human purposes.
2. Richness and diversity of life forms are values in themselves and contribute to the flourishing of human and non-human life on Earth.
3. Humans have no right to reduce this richness and diversity except to satisfy vital needs.
4. Present human interference with the non-human world is excessive, and the situation is rapidly worsening.
5. The flourishing of human life and cultures is compatible with a substantial decrease of the human population. The flooring of non-human life requires such a decrease.
6. Significant change of life conditions for the better requires change in policies. These affect basic economic, technological, and ideological structures.
7. The ideological change is mainly that of appreciating life quality (dwelling in situations of intrinsic value) rather than adhering to a high standard of living. There will be a profound awareness of the difference between big and great.
8. Those who subscribe to the forgoing points have an obligation directly or indirectly to participate in the attempt to implement necessary changes.

STAGES OF MONEY MINDFULNESS[4]

1. Awareness of the divide
2. Mapping the Mind Field (Landscaping)
3. Exploration of external options
4. Process of Internal Journey/Exploration
5. Capital Centering
6. Identifying Capital Energy Flows, Blocks and Synergies
7. Outlining a Practice
8. Committing to a Process
9. Consciousness of Experience and securing feedback loops and input
10. Evolving Mindset and Strategy

IN *ETHICS*,
ARISTOTLE OFFERS FIVE STEPS TO UNDERSTANDING[5]

1. Human life is purposive
2. There is a highest purpose or good
3. This is happiness
4. In order to understand happiness one must comprehend human function, which in turn discloses our appropriate excellence or virtue
5. This function is a rational activity.

Two Talks in Autumn

I first began "going public" with some of these thoughts and research in the fall of 2017 after having written a 420-page research manuscript.

Here is a link to a video of the first talk, during which I actually begin to cry when speaking about the Purpose of Capital—no doubt a first! This talk was given at SOCAP2017 in San Francisco.

https://www.youtube.com/watch?v=PwsAk--31-A

The second talk was given at the 2017 SRI Conference in San Diego. Here is the link for that talk, but be forewarned that about ten minutes in a fire alarm goes off, which actually helped relax me during the reflection.

https://www.youtube.com/watch?v=Ku-5MyPpD48&feature=youtu.be

Selected Writings by Emerson and Various Collaborators

BOOKS

1. The Impact Assets Investor Handbook (2017)
2. Collaborative Capitalism and the Rise of Impact Investing (2014)
3. The Impact Investor: Lessons in Leadership and Strategy for Collaborative Capitalism (2014)
4. Impact Investing: Transforming How We Make Money While Making a Difference (2011)
5. Enterprising Non-Profits: A Toolkit for Social Entrepreneurs (2001)
6. The New Social Entrepreneurs: Success, Challenge and Lessons of Nonprofit Enterprise Creation (1996)
7. Strategic Tools for Social Entrepreneurs: Enhancing the Performance of Your Enterprising Nonprofit (2002)

ARTICLES AND PAPERS OF NOTE
(All Available at the Blended Value Website, www.blendedvalue.org)

1. Total Portfolio Management: Construction of an Impact Portfolio (2015)
2. The Metrics Myth: Why Quantitative Presentation of Qualitative Value Matters (2015)
3. The Blended Value Map (2003)
4. Mutual Accountability And The Wisdom of Frank Capra (2001)
5. Where Money Meets Mission (2003)
6. The Nature of Returns: A Social Capital Markets Inquiry Into Elements of Investment and The Blended Value Proposition (2000)
7. REDF Papers: Between 1996 and 2000, Emerson authored, co-authored and edited a wide range of papers on Social Return on Investment, Social Enterprise, Venture Philanthropy and a range of related topics.

Image Credits

Part One: yin yang tree - Alex Illi/Shutterstock.com;

Chapter One: **pg xiv**: maze - Lucky_Cat/Shutterstock.com, path - ArtMari/Shutterstock.com, geese - Uncle Leo/Shutterstock.com; **pg 6**: meditator - Wision/Shutterstock.com, diamond - Klaus Kunstler/Shutterstock.com; **pg 21**: wolverine - aleks1949/Shutterstock.com; **pg 29**: quail nest - Dinkoobraz/Shutterstock.com; **pg 31**: trail stones - kominque/Shutterstock.com.

Chapter Two: **pg 36**: coral - Val_Iva/Shutterstock.com, ear - Artur Balytskyi/Shutterstock.com.

Chapter Three: **pg 52**: motherboard - pzAxe/Shutterstock.com, stone henge - BORTEL Pavel - Pavelmidi/Shutterstock.com; **pg 56**: boat - MoreVector/Shutterstock.com, wheat - KateMacate/Shutterstock.com; **pg 62**: suitcase - MaKars/Shutterstock.com, lemming - Morphart Creation/Shutterstock.com.

Part Two: **pg 68**: triple spiral - artdock/Shutterstock.com.

Chapter Four: **pg 70**: rhino - Cactus Studio/Shutterstock.com, oil rig - astudio/Shutterstock.com; **pg 80**: pika - Hein Nouwens/Shutterstock.com, iceberg - Morphart Creation@Shutterstock.com; **pg 84**: drone -Vectorcarrot/Shutterstock.com, talon - simpleBE/Shutterstock.com.

Chapter Five: **pg 94**: heart - Hein Nouwens/Shutterstock.com, brain - Hein Nouwens/Shutterstock.com; **pg 106**: octopus - Alexander_P/Shutterstock.com; **pg 109**: doves - Amili/Shutterstock.com; **pg 115**: ants - DnBr/Shutterstock.com, map - pio3/Shutterstock.com; **pg 116**: moth - Inna Sinano/Shutterstock.com.

Chapter Six: **pg 118**: egg -zhekakopylov/Shutterstock.com, mountains - marinat197/Shutterstock.com; **pg 127**: moose - Hein Nouwens/Shutterstock.com, tracks - wawritto/Shutterstock.com; **pg 135**: cormorant - isaxar/Shutterstock.com, traffic - rob zs/Shutterstock.com.

Chapter Seven: **pg 138**: houses - lookus/Shutterstock.com, tree - Macrovector/Shutterstock.com; **pg 143**: sheep - DnBr/Shutterstock.com, data - Funny Drew/Shutterstock.com; **pg 148**: eye - Gorbash Varvara/Shutterstock.com, buildings- Cerama_ama/Shutterstock.com; **pg 165**: climber - Mount Elbrus/Shutterstock.com.

Chapter Eight: **pg 166**: tree rings - Toluk/Shutterstock.com, fingerprint - lestyan/Shutterstock.com; **pg 171**: snakes egorkeon/Shutterstock.com; **pg 172**: birds - OlenyatkO/Shutterstock.com, powerline - Liubov Dmitrieva/Shutterstock.com; **pg 175**: clock - Babich Alexander/Shutterstock.com, spiral - wongstock/Shutterstock.com; **pg 176**: raven onskull - Cimmerian/Shutterstock.com.

Chapter Nine: **pg 182**: seal - Nosyrevy/Shutterstock.com, thumb - MadSnail/Shutterstock.com; **pg 185**: cowrie - Sabelskaya/Shutterstock.com;

Part Three: **pg 196**: star shape - polosatik/Shutterstock.com, green man face - Del Boy/Shutterstock.com.

Chapter Ten: **pg 198**: nautilus - Morphart Creation/Shutterstock.com, wave - Nadezhda Molkentin/Shutterstock.com; **pg 200**: guitars - MoreVector/Shutterstock.com; **pg 206**: bison - antoninaart/Shutterstock.com; **pg 210**: waterfall - Danussa/Shutterstock.com;

Chapter Eleven: **pg 214**: lantern - Channarong Pherngjanda/Shutterstock.com, sun - Channarong Pherngjanda//Shutterstock.com; **pg 222**: camel - Morphart Creation/Shutterstock.com, needles - Babich Alexander/Shutterstock.com; **pg 228**: stump - Channarong Pherngjanda/Shutterstock.com, truck - Dmitry Natashin/Shutterstock.com.

Chapter Twelve: **pg 244**: wolf - Sunny Whale/Shutterstock.com. wireframe - tomhathaway/Shutterstock.com; **pg 249**: cell – Morphart Creation/Shutterstock.com; **pg 254**: sunflower - Tatiana Davidova/Shutterstock.com, lungs - Morphart Creation/Shutterstock.com

Afterword: **pg 268**: owl & partridges – Morphart Creation/Shutterstock.com; songbirds – Dn Br/Shutterstock.com.

Addendum: **pg 275**: Dock – intueri/Shutterstock.com.

Turtle: Bodor Tivadar/Shutterstock.com;

Endnotes

Chapter One:

Books most relevant to my reflections on this theme include *What Money Can't Buy: the Moral Limits of Markets*, by Michael Sandel; *Dancing Standing Still: Healing the World from a Place of Prayer*, by Richard Rohr; *No Rising Tide: Theology, Economics and the Future*, by Joerg Rieger; *The Dream of Enlightenment: The Rise of Modern Philosophy*, by Anthony Gottlieb; *The Myth of Enlightenment: Seeing Through the Illusion of Separation*, by Karl Renz; *Sapiens: A Brief History of Humankind*, by Yuval Noah Harari; and *The Economics of Good and Evil: The Quest of Economic Meaning From Gilgamesh to Wall Street*.

1. To paraphrase Kafka, as cited by Orner…!
2. Am I Alone Here? Notes on Living to Read and Reading to Live, Peter Orner, Catapult Press: New York, 2016, 158.
3. Imagined Communities: Reflections on the Origin and Spread of Nationalism, Benedict Anderson, Verso Press: London, 1983/2016., 193.
4. John Prine, Angel From Montgomery.
5. Mindfulness and Money: The Buddhist Path of Abundance, Kulananda and Dominic Houlder, Broadway Books: New York City, NY, 2002, 210.
6. Informed by this passage: Beauregard, Mario and Denyse O'Leary, The Spiritual Brain: A Neuroscientist's Case for the Existence of the Soul, Harper One: New York, 2007, xi.
7. Democracy In America, de Tocqueville, Literary Classics of America, New York: NY, 2004, 13.
8. Retrieving the Ancients: An Introduction to Greek Philosophy, David Roochnik, Blackwell Publishing: Malden, MA, 2004, 227.
9. Beauregard, Mario and Denyse O'Leary, The Spiritual Brain: A Neuroscientist's Case for the Existence of the Soul, Harper One: New York, 2007, 4.
10. The Evolution of Everything: How Selection Shapes Culture, Commerce and Nature, Mark Summer, PoliPoint Press: Sausalito, CA, 2010, 74.

11. It's important to emphasize that Darwin's key concept was natural selection and not survival of the fittest. When asked, many would cite the phrase "survival of the fittest" as originating with Darwin; in fact, the term was coined and popularized by Hubert Spencer, whose work fit well with our quest for organization, ranking and hierarchy. In fact, the notion that the strongest survive—and the thinking of Social Darwinists, many of whom later advocated sterilization programs and the theory that the size of one's cranium differed relative to race and intelligence—were notions Darwin most likely would not have recognized nor promoted. For more on this, please see: The Evolution of Everything: How Selection Shapes Culture, Commerce and Nature, Mark Summer, PoliPoint Press: Sausalito, CA, 2010, 88, 117.

12. The Systems View of Life: A Unifying Vision, Fritjof Capra and Pier Luigi Luisi, Cambridge University Press: Cambridge, UK, 2014, 38.

13. Systems Thinking for Social Change: A Practical Guide to Solving Complex Problems, Avoiding Unintended Consequences, and Achieving Lasting Results, David Peter Stroh, Chelsea Green Publishing: White River Green, VT, 2015, 74.

14. The Courtier and the Heretic: Leibniz, Spinoza and the Fate of God in the Modern World, Matthew Stewart, Norton: New York, 2006, 36.

15. The Courtier and the Heretic: Leibniz, Spinoza and the Fate of God in the Modern World, Matthew Stewart, Norton: New York, 2006, 54.

16. The Myth of Enlightenment: Seeing Through the Illusion of Separation, Karl Renz, Inner Directions Press, 2005, 195.

17. The Four Nobel Truths of Wealth: A Buddhist View of Economic Live, Layth Matthews, Enlightened Economy Books: US, 2014, 65.

18. Each Moment is the Universe: Zen and the way of Being Time, Dainin Katagiri, 2007, page 16

19. The notion we are living in minuscule moments is taken from Richard Rohr's passage here...Dancing Standing Still: Healing the World from a Place of Prayer, Richard Rohr, Paulist Press: New York City, NY, 2014, 81.

20. Cosmopolitanism: Ethics in a World of Strangers, Kwame Anthony Appiah, Norton and Company: New York City, NY, 2006, 168.

21. This connection between Deep Thought and "the answer" is one I also had; and found the reference in two different books, but this was the first I came upon. Beauregard, Mario and Denyse O'Leary, The Spiritual Brain: A Neuroscientist's Case for the Existence of the Soul, Harper One: New York, 2007, 19.

22. This following section was included in my original research manuscript as well as used as part of my plenary talk at SOCAP2017, referenced at the end of this document in Two Talks in Autumn.

23. For a discussion of considerations regarding a new economic paradigm linking reflection with impact investment practice, please see my

ImpactAlpha blog on that idea: https://impactalpha.com/toward-a-new-economic-paradigm-jed-emerson-on-theory-practice-and-community/

24. http://quoteinvestigator.com/2014/05/22/solve/

25. The Silk Roads: A New History of the World, Peter Frankopan, Alfred Knopf: New York, NY, 2016, 96.

26. Economics of Good and Evil: The Quest of Economic Meaning from Gilgamesh to Wall Street, Tomas Sedlacek, Oxford University Press, Oxford: England, 2011, page 171.

27. The Dream of Enlightenment: The Rise of Modern Philosophy, Anthony Gottlieb, Liverlight Publishing Corporation: New York, 2016, 29.

28. A later author built upon Kant's division and placed Locke, Berkeley and Hume into the realm of the empiricists with the rationalists consisting of Leibniz, Spinoza and Descartes (The Dream of Enlightenment: The Rise of Modern Philosophy, Anthony Gottlieb, Liverlight Publishing Corporation: New York, 2016, 33.) The irony, of course, is that as one reads the work of these various philosophers the actual positions of the authors hardly lend themselves to such an easy division and would have been baffling to those so named (The Dream of Enlightenment: The Rise of Modern Philosophy, Anthony Gottlieb, Liverlight Publishing Corporation: New York, 2016, 33.)

29. Beauregard, Mario and Denyse O'Leary, The Spiritual Brain: A Neuroscientist's Case for the Existence of the Soul, Harper One: New York, 2007, 24.

30. Beauregard, Mario and Denyse O'Leary, The Spiritual Brain: A Neuroscientist's Case for the Existence of the Soul, Harper One: New York, 2007, 24.

31. The Practice of the Wild, Gary Snyder, Counterpoint Press: Berkeley, CA., 1990, page 8.

32. The Lessons of History, Will & Ariel Durant, Simon and Schuster: New York City, NY, 1968, 95.

33. Consilience: The Unity of Knowledge, Edward O. Wilson, Vintage Books: New York City, NY, 1998, 31

34. A Responsible Life: The Spiritual Path of Mussar, Ira Stone, Wipf & Stock: Eugene, OR, 2006, xxxi.

35. Dancing Standing Still: Healing the World from a Place of Prayer, Richard Rohr, Paulist Press: New York City, NY, 2014, 31.

36. Dancing Standing Still: Healing the World from a Place of Prayer, Richard Rohr, Paulist Press: New York City, NY, 2014, 33.

37. Nature's God: The Heretical Origins of the American Republic, Matthew Stewart, Norton Press: New York, 2014, 153.

38. I am paraphrasing Karen Armstrong's reflection on the nature of mythology here, placing her thoughts in the context of impact investing's journey. A Short History of Myth, Karen Armstrong, Canongate Press: Edinburgh/New York, 2005, 10.

39. Dancing Standing Still: Healing the World from a Place of Prayer, Richard Rohr, Paulist Press: New York City, NY, 2014, 3.

40. What Money Can't Buy: The Moral Limits of Markets, Michael Sandel, Farrar, Straus and Giroux: New York City, NY, 2012, 13.

41. No Rising Tide: Theology, Economics and the Future, Joerg Rieger, Fortress Press: Minneapolis, MN. 2009, 33.

42. How to Do Good and Avoid Evil: A Global Ethic from the Sources of Judaism, Hans Kung and Rabbi Walter Homolka, Skylight Paths Publishing: Woodstock, VT, 2009, 117.

43. The Alchemist, Paulo Coelho, Harper One: New York City, NY, 1993.

44. The Practice of the Wild, Gary Snyder, Counterpoint Press: Berkeley, CA., 1990., page 155.

45. The Myth of Enlightenment: Seeing Through the Illusion of Separation, Karl Renz, Inner Directions Press, 2005, 2.

46. Ecology, Community and Lifestyle, Arne Naess as Translated by David Rothenberg, Cambridge University Press: Cambridge, UK. 1989, 9.

47. See Giles Hutchins excellent book, The Illusion of Separation. Also, see Loy for more on the notion of dualism and, interestingly enough, how the rejection of intentionality is the first step in our movement toward becoming One. First chapter and subsequent ones bring these ideas forward.

48. What Money Can't Buy: The Moral Limits of Markets, Michael Sandel, Farrar, Straus and Giroux: New York City, NY, 2012, 8.

49. What Money Can't Buy: The Moral Limits of Markets, Michael Sandel, Farrar, Straus and Giroux: New York City, NY, 2012, 9-10.

50. As framed in that great book, Sapiens: A Brief History of Humankind, Yuval Noah Harari, Vintage Books: London, 2011, 5.

Chapter Two:

Books most relevant to my reflections on this theme include *The Four Nobel Truths of Wealth: A Buddhist View of Economic Life*, by Layth Matthews; *The Conquest of America: The Question of the Other*, by Tzvetan Todorov; *The Wisdom of Sustainability: Buddhist Economics for the 21ˢᵗ Century*, by Sulak Sivaraksa.

1. To be clear, my editor, Herb, was adamant that I NOT capitalize Other, Broad, Deep and Mutual Impact, but I just couldn't help my self...Sorry, Herb! 😊

2. The Four Nobel Truths of Wealth: A Buddhist View of Economic Live, Layth Matthews, Enlightened Economy Books: US, 2014, 66

3. For a rich, but dense, exploration of the concept of the Other, see: The Conquest of America: The Question of the Other, Tzvetan Todorov,

University of Oklahoma Press: Norman, OK, 1982, 185 onward. See also, Time and The Other, by Emanuel Levinas and Richard Cohen.

4. The Conquest of America: The Question of the Other, Tzvetan Todorov, University of Oklahoma Press: Norman, OK, 1982, 130.
5. Dietrich Bonhoeffer, The Cost of Discipleship, Simon and Shuster: New York City, NY, 1959
6. Mindfulness and Money: The Buddhist Path of Abundance, Kulananda and Dominic Houlder, Broadway Books: New York City, NY, 2002, 73.
7. A Responsible Life: The Spiritual Path of Mussar, Ira Stone, Wipf & Stock: Eugene, OR, 2006, xxvii.

Chapter Three:

Books most relevant to my reflections on this theme include *The Origin of Wealth: Evolution, Complexity and the Radical Remaking of Economics*, by Eric Beinhacker; *The Evolution of Minds: From Bacteria to Bach and Back*, by Daniel Dennett; *Imagined Communities: Reflections on the Origin and Spread of Nationalism*, by Benedict Anderson; *Retrieving the Ancients: An Introduction to Greek Philosophy*, by David Roochnik; *The Dynamics of Transformation: Tracing An Emerging World View*, by Grant Maxwell; *Deep Ecology for the 21ˢᵗ Century*, edited by George Sessions; *Nature's God: The Heretical Origins of the American Republic*, by Matthew Stewart; *A Responsible Life: The Spiritual Path of Mussar*, by Ira Stone; *Prelude in Economics: A New Approach to Economics*, by Christopher Budd; and *The Reformation*, by Owen Chadwick.

1. Learning to Die in the Anthropocene: Reflections on the End of Civilization, Roy Scranton, City Lights Books: San Francisco, CA, 2015, 56.
2. A Short History of Myth, Karen Armstrong, Canongate Press: Edinburgh/ New York, 2005, Table of Contents.
3. Extinction: A Radical History, Ashley Dawson, OR Books: New York City, NY, 2016, 27.
4. Imagined Communities: Reflections on the Origin and Spread of Nationalism, Benedict Anderson, Verso Press: London, 1983/2016, 56.
5. The Origin of Wealth: Evolution, Complexity and the Radical Remaking of Economics, Eric Beinhacker, Harvard Business School Press: Boston, MA, 2006, 15.
6. The Reformation, Owen Chadwick, Penguin Books: London, UK, 1964, 67.
7. The Evolution of Minds: From Bacteria to Bach and Back, Daniel Dennett, Norton & Co.: New York City, 2017, 9.

8. The Evolution of Minds: From Bacteria to Bach and Back, Daniel Dennett, Norton & Co.: New York City, 2017, 10.

9. Imagined Communities: Reflections on the Origin and Spread of Nationalism, Benedict Anderson, Verso Press: London, 1983/2016, 193.

10. Retrieving the Ancients: An Introduction to Greek Philosophy, David Roochnik, Blackwell Publishing: Malden, MA, 2004, 20-21.

11. The Dynamics of Transformation: Tracing An Emerging World View, Grant Maxwell, Persistent Press: Nashville, TN, 2017, 21.

12. Silence: The Mystery of Wholeness, Robert Sardello, Goldstone Press: Benson, North Carolina, 2006/2008, xvii.

13. Nature's God: The Heretical Origins of the American Republic, Matthew Stewart, Norton Press: New York, 2014, 130.

14. Nature's God: The Heretical Origins of the American Republic, Matthew Stewart, Norton Press: New York, 2014, 131.

15. A Responsible Life: The Spiritual Path of Mussar, Ira Stone, Wipf & Stock: Eugene, OR, 2006, 49.

16. The Conquest of America: The Question of the Other, Tzvetan Todorov, University of Oklahoma Press: Norman, OK, 1982, 254.

17. Imagined Communities: Reflections on the Origin and Spread of Nationalism, Benedict Anderson, Verso Press: London, 1983/2016., 11.

18. Prelude in Economics: A New Approach to Economics, Christopher Budd, Johanus Academy of Sociology and Economics: West Sussex, UK, 1979, 61.

19. The Power of Meaning: Crafting A Life That Matters, Emily Esfahani Smith, Crown Publishing: New York City, NY, 20174

20. The Reformation, Owen Chadwick, Penguin Books: London, UK, 1964 36.

Chapter Four:

Books which most influenced my reflections on this theme include *The Axial Age and Its Consequences*, edited by Robert Bellah and Hans Joas— though I drew upon and was intrigued by many of the authors who submitted writings to this volume; *A Short History of Myth*, by Karen Armstrong; *The Age of the Sages: The Axial Age in Asia and the Near East*, by Mark Muesse; *The Birth of the Anthropocene*, by Jeremy Davis; *A Redder Shade of Green*, by Ian Angus; *Dark Ecology: For a Logic of Future Coexistence*, by Timothy Morton; and *The Myth of Human Supremacy*, by Derrick Jensen.

1. The Axial Age and Its Consequences, Robert Bellah and Hans Joas, Eds., Belknap Press: Cambridge, MA, 2012, 367.

2. As ever, the reader will find various citations for the Axial Age in the bibliography of this document.

3. A Short History of Myth, Karen Armstrong, Canongate Press: Edinburgh/New York, 2005., 78.
4. A Short History of Myth, Karen Armstrong, Canongate Press: Edinburgh/New York, 2005., 79.
5. A Short History of Myth, Karen Armstrong, Canongate Press: Edinburgh/New York, 2005., 80.
6. Buddha, Karen Armstrong, Penguin Books: New York City, NY, 2001, 11.
7. The Axial Age and Its Consequences, Robert Bellah and Hans Joas, Eds., Belknap Press: Cambridge, MA, 2012, 30/31.
8. The Axial Age and Its Consequences, Robert Bellah and Hans Joas, Eds., Belknap Press: Cambridge, MA, 2012, 71.
9. The Axial Age and Its Consequences, Robert Bellah and Hans Joas, Eds., Belknap Press: Cambridge, MA, 2012, 106.
10. Sapiens: A Brief History of Humankind, Yuval Noah Harari, Vintage Books: London, 2011. This concept is a central one explored throughout his text.
11. The Axial Age and Its Consequences, Robert Bellah and Hans Joas, Eds., Belknap Press: Cambridge, MA, 2012, 73.
12. The Age of the Sages: The Axial Age in Asia and the Near East, Mark Muesse, Fortress Press: Minneapolis, MN, 2013, 4-5.
13. The Age of the Sages: The Axial Age in Asia and the Near East, Mark Muesse, Fortress Press: Minneapolis, MN, 2013, 227.
14. This is basically a summation of the closing comments from: The Age of the Sages: The Axial Age in Asia and the Near East, Mark Muesse, Fortress Press: Minneapolis, MN, 2013, 188.
15. The Birth of the Anthropocene, Jeremy Davies, University of California Press: Oakland, CA, 2016, 6.
16. The Birth of the Anthropocene, Jeremy Davies, University of California Press: Oakland, CA, 2016, 7.
17. Learning to Die in the Anthropocene: Reflections on the End of Civilization, Roy Scranton, City Lights Books: San Francisco, CA, 2015, 34.
18. Purdy, Jedidiah, After Nature: A Politics for the Anthropocene, Harvard University Press: Cambridge, MA, 2015, 2.
19. Dark Ecology: For a Logic of Future Coexistence, Timothy Morton, Columbia University Press: New York, 2016, 8.
20. I'd be curious to know it they've thought about it at all, though if so, I'd imagine them landing more on the "denier" side of the discussion.
21. https://www.nps.gov/meve/index.htm
22. The Birth of the Anthropocene, Jeremy Davies, University of California Press: Oakland, CA, 2016, 9.
23. The Birth of the Anthropocene, Jeremy Davies, University of California Press: Oakland, CA, 2016, 10.
24. The Birth of the Anthropocene, Jeremy Davies, University of California Press: Oakland, CA, 2016, 12.

25. The Birth of the Anthropocene, Jeremy Davies, University of California Press: Oakland, CA, 2016, 20.
26. The Birth of the Anthropocene, Jeremy Davies, University of California Press: Oakland, CA, 2016, 61-62.
27. Anthropocene or Capitalocene? Nature, History and the Crisis of Capitalism, Jason Moore, Editor, PM Press: Oakland, CA, 2016, 16
28. Anthropocene or Capitalocene? Nature, History and the Crisis of Capitalism, Jason Moore, Editor, PM Press: Oakland, CA, 2016, 21.
29. Anthropocene or Capitalocene? Nature, History and the Crisis of Capitalism, Jason Moore, Editor, PM Press: Oakland, CA, 2016.
30. Angus, Ian, A Redder Shade of Green: Intersections of Science and Socialism, Monthly Review Press: New York City, NY, 2017.
31. The following section was written by me and published in ImpactAlpha at this link: https://impactalpha.com/toward-a-new-economic-paradigm-jed-emerson-on-theory-practice-and-community/, which I appreciated, although they did not print a very complimentary photo of the author...
32. Dark Ecology: For a Logic of Future Coexistence, Timothy Morton, Columbia University Press: New York, 2016, 23.

Chapter Five:

Books which most influenced my reflections on this theme include *The Courtier and the Heretic: Leibniz, Spinoza and the Fate of God in the Modern World*, by Matthew Stewart; *The Dream of Enlightenment: The Rise of Modern Philosophy*, by Anthony Gottlieb; *Sacred Economics: Money, Gift & Society in the Age of Transition*, by Charles Eisenstein; *The Illusion of Separation: Exploring the Cause of Our Current Crisis*, by Giles Hutchins; *The Practice of the Wild*, by Gary Snyder; *Landscapes of Capital: Representing Time, Space and Globalization in Corporate Advertising*, by Robert Goldman and Stephen Papson; *Ecology, Community and Lifestyle*, by Arne Naess; *Systems Thinking for Social Change: A Practical Guide to Solving Complex Problems, Avoiding Unintended Consequences and Achieving Lasting Results*, by David Peter Stroh.

1. The Age of the Sages: The Axial Age in Asia and the Near East, Mark Muesse, Fortress Press: Minneapolis, MN, 2013, 42.
2. Change and Habit: The Challenge of our Time, Arnold Toynbee, One World: Oxford University Press, 1966, 162.
3. Change and Habit: The Challenge of our Time, Arnold Toynbee, One World: Oxford University Press, 1966, 162.

4. Retrieving the Ancients: An Introduction to Greek Philosophy, David Roochnik, Blackwell Publishing: Malden, MA, 2004, 19.

5. Retrieving the Ancients: An Introduction to Greek Philosophy, David Roochnik, Blackwell Publishing: Malden, MA, 2004, 19.

6. The Illusion of Separation: Exploring the Cause of our Current Crisis, Giles Hutchins, Floris Books, 2014, page 31.

7. While Descartes is known for stating "I think, therefore I am" in fact his understanding of thought was really simply a hyper-focus upon mathematics as a structure of thinking. "...Fascinated by the technical progress of the time, the new period introduces the concept of mathematical mechanics as the ontological texture of reality. Mechanics then is promoted from a relatively narrow use in machinery to the hight rung on the ontological ladder. If morals are the main texture of reality in the notions of the Hebrews, mercy for the Christians, and love for Augustine, mocha nice becomes the main building block in Descartes hands...'Despite his superficial emphasis on thinking, Descartes really assigned to thought only a very meager role. The roads to discovery are many but he acknowledged only one—the mathematical one." Economics of Good and Evil: The Quest of Economic Meaning from Gilgamesh to Wall Street, Tomas Sedlacek, Oxford University Press, Oxford: England, 2011, page 173.

8. Margaret Wheatley, Leadership and the New Science: Discovering Order in a Chaotic World, Burrett-Koehler Publishers, San Francisco, page 29.

9. The Illusion of Separation: Exploring the Cause of our Current Crisis, Giles Hutchins, Floris Books, 2014, page 33.

10. The Illusion of Separation: Exploring the Cause of our Current Crisis, Giles Hutchins, Floris Books, 2014, page 35.

11. The Courtier and the Heretic: Leibniz, Spinoza and the Fate of God in the Modern World, Matthew Stewart, Norton: New York, 2006.

12. The Courtier and the Heretic: Leibniz, Spinoza and the Fate of God in the Modern World, Matthew Stewart, Norton: New York, 2006, 164.

13. The Courtier and the Heretic: Leibniz, Spinoza and the Fate of God in the Modern World, Matthew Stewart, Norton: New York, 2006l, 167.

14. The Courtier and the Heretic: Leibniz, Spinoza and the Fate of God in the Modern World, Matthew Stewart, Norton: New York, 2006, 168.

15. The Dream of Enlightenment: The Rise of Modern Philosophy, Anthony Gottlieb, Liverlight Publishing Corporation: New York, 2016, 20.

16. The Dream of Enlightenment: The Rise of Modern Philosophy, Anthony Gottlieb, Liverlight Publishing Corporation: New York, 2016, 22.

17. The Evolution of Minds: From Bacteria to Bach and Back, Daniel Dennett, Norton & Co.: New York City, 2017, 16.

18. Through the Eye of a Needle: Wealth, the Fall of Rome, and the Making of Christianity in the West, 350—550 AD, Peter Brown, Princeton University Press: Princeton, New Jersey, 2012, 57.

19. Through the Eye of a Needle: Wealth, the Fall of Rome, and the Making of Christianity in the West, 350—550 AD, Peter Brown, Princeton University Press: Princeton, New Jersey, 2012, 8.

20. For a discussion of how the VOC was ultimately reformed to improve its governance, see: The Ascent of Money: A Financial History of the World, Niall Ferguson, Penguin Books Group: New York City, 2008, 134.

21. The Ascent of Money: A Financial History of the World, Niall Ferguson, Penguin Books Group: New York City, 2008, page 132.

22. The Ascent of Money: A Financial History of the World, Niall Ferguson, Penguin Books Group: New York City, 2008, page 132.

23. The Ascent of Money: A Financial History of the World, Niall Ferguson, Penguin Books Group: New York City, 2008, 135. Sapiens also offers a lengthy description of the way VOC engaged in battles and warfare in pursuit of its wealth generated for shareholders, etc. See pages 357 to 359.

24. The Ascent of Money: A Financial History of the World, Niall Ferguson, Penguin Books Group: New York City, 2008, page 363.

25. The Impact Investor: Lessons in Leadership and Strategy for Collaborative Capitalism, Cathy Clark, Jed Emerson and Ben Thornley, Jossey Bass: Hoboken, NJ, 2015.

26. The Myth of the Rational Market: A History of Risk, Reward, and Delusion on Wall Street, Justin Fox, Harper Business: New York, 2009, 154.

27. The Myth of the Rational Market: A History of Risk, Reward, and Delusion on Wall Street, Justin Fox, Harper Business: New York, 2009, 159-160.

28. No Rising Tide: Theology, Economics and the Future, Joerg Rieger, Fortress Press: Minneapolis, MN. 2009, 134.

29. http://www.law.nyu.edu/sites/default/files/ECM_PRO_060892.pdf
See: https://www.cnbc.com/2018/06/12/capitalism-may-need-modernizing-says-billionaire-hedge-fund-manager-paul-tudor-jones.html

30. https://www.thinkadvisor.com/2018/06/13/gmos-grantham-its-a-toxic-world/?kw=GMO%27s%20Grantham:%20%27We%27ve%20Created%20a%20Toxic%20World%27&et=editorial&bu=TA&cn=20180614&src=EMC-Email&pt=EarlyWire and also,
https://www.nytimes.com/2018/01/15/business/dealbook/blackrock-laurence-fink-letter.html

31. No Rising Tide: Theology, Economics and the Future, Joerg Rieger, Fortress Press: Minneapolis, MN. 2009, 134.

32. Frozen Desire: The Meaning of Money, James Buchan, Farrar, Straus and Giroux: New York, NY, 1997, 177.

33. Frozen Desire: The Meaning of Money, James Buchan, Farrar, Straus and Giroux: New York, NY, 1997, 177.

34. Nonduality: A Study in Comparative Philosophy, David Loy, Humanity Books: Amherst, NY, 1988, 114.

35. The Dream of Enlightenment: The Rise of Modern Philosophy, Anthony Gottlieb, Liverlight Publishing Corporation: New York, 2016.

36. No Rising Tide: Theology, Economics and the Future, Joerg Rieger, Fortress Press: Minneapolis, MN. 2009, 20, 21.
37. Nonduality: A Study in Comparative Philosophy, David Loy, Humanity Books: Amherst, NY, 1988, 1.
38. Sacred Economics: Money, Gift & Society in the Age of Transition, Charles Eisenstein, Evolver Editions: Berkeley, CA., 2011, 2.
39. The Illusion of Separation: Exploring the Cause of our Current Crisis, Giles Hutchins, Floris Books, 2014, page 43.
40. Mindfulness and Money: The Buddhist Path of Abundance, Kulananda and Dominic Houlder, Broadway Books: New York City, NY, 2002, 41.
41. This quote is exactly as presented in the original text, but I think there may be an error. Economics of Good and Evil: The Quest of Economic Meaning from Gilgamesh to Wall Street, Tomas Sedlacek, Oxford University Press, Oxford: England, 2011, pages 30 and 31.
42. Landscapes of Capital: Representing Time, Space and Globalization in Corporate Advertising. Robert Goldman and Stephen Papson, Polity Press: Cambridge, UK; 2011, 14.
43. Nonduality: A Study in Comparative Philosophy, David Loy, Humanity Books: Amherst, NY, 1988, 115.
44. Landscapes of Capital: Representing Time, Space and Globalization in Corporate Advertising, Robert Goldman and Stephan Papson, Polity Press, 2011, 138.

Chapter Six:

Books which most influenced my reflections on this theme include *Losing Ground: American Environmentalism at the Close of the 21ˢᵗ Century*, by Mark Dowie; *Mankind and Mother Earth: A Narrative History of the World*, by Arnold Toynbee; *Against Empire*, by Michael Parenti; *After Nature: A Politics for the Anthropocene*, by Jedidiah Purdy; *The Illusion of Separation: Exploring the Cause of our Current Crisis*, by Giles Hutchins; *Deep Ecology for the 21ˢᵗ Century*, edited by George Sessions; *Sapiens: A Brief History of Humankind*, by Yuval Noah Harari; *Four Futures: Life After Capitalism*, by Peter Frase; *Aldo Leopold's Odyssey*, by Julianne Lutz Warren.

1. Mankind and Mother Earth: A Narrative History of the World, Arnold Toynbee, Oxford University Press: Oxford, UK, 1976.
2. Against Empire, Michael Parenti, City Lights Books: San Francisco, CA, May, 1995.
3. The Illusion of Separation: Exploring the Cause of our Current Crisis, Giles Hutchins, Floris Books, 2014, page 28.

4. Purdy, Jedidiah, After Nature: A Politics for the Anthropocene, Harvard University Press: Cambridge, MA, 2015, 34-35.
5. Retrieving the Ancients: An Introduction to Greek Philosophy, David Roochnik, Blackwell Publishing: Malden, MA, 2004, 7.
6. Purdy, Jedidiah, After Nature: A Politics for the Anthropocene, Harvard University Press: Cambridge, MA, 2015, 78.
7. The Myth of Human Supremacy, Derrick Jensen, Seven Stories Press: New York, 2016, 17.
8. Rainforest Shamans: Essays on the Tufano Indians of the Northwest Amazon, Gerardo Reichel-Dolmatoff, Themis Books: Devon, UK, 1997, 74.
9. The Myth of Human Supremacy, Derrick Jensen, Seven Stories Press: New York, 2016, 302.
10. Mindfulness and Money: The Buddhist Path of Abundance, Kulananda and Dominic Houlder, Broadway Books: New York City, NY, 2002, 43.
11. Deep Ecology for the 21st Century, edited by George Sessions, Shambhala Press, Boston, 1995, Four Forms of Ecological Consicousness., John Rodman, 129.
12. Dowie, Mark, Losing Ground: American Environmentalism at the Close of the 21st Century, The MIT Press, Cambridge, Massachusetts, 1995, page 12.
13. Dowie, Mark, Losing Ground: American Environmentalism at the Close of the 21st Century, The MIT Press, Cambridge, Massachusetts, 1995, page 13.
14. Extinction: A Radical History, Ashley Dawson, OR Books: New York City, NY, 2016, 35.
15. Deep Ecology for the 21st Century, edited by George Sessions, Shambhala Press, Boston, 1995, Ecocentrism and the Anthropocentric Detour, Goerge Sessions, page 159.
16. The Practice of the Wild, Gary Snyder, Counterpoint Press: Berkeley, CA., 1990, page 20.
17. Deep Ecology for the 21st Century, edited by George Sessions, Shambhala Press, Boston, 1995, Deep Ecology: A New Paradigm, Fritjof Capra, page 21.
18. Change and Habit: The Challenge of our Time, Arnold Toynbee, One World: Oxford University Press, 1966, 26.
19. Ecology, Community and Lifestyle, Arne Naess as Translated by David Rothenberg, Cambridge University Press: Cambridge, UK. 1989, 167.
20. Change and Habit: The Challenge of our Time, Arnold Toynbee, One World: Oxford University Press, 1966, 172.
21. A Short History of Myth, Karen Armstrong, Canongate Press: Edinburgh/ New York, 2005, 15-16.
22. A Short History of Myth, Karen Armstrong, Canongate Press: Edinburgh/ New York, 2005, 5.
23. A Short History of Myth, Karen Armstrong, Canongate Press: Edinburgh/ New York, 2005, 5.
24. A Short History of Myth, Karen Armstrong, Canongate Press: Edinburgh/ New York, 2005, 43.

25. Mankind and Mother Earth: A Narrative History of the World, Arnold Toynbee, Oxford University Press: Oxford, UK, 1976, 588.

26. Dark Ecology: For a Logic of Future Coexistence, Timothy Morton, Columbia University Press: New York, 2016, 52.

27. Four Futures: Life After Capitalism, Peter Frase, Verso Press: London/New York, 2016, 105.

28. Antecedent to the Fourth-wave environmentalist were activists such as Bob Marshall of the Wilderness Society. He was chief of the Forest Service's Division of Recreation and Lands, writing the 1940s regulation that brought wilderness into law and promoting a vision of our relationship with the earth that positioned us not as dominator but subject of the Earth. "Like later environmentalists of the ecological age, they cared about the wild, tangled fabric of nature as such, just because it existed, apart from its service to human beings. These two values—human consciousness and inhuman nature—were linked…because the consciousness they prized was precisely awareness of, and attunement to, indifferent, alien nature. They came to describe this as an attitude of "humility"—a word that connoted, in its etymology, at-homeness, but also smallness and modesty, as if to say that the world is our home, but not one that we own or master in any simple or complete way. As they set out these ideas, wilderness activists became, quite unknowingly, a bridge between the Romantics of the Sierra Club, for whom encountering nature elevated consciousness, and the ecologically minded environmentalists, for whom nature was a difficult but precious home." As cited by Purdy, Jedidiah, After Nature: A Politics for the Anthropocene, Harvard University Press: Cambridge, MA, 2015,192.

29. Dowie, Mark, Losing Ground: American Environmentalism at the Close of the 21st Century, The MIT Press, Cambridge, Massachusetts, 1995, page 234.

30. Change and Habit: The Challenge of our Time, Arnold Toynbee, One World: Oxford University Press, 1966, 11.

Chapter Seven:

Books which most influenced my reflections on this theme include *The Myth of Human Supremacy*, by Derrick Jensen; *No Rising Tide: Theology, Economics, and the Future*, by Joerg Rieger; *Economics of Good and Evil: The Quest of Economic Meaning from Gilgamesh to Wall Street*, by Tomas Sedlacek; *Change and Habit: The Challenge of our Time*, by Arnold Toynbee; *The Dynamics of Transformation: Tracing an Emerging World View*, by Grant Maxwell; *Cosmopolitan: Ethics in a World of Strangers*, by Kwame Anthony Appiah.

1. The Illusion of Separation: Exploring the Cause of our Current Crisis, Giles Hutchins, Floris Books, 2014, page 22.
2. Sapiens: A Brief History of Humankind, Yuval Noah Harari, Vintage Books: London, 2011, 184.
3. https://www.wildmind.org/blogs/quote-of-the-month/quote-anais-nin
4. I believe this is what Richard Rohr writes and reflects upon, but I don't know that I have a specific quote, per se. Much of his writing is on this topic and is worth your review.
5. Psalm 46:10
6. The Alchemist, Paulo Coelho, Harper One: New York City, NY, 1993, 138.
7. https://medium.com/@bcassano/on-purpose-ness-b73e137f8127
8. The Dynamics of Transformation: Tracing An Emerging World View, Grant Maxwell, Persistent Press: Nashville, TN, 2017
9. Dancing Standing Still: Healing the World from a Place of Prayer, Richard Rohr, Paulist Press: New York City, NY, 2014, 12.
10. Hanna Arendt, as quoted in Culture and Imperialism, Edward Said, Vintage Press: New York City, NY, 1993, 25.
11. The Metaphysical Club: A Story of Ideas in America, Louis Menand, Farrar, Straus and Girox: 2001, 64.
12. The Dynamics of Transformation: Tracing An Emerging World View, Grant Maxwell, Persistent Press: Nashville, TN, 2017, 8.
13. https://en.wikipedia.org/wiki/The_Kasidah
14. Sapiens: A Brief History of Humankind, Yuval Noah Harari, Vintage Books: London, 2011, 126.
15. A Short History of Myth, Karen Armstrong, Canongate Press: Edinburgh/ New York, 2005, 2-3.
16. A Short History of Myth, Karen Armstrong, Canongate Press: Edinburgh/ New York, 2005., 7.
17. The Evolution of Everything: How Selection Shapes Culture, Commerce and Nature, Mark Summer, PoliPoint Press: Sausalito, CA, 2010, 37.
18. The Myth of Human Supremacy, Derrick Jensen, Seven Stories Press: New York, 2016, 27.
19. The Myth of Human Supremacy, Derrick Jensen, Seven Stories Press: New York, 2016, 27.
20. The Myth of Human Supremacy, Derrick Jensen, Seven Stories Press: New York, 2016, 63.
21. No Rising Tide: Theology, Economics and the Future, Joerg Rieger, Fortress Press: Minneapolis, MN. 2009, 68.
22. No Rising Tide: Theology, Economics and the Future, Joerg Rieger, Fortress Press: Minneapolis, MN. 2009, 79.
23. No Rising Tide: Theology, Economics and the Future, Joerg Rieger, Fortress Press: Minneapolis, MN. 2009, 80.
24. No Rising Tide: Theology, Economics and the Future, Joerg Rieger, Fortress Press: Minneapolis, MN. 2009, 130.

25. Sapiens: A Brief History of Humankind, Yuval Noah Harari, Vintage Books: London, 2011, 31.
26. Culture and Imperialism, Edward Said, Vintage Press: New York City, NY, 1993, 11.
27. Landscapes of Capital: Representing Time, Space and Globalization in Corporate Advertising. Robert Goldman and Stephen Papson, Polity Press: Cambridge, UK; 2011, 203.
28. Retrieving the Ancients: An Introduction to Greek Philosophy, David Roochnik, Blackwell Publishing: Malden, MA, 2004, 4-5.
29. Landscapes of Capital: Representing Time, Space and Globalization in Corporate Advertising. Robert Goldman and Stephen Papson, Polity Press: Cambridge, UK; 2011.
30. Culture and Imperialism, Edward Said, Vintage Press: New York City, NY, 1993, 14.
31. Culture and Imperialism, Edward Said, Vintage Press: New York City, NY, 1993, 23.
32. In conducting my research on community-based business ventures in 1989, I spent a good amount of time with the folks at the National Economic Development and Law Center in Oakland, where James Head was the executive director. At the time, there were just three volumes of studies conducted on the success and lessons of community ventures—and that was it! The studies dated from the mid-1970s and were the most current research available at the Center.
33. See the early writings of REDF, in particular, New Social Entrepreneurs: The Success, Challenge and Lessons of Nonprofit Enterprise Creation, 1996.
34. The Discovery of Chance: The Life and Thought of Alexander Herzen, Aileen Kelly, Harvard University Press: Harvard, MA, 2016, 212.
35. The Voice of Knowledge, Don Miguel Ruiz with Janet Mills, Amber-Allen Publishing: San Rafael, CA, 2004, 23.
36. The Voice of Knowledge, Don Miguel Ruiz with Janet Mills, Amber-Allen Publishing: San Rafael, CA, 2004, 67.
37. The Dynamics of Transformation: Tracing An Emerging World View, Grant Maxwell, Persistent Press: Nashville, TN, 2017, 41.
38. Dancing Standing Still: Healing the World from a Place of Prayer, Richard Rohr, Paulist Press: New York City, NY, 2014, 16.
39. The Evolution of Everything: How Selection Shapes Culture, Commerce and Nature, Mark Summer, PoliPoint Press: Sausalito, CA, 2010, 135.

Chapter Eight:

Books which most influenced my reflections on this theme include *Medicine Wheels: Ancient Teachings for Modern Times*, by Roy Wilson; *The Moral Imagination: The Art and Soul of Building Peace*, by John Paul

Lederach; *Each Moment is the Universe: Zen and the Way of Being*, by Dainin Katagiri; *Through the Eye of the Needle: Wealth, the Fall of Rome, and the Making of Christianity in the West*, by Peter Brown; *Travels with Epicurus: A Journey to a Greek Island in Search of a Fulfilled Life*, by Daniel Klein; *Seven Brief Lessons on Physics*, by Carlo Rovelli; and *The Wonder Box: Curious Histories of How to Live*, by Roman Krznaric.

1. Medicine Wheels: Ancient Teachings for Modern Times, Roy Wilson, Crossroad Publishing Company: New York, 1994, 65.
2. The Moral Imagination: The Art and Soul of Building Peace, John Paul Lederach, Oxford University Press: Oxford, England, 2005, 136.
3. As discussed in The Moral Imagination: The Art and Soul of Building Peace, John Paul Lederach, Oxford University Press: Oxford, England, 2005, 22-23.
4. The Moral Imagination: The Art and Soul of Building Peace, John Paul Lederach, Oxford University Press: Oxford, England, 2005, 23.
5. The Age of the Sages: The Axial Age in Asia and the Near East, Mark Muesse, Fortress Press: Minneapolis, MN, 2013, 33.
6. Economics of Good and Evil: The Quest of Economic Meaning from Gilgamesh to Wall Street, Tomas Sedlacek, Oxford University Press, Oxford: England, 2011, page 47.
7. Economics of Good and Evil: The Quest of Economic Meaning from Gilgamesh to Wall Street, Tomas Sedlacek, Oxford University Press, Oxford: England, 2011, page 48.
8. Frozen Desire: The Meaning of Money, James Buchan, Farrar, Straus and Giroux: New York, NY, 1997, 61.
9. Seven Brief Lessons on Physics, Carlo Rovelli, Riverhead Books: New York, 2016, 60.
10. Through the Eye of a Needle: Wealth, the Fall of Rome, and the Making of Christianity in the West, 350—550 AD, Peter Brown, Princeton University Press: Princeton, New Jersey, 2012, 14.
11. For a really interesting discussion of time-space compression, please see: Page 106 of Landscapes of Capital: Representing Time, Space and Globalization in Corporate Advertising. Robert Goldman and Stephen Papson, Polity Press: Cambridge, UK; 2011.
12. Landscapes of Capital: Representing Time, Space and Globalization in Corporate Advertising. Robert Goldman and Stephen Papson, Polity Press: Cambridge, UK; 2011, 2.
13. Each Moment is the Universe: Zen and the way of Being Time, Dainin Katagiri, 2007, page 8
14. One is reminded of the following:"You are a function of what the whole universe is doing in the same way that a wave is a function of what the whole ocean is doing."– Alan Watts

15. Each Moment is the Universe: Zen and the way of Being Time, Dainin Katagiri, 2007, page 8

16. "In human society, the adult generation can choose what it will transmit to the rising generation and what it will discard, and the rising generation can choose, though this to a lesser degree, to be more or less receptive to its education or to be more or less recalcitrant to it. Actually, a social and culture tradition is never transmitted from one generation to another without some involuntary change in it, even when both generations concur in wanting the tradition to be transmitted intact. it is impossible, for instance, to freeze a language at some arbitrarily chosen stage of its development…History is the process of change; in the subjective meaning, it is the study of how and why one generation changes into another. History is the 'living garment' that Time-Spirit is always weaving for mankind on the 'humming loom of Time."Change and Habit: The Challenge of our Time, Arnold Toynbee, One World: Oxford University Press, 1966,18-19.

17. Robinson, Marilynne, The Givenness of Things: Essays, Farrar, Straus and Giroux: New York, 2015, 4-5.

18. Robinson, Marilynne, The Givenness of Things: Essays, Farrar, Straus and Giroux: New York, 2015, 4-5.

19. Robinson, Marilynne, The Givenness of Things: Essays, Farrar, Straus and Giroux: New York, 2015, 5.

20. Philosophy, David Papineau, Oxford University Press: Oxford, UK, 2009, 41

21. The Wonder Box: Curious Histories of How to Live, Roman Krznaric, Profile Books: London, UK, 2012, 114.

Chapter Nine:

Books which most influenced my reflections on this theme include *The Ascent of Money: A Financial History of the World*, by Niall Ferguson; *Economics of Good and Evil: The Quest for Economic Meaning from Gilgamesh to Wall Street*, by Tomas Sedlacek; *No Rising Tide: Theology, Economics and the Future*, by Joerg Rieger; *Religions, Values and Peak Experiences*, by A.H. Maslow; *The Givenness of Things: Essays*, by Marilynne Robinson.

1. http://www.gotquestions.org/definition-of-faith.html

2. No Rising Tide: Theology, Economics and the Future, Joerg Rieger, Fortress Press: Minneapolis, MN. 2009 9.

3. Economics of Good and Evil: The Quest of Economic Meaning from Gilgamesh to Wall Street, Tomas Sedlacek, Oxford University Press, Oxford: England, 2011, 81.

4. The Ascent of Money: A Financial History of the World, Niall Ferguson, Penguin Books Group: New York City, 2008, page 30.

5. Sapiens: A Brief History of Humankind, Yuval Noah Harari, Vintage Books: London, 2011, 199.
6. No Rising Tide: Theology, Economics and the Future, Joerg Rieger, Fortress Press: Minneapolis, MN. 2009, 6.
7. Change and Habit: The Challenge of our Time, Arnold Toynbee, One World: Oxford University Press, 1966, 171.
8. Economics of Good and Evil: The Quest of Economic Meaning from Gilgamesh to Wall Street, Tomas Sedlacek, Oxford University Press, Oxford: England, 2011, page 178.
9. Religions, Values, and Peak-Experiences, A. H. Maslow, Penguin Compass: New York City, NY, 1964/1970, 40-43.
10. Frozen Desire: The Meaning of Money, James Buchan, Farrar, Straus and Giroux: New York, NY, 1997, 180.
11. Consilience: The Unity of Knowledge, Edward O. Wilson, Vintage Books: New York City, NY, 1998, 53.
12. No Rising Tide: Theology, Economics and the Future, Joerg Rieger, Fortress Press: Minneapolis, MN. 2009, 15.
13. Sapiens: A Brief History of Humankind, Yuval Noah Harari, Vintage Books: London, 2011, 391.
14. Jacob Weisberg, The Digital Poorhouse, a review of Algorithms of Oppression: How Search Engines Reinforce Racisicm, by Safiya Noble, and Automating Inequality: How High-Tech Tools Profile, Police and Punish the Poor, by Virginia Eubanks, New York Review of Books, June 7, 2018
15. No Rising Tide: Theology, Economics and the Future, Joerg Rieger, Fortress Press: Minneapolis, MN. 2009, 74.
16. No Rising Tide: Theology, Economics and the Future, Joerg Rieger, Fortress Press: Minneapolis, MN. 2009, 12.
17. Sacred Economics: Money, Gift & Society in the Age of Transition, Charles Eisenstein, Evolver Editions: Berkeley, CA., 2011, xiv.
18. Seven Brief Lessons on Physics, Carlo Rovelli, Riverhead Books: New York, 2016, 37.

Chapter Ten:

Books which most influenced my reflections on this theme include *The Myth of the Rational Market: A History of Risk, Reward and Delusion on Wall Street*, by Justin Fox; *Anti-Education: On the Future of Our Educational Institutions*, by Frederich Nietzsche; *Learning to Die in the Anthropocene: Reflections on the End of Civilization*, by Roy Scranton; *The Knowledge Illusion: Why We Never Think Alone*, by Steven Sloman and Philip Fernbach; *The Ascent of Money: A Financial History of the World*, by Niall Ferguson; *Concerned Markets: Economic Ordering of Multiple*

Values, by Susie Geiger, Debbie Harrison, et. al.; *The Conquest of America: The Question of the Other*, by Tzvetan Todorov; *The Metaphysical Club: A Story of Ideas in America*, by Louis Menand; *The Ascent of Money: A Financial History of the World*, by Niall Ferguson; *Economics: The World as One Economy*, by Rudolph Steiner; *Frozen Desire: The Meaning of Money*, by James Buchan; *The Myth of the Rational Market: A History of Risk, Reward and Delusion on Wall Street*, by Justin Fox.

1. Economics: The World as One Economy, Rudolph Steiner, New Economy Publications/Rudolph Steiner Press: London, UK, 1972, 122.
2. The Dynamics of Transformation: Tracing An Emerging World View, Grant Maxwell, Persistent Press: Nashville, TN, 2017, 15-16.
3. Frozen Desire: The Meaning of Money, James Buchan, Farrar, Straus and Giroux: New York, NY, 1997, 183.
4. A good overview is presented, starting on page 31, of The Practice of the Wild, Gary Snyder, Counterpoint Press: Berkeley, CA., 1990; as well as here http://www.onthecommons.org/about and, with a focus on intellectual property rights and the Commons starting on page 75 in Four Futures: Life After Capitalism, Peter Frase, Verso Press: London/New York, 2016. For a conservative perspective on the idea of The Commons, see The Birth of Plenty: How the Prosperity of the Modern World was Created, William Bernstein, McGraw-Hill: New York, NY, 2004, 88.
5. Dowie, Mark, Losing Ground: American Environmentalism at the Close of the 21st Century, The MIT Press, Cambridge, Massachusetts, 1995, page 11.
6. As quoted in Through the Eye of a Needle: Wealth, the Fall of Rome, and the Making of Christianity in the West, 350—550 AD, Peter Brown, Princeton University Press: Princeton, New Jersey, 2012, 133; Ecclesiastics 4:8.
7. Ambrose as quoted in Through the Eye of a Needle: Wealth, the Fall of Rome, and the Making of Christianity in the West, 350—550 AD, Peter Brown, Princeton University Press: Princeton, New Jersey, 2012, 131.
8. Through the Eye of a Needle: Wealth, the Fall of Rome, and the Making of Christianity in the West, 350—550 AD, Peter Brown, Princeton University Press: Princeton, New Jersey, 2012, 132.
9. The Conquest of America: The Question of the Other, Tzvetan Todorov, University of Oklahoma Press: Norman, OK, 1982, 39.
10. The Conquest of America: The Question of the Other, Tzvetan Todorov, University of Oklahoma Press: Norman, OK, 1982, 39.
11. The Conquest of America: The Question of the Other, Tzvetan Todorov, University of Oklahoma Press: Norman, OK, 1982, 40.
12. The Conquest of America: The Question of the Other, Tzvetan Todorov, University of Oklahoma Press: Norman, OK, 1982, 40.

13. Deep Ecology for the 21st Century, edited by George Sessions, Shambhala Press, Boston, 1995, The Viable Human, page 13.
14. Four Futures: Life After Capitalism, Peter Frase, Verso Press: London, 2016, 75.
15. Purdy, Jedidiah, After Nature: A Politics for the Anthropocene, Harvard University Press: Cambridge, MA, 2015, 83.
16. For an excellent—though very sobering—overview of this topic, please see: Peter Cozzens, The Earth is Weeping: The Epic Story of the Indian Wars for the American West, Alfred Knopf: New York, NY, 2016.
17. The Myth of Human Supremacy, Derrick Jensen, Seven Stories Press: New York, 2016, 158.
18. The Practice of the Wild, Gary Snyder, Counterpoint Press: Berkeley, CA., 1990., page 86.
19. The Metaphysical Club: A Story of Ideas in America, Louis Menand, Farrar, Straus and Girox: 2001, 304.
20. The Metaphysical Club: A Story of Ideas in America, Louis Menand, Farrar, Straus and Girox: 2001, 306.
21. An excellent piece addressing this theme was recently produced by Tribe Impact Capital, entitled The Evolution of Wealth.
22. The Knowledge Illusion: Why We Never Think Alone, Steven Sloman and Philip Fernbach, Riverhead Books: New York City, NY, 2017, 213-214.
23. https://en.wikipedia.org/wiki/Freedom_to_roam
24. Philosophy, David Papineau, Oxford University Press: Oxford, UK, 2009, 206.

Chapter Eleven:

Books which most influenced my reflections on this theme include *In the Absence of the Sacred: The Failure of Technology and the Survival of the Indian Nations*, by Jerry Mander; *Money and Possessions*, by Walter Brueggemann; *A Socially Responsible Islamic Finance: Character and Common Good*, by Umar Moghul; *Mindfulness and Money: The Buddhist Path of Abundance*, by Kulananda and Dominic Houlder; *After Nature: A Politics for the Anthropocene*, by Jedidiah Purdy.

1. In the Absence of the Sacred: The Failure of Technology and the Survival of the Indian Nations, Jerry Mander, Sierra Club Books: San Francisco CA, 1991, 161.
2. Money and Possessions, Walter Brueggemann, Westminster John Knox Press: Louisville, KY, 2016, 211.
3. A Socially Responsible Islamic Finance: Character and the Common Good, Umar Moghul, Palgrave McMillan: Brooklyn, NY, 2017, 27.
4. Mindfulness and Money: The Buddhist Path of Abundance, Kulananda and Dominic Houlder, Broadway Books: New York City, NY, 2002, 9-10.

5. Its interesting to note that while this line is in the bible and has been the basis for countless Sunday morning sermons regarding how the "eye of the needle" was a reference to a gate into Jerusalem, this is actually not the case and no such gate ever existed that historians or archaeologists can document. See Peter Brown's book for more on this…See also, The Evolution of Everything: How Selection Shapes Culture, Commerce and Nature, Mark Summer, PoliPoint Press: Sausalito, CA, 2010, 126.

6. Dancing Standing Still: Healing the World from a Place of Prayer, Richard Rohr, Paulist Press: New York City, NY, 2014, 45.

7. Dancing Standing Still: Healing the World from a Place of Prayer, Richard Rohr, Paulist Press: New York City, NY, 2014, 63.

8. One of the "best" pieces I believe I ever wrote was based on It's a Wonderful Life and its implications for our mutual accountability, one to the other. Perhaps you'll like it! http://www.blendedvalue.org/wp-content/uploads/2001/03/Mutual-Accountability.pdf

9. The Nothing That Is: A Natural History of Zero, Robert Kaplan, Oxford University Press: Oxford, UK, 1999, 101.

10. For more on the Golden Age, see this citation: The Dream of Enlightenment: The Rise of Modern Philosophy, Anthony Gottlieb, Liverlight Publishing Corporation: New York, 2016, page 56.

11. Ecology, Community and Lifestyle, Arne Naess as Translated by David Rothenberg, Cambridge University Press: Cambridge, UK. 1989, 105.

12. The Courtier and the Heretic: Leibniz, Spinoza and the Fate of God in the Modern World, Matthew Stewart, Norton: New York, 2006, 102.

13. A Short History of Myth, Karen Armstrong, Canongate Press: Edinburgh/New York, 2005, 59.

14. The Moral Imagination: The Art and Soul of Building Peace, John Paul Lederach, Oxford University Press: Oxford, England, 2005, 42.

15. The Moral Imagination: The Art and Soul of Building Peace, John Paul Lederach, Oxford University Press: Oxford, England, 2005, 40.

16. The Silk Roads: A New History of the World, Peter Frankopan, Alfred Knopf: New York, NY, 2016, 4.

17. Mankind and Mother Earth: A Narrative History of the World, Arnold Toynbee, Oxford University Press: Oxford, UK, 1976, 564.

18. Philosophy, David Papineau, Oxford University Press: Oxford, UK, 2009, 208.

19. Just for starters, please see:
    http://money.cnn.com/2018/01/21/news/economy/davos-oxfam-inequality-wealth/index.html
    http://time.com/money/5112462/billionaires-made-so-much-money-last-year-they-could-end-extreme-poverty-seven-times/
    https://www.theatlantic.com/magazine/archive/2018/06/the-birth-of-a-new-american-aristocracy/559130/?utm_source=newsletter&utm_medium=email&utm_campaign=atlantic-weekly-newsletter&utm_content=20180518&silverid-ref=Mzc0MTYyMzY3ODQ0S0

20. No Rising Tide: Theology, Economics and the Future, Joerg Rieger, Fortress Press: Minneapolis, MN. 2009, 3.
21. Purdy, Jedidiah, After Nature: A Politics for the Anthropocene, Harvard University Press: Cambridge, MA, 2015, 46.
22. Purdy, Jedidiah, After Nature: A Politics for the Anthropocene, Harvard University Press: Cambridge, MA, 2015,46.
23. The Great Leveler: Violence and the History of Inequality from the Stone Age to the Twenty-First Century, Walter Scheidel, Princeton University Press: Princeton, New Jersey, 2017.

Chapter Twelve:

Books which most influenced my reflections on this theme include *Ecology, Community and Lifestyle*, by Arne Naess; *The Genius of Money: Essays and Interviews Reimagining the Financial World*, by John Bloom; *The Moral Imagination: The Art and Soul of Building Peace*, by John Paul Lederach; *The Silk Roads: A New History of the World*, by Peter Frankopan; *The Lessons of History, by Will and Ariel Durant; Philosophy*, by David Papineau; *The Great Leveler: Violence and the History of Inequality from the Stone Age to the Twenty-First Century*, by Walter Scheidel; *Dancing While Standing Still: Healing the World from a Place of Prayer*, by Richard Rohr; *The Power of Meaning: Crafting A Life That Matters*, by Emily Esfahani Smith; *The Practice of the Wild*, by Gary Snyder; *How to Do Good and Avoid Evil: A Global Ethic from the Sources of Judaism*, by Hans Kung and Rabbi Walter Homolka; *The Wisdom of Sustainability: Buddhist Economics for the 21st Century*, by Sulak Sivaraksa; *The Systems View of Life: A Unifying Vision*, by Fritjof Capra and Pier Luigi; *Sapiens: A Brief History of Humankind*, by Yuval Noah Harari; *The Birth of the Anthropocene*, by Jeremy Davies.

1. The Axial Age and Its Consequences, Robert Bellah and Hans Joas, Eds., Belknap Press: Cambridge, MA, 2012, 369.
2. Deep Ecology for the 21st Century, edited by George Sessions, Shambhala Press, Boston, 1995, The Viable Human, page 14.
3. Deep Ecology for the 21st Century, edited by George Sessions, Shambhala Press, Boston, 1995, Simple in Means, Rick in Ends: An interview with Arne Naess, StephanBodian, page 32.
4. Ecology, Community and Lifestyle, Arne Naess as Translated by David Rothenberg, Cambridge University Press: Cambridge, UK. 1989, 72.

5. Mankind and Mother Earth: A Narrative History of the World, Arnold Toynbee, Oxford University Press: Oxford, UK, 1976, 591-592.
6. The Wisdom of Sustainability: Buddhist Economics for the 21st Century, Sulak Sivaraksa, Koa Books/Chiron Publications: North Carolina, 2016, 20.
7. The Wisdom of Sustainability: Buddhist Economics for the 21st Century, Sulak Sivaraksa, Koa Books/Chiron Publications: North Carolina, 2016, vii.
8. Sapiens: A Brief History of Humankind, Yuval Noah Harari, Vintage Books: London, 2011, 374.
9. Four Futures: Life After Capitalism, Peter Frase, Verso Press: London, 2016, 95.
10. The Birth of the Anthropocene, Jeremy Davies, University of California Press: Oakland, CA, 2016, 198.
11. Ecology, Community and Lifestyle, Arne Naess as Translated by David Rothenberg, Cambridge University Press: Cambridge, UK. 1989, 112.
12. As quoted in The Wisdom of Sustainability: Buddhist Economics for the 21st Century, Sulak Sivaraksa, Koa Books/Chiron Publications: North Carolina, 2016, 36.
13. Money and Magic: A Critique of the Modern Economy in Light of Goethe's Faust, Hans Christoph Binswanger, University of Chicago Press: Chicago, IL, 1985 36.
14. Ecology, Community and Lifestyle, Arne Naess as Translated by David Rothenberg, Cambridge University Press: Cambridge, UK. 1989, 28.
15. Keith Makoto Woodhouse, The Ecocentrists: A History of Radical Environmentalism, Columbia University Press: New York, NY, 2018, 106, also see Chapter 5 discussion beginning on page 184.
16. Dancing Standing Still: Healing the World from a Place of Prayer, Richard Rohr, Paulist Press: New York City, NY, 2014, 65.
17. Economics: The World as One Economy, Rudolph Steiner, New Economy Publications/Rudolph Steiner Press: London, UK, 1972, 5.
18. The Moral Imagination: The Art and Soul of Building Peace, John Paul Lederach, Oxford University Press: Oxford, England, 2005, 36.
19. Nature's God: The Heretical Origins of the American Republic, Matthew Stewart, Norton Press: New York, 2014, 277.
20. The Moral Imagination: The Art and Soul of Building Peace, John Paul Lederach, Oxford University Press: Oxford, England, 2005, 33.
21. Consilience: The Unity of Knowledge, Edward O. Wilson, Vintage Books: New York City, NY, 1998, 59.
22. See introductory pages of the first chapter for a great discussion of this process Darwin underwent. Angus, Ian, A Redder Shade of Green: Intersections of Science and Socialism, Monthly Review Press: New York City, NY, 2017.
23. Ecology, Community and Lifestyle, Arne Naess as Translated by David Rothenberg, Cambridge University Press: Cambridge, UK. 1989, 6.

24. Deep Ecology for the 21st Century, edited by George Sessions, Shambhala Press, Boston, 1995, Self Realization: An Ecological Approach to Being in the World, Arne Naess, page 234.

25. Dancing Standing Still: Healing the World from a Place of Prayer, Richard Rohr, Paulist Press: New York City, NY, 2014, 38.

26. The Wisdom of Sustainability: Buddhist Economics for the 21st Century, Sulak Sivaraksa, Koa Books/Chiron Publications: North Carolina, 2016, 22.

27. The Diamond Cutter: The Buddha on Managing Your Business and Your Life, Geshe Michael Roach, Double Day Press: New York City, NY, 2000, 89.

28. Medicine Wheels: Ancient Teachings for Modern Times, Roy Wilson, Crossroad Publishing Company: New York, 1994, 31.

29. For a lengthy historical review on this topic, please see Scott Martelle, Blood Passion: The Ludlow Massacre and Class War in the American West, Rutgers University Press: New Brunswick, NJ, 2007.

30. Leadership and the New Science: Discovering Order in a Chaotic World, Burrett-Koehler Publishers, San Francisco, 2006, page 65.

31. The Power of Meaning: Crafting A Life That Matters, Emily Esfahani Smith, Crown Publishing: New York City, NY, 2017, 77.

32. The Practice of the Wild, Gary Snyder, Counterpoint Press: Berkeley, CA., 1990., page 127.

33. How to Do Good and Avoid Evil: A Global Ethic from the Sources of Judaism, Hans Kung and Rabbi Walter Homolka, Skylight Paths Publishing: Woodstock, VT, 2009, 139.

34. Trophic is from the Greek word trophe for food; trophic level refers to where an animal sits in the food chain. The Systems View of Life: A Unifying Vision, Fritjof Capra and Pier Luigi Luisi, Cambridge University Press: Cambridge, UK, 2014, 343.

Afterword: The Reading Life: Limitations of Self

1. Nonduality: A Study in Comparative Philosophy, David Loy, Humanity Books: Amherst, NY, 1988, 13.

2. Am I Alone Here? Notes on Living to Read and Reading to Live, Peter Orner, Catapult Press: New York, 2016, 23.

3. Am I Alone Here? Notes on Living to Read and Reading to Live, Peter Orner, Catapult Press: New York, 2016, 80.

4. Pirke Avot (Sayings of Our Fathers, 2:4)

Six Lists to Live By

1. The Wisdom of Sustainability: Buddhist Economics for the 21st Century, Sulak Sivaraksa, Koa Books/Chiron Publications: North Carolina, 2016, 24.

2. How to Do Good and Avoid Evil: A Global Ethic from the Sources of Judaism, Hans Kung and Rabbi Walter Homolka, Skylight Paths Publishing: Woodstock, VT, 2009, 116.
3. Ecology, Community and Lifestyle, Arne Naess as Translated by David Rothenberg, Cambridge University Press: Cambridge, UK. 1989, 29.
4. The Four Nobel Truths of Wealth: A Buddhist View of Economic Live, Layth Matthews, Enlightened Economy Books: US, 2014, 102. Confirm Citation
5. Retrieving the Ancients: An Introduction to Greek Philosophy, David Roochnik, Blackwell Publishing: Malden, MA, 2004, 203.

Index

About Jed Emerson

A senior strategic advisor to leading family offices and investment firms, *Conscious Company Magazine* called Jed Emerson, "The Godfather of Impact Investing," and ImpactAlpha labeled him "...an Original Gangster of Impact Investing."

He co-authored an award wining, first book on the topic and has co-authored/edited seven books on social entrepreneurship and impact investing.

Emerson serves as a Senior Research Fellow at the University of Heidelberg's Center on Social Investing and has held faculty appointments at Stanford, Harvard and Oxford Business Schools, along with teaching appointments at Northwestern University and NYU-Abu Dhabi.

He is an internationally recognized thought leader, having presented at The World Economic Forum, Skoll World Forum and the Impact Investing Summit/Asia Pacific, among countless other conferences and events around the world.

The Purpose of Capital Project

...is a field building effort to support and shine a light upon diverse explorations into the topic from a variety of perspectives, timeframes, cultures and viewpoints.

The Project is a charitable initiative operating through its fiscal sponsor, Impact Assets, a nonprofit financial services group with a mandate to advance impact investing and innovative uses of capital to support the creation of a more just, equitable and sustainable world.

The Blended Value Group is an advisory and thought leadership firm consisting of Jed Emerson.

Our intention is to create a web site and periodic newsletter promoting the good work of not only the authors cited in this initial research, but a host of other thought leaders, organizations and networks active in promoting a new vision of the purpose of capital.

Both organizations' web sites offer free resources and background information on impact investing and value creation.

Over coming months, future publications of The Purpose of Capital Project will be distributed, free of charge, to those interested in continuing to explore these themes, history, and the implications of the ideas presented in this initial book, as well as related books and resources offered by others.

If you would like to receive notification of these offerings, please register your email address at The Purpose of Capital Project web site.

www.purposeofcapital.org

Onward!
(or simply be fully present where you are...)

CPSIA information can be obtained
at www.ICGtesting.com
Printed in the USA
FSHW02n2331210918